Margaret Morris

Gyda'i Dymuniadau Gorau
all good wishes

D1615541

PAGES FROM
MEMORY

PAGES FROM
MEMORY

JAMES GRIFFITHS

J. M. DENT & SONS LTD

LONDON

SBN: 460 03850 8

To Win

on the fiftieth anniversary
of our wedding 1918–1968

CONTENTS

LIST OF ILLUSTRATIONS

ACKNOWLEDGMENTS

I would like to express my sincere thanks to all those who
have helped me in recalling the past and in writing these
pages from memory. To the diminished band of contemporaries
who shared my nostalgia as we recalled all our yesterdays;
my friend Gwilym Prys Davies for his guidance and
encouragement; to my son Harold, and niece May Harris;
and, most of all, to my wife, to whom I dedicate this book,
the writing of which was for us a joyous sharing of memories.

I also wish to acknowledge my indebtedness to the staff of
the House of Commons Library for their courteous response
to every request and to the Editor of the *Western Mail* for
his permission to reprint from its columns the story of my
first day down the mine.

1

ROOTS

ON SUNDAY evenings in the winter—when it was too cold, or wet, to go to chapel, Mother would gather us around her before the fire and show us the pictures in the album. As she turned the pages we would see the likenesses of Dadcu and Mamgu Llanddarog, Mother's father and mother who had died before I was born, and then of Dadcu and Mamgu Pontamman, Father's parents, one of whom, Mamgu, was still alive and living in the old home. Then there were the host of pictures of uncles and aunts and cousins and of my own brothers and sisters at varying stages on life's journey. Now I am old I too have an album and, being a nostalgic Welshman, I like to turn the pages and live life over again. This is my album as memory turns the pages.

I

Whenever one Welshman meets another away from their native land the first question they will ask each other is: 'Where are you from?' For every Welshman belongs to a village and a valley and a town. And I belong to the village of Betws, in the valley of the Amman and near to the town of Llanelli.

There are many villages called Betws in Wales. Everybody knows of Betws-Y-Coed with its Swallow Falls. Very few people know of my Betws except those like me for whom it is home. The learned have argued for years, and still go on arguing about the origin and meaning of the name 'Betws'. I like the story which links all our Betwses with long ago. In olden days, before Henry VIII and all that, the Church would provide a sacred place where the folk could come and count their beads—and in time a village would grow around the 'Beads-house' and become another Betws as mine did. To distinguish it from all the others my Betws was known as 'Betws-mas-o'r-Byd' ('Betws-beyond-the-World'). My Betws is set by the side of the River Amman, which gives its name to my valley. The river begins its journey from the Black Mountains which stand at the head of the valley behind Brynamman. It flows in summer, and rushes in winter, down the valley to join the River Loughor at the bottom, on its way down to my town Llanelli. These are the three—the village, valley and town in which my life has been rooted all the seventy-odd years of my journey.

Father and Mother had made their home in a thatched cottage —the nearest to the river—and it was there that I was born on what Mother told me was a lovely Indian-summer day (*haf bach Mihangel*) in September of 1890. By the side of the cottage Father had built his smithy (*yr efail*), that is why I am still known as '*Jim-yr-efail*' to those who grew up with me in our village.

My father belonged to a family with its roots deep in the life of our valley. One of my compatriots, the writer D. J. Williams of Fishguard, who worked and lived in Betws for a while, has painted a word-picture of my father and our family. In his auto-biography *Yn Chwech Ar Hugain Oed* ('When I was Twenty-six') he tells the story he had heard that my father's family were the descendants of a race of people born of the intermarriage of the women who belonged to the 'little dark people' of the Black Mountains with the warriors of the Roman Legion. And I can believe him, for that explains the Roman nose which marked out the faces of the Griffiths. D. J. Williams, not content with this discovery, goes on to say that Father was the very likeness of Joseph Stalin. My Griffiths grandfather was a smith and my father and two of his brothers followed him in his craft. I do not remember 'Dadcu Pontamman', as we called him, but I heard so much about him from old Twmi Hopkin that I feel as if I must have known him. Twmi was a regular visitor to our cottage. As soon as he entered our kitchen (*y gegin fach*) Mother would say 'Make room for Twmi by the fireside'. Seated in the big chair, Twmi would beg a cigarette (*pib-bapur*—paper pipe, he would call it) from one of my elder brothers and turn to me and ask me to peel off the paper so that he could put the tobacco in his clay pipe. That done, he would settle down to tell us once more of the time when he had gone away with my grandfather to work at the ironworks at Ystalyfera making munitions for the Crimean War. At the works Grandfather followed his craft and Twmi worked as his mate. They would walk the twelve miles to the works, toil long hours for 'good money' and once a month they would come home for a Sunday, walking the twenty-four miles there and back. Twmi's most vivid memories were of 'Fifty-Nine'—the cholera and the revival . . . and the story would end with Twmi singing one of the old revival hymns in his still sweet (if broken) tenor voice. My grandmother, Mamgu Pontamman, was still alive and survived till her ninety-fifth year. She had been Susannah Rhys, and was known to all as Susannah Rhysi. There were times when she and Twmi would sit together at our fireside and join in the story of the Crimea. But she had her own story of those days when she would walk all the way up the valleys and over the hills to faraway Merthyr to buy iron, straight from the ironworks, for use at the smithy, a journey of fifty miles, bringing back with her samples of what she had bought. She was proud of Dadcu's skill and would tell me, 'If ever you go as far as Ynyscedwyn [Ystradgynlais today] look at the gates of Sardis Chapel and you will be proud of your Dadcu.' Mamgu did not have to depend on the fame of Dadcu—she herself was known, and revered, for her skill as a 'doctor'. People for miles around would come to her cottage to seek a cure for burns and other ailments. She made a special ointment—from what she described as 'a mixture of what is in every woman's pantry'—and the ointment worked wonders. Sometimes when the malady was not to be seen with the eye there were ways of taking out the evil in the blood which were among the secrets of Susannah Rhysi. She bequeathed her secrets and her skills to her son, my Uncle Jerry, whose fame still survives at Penygroes, where he worked at the Emlyn Colliery for fifty years and on his retirement was made a presentation for his services to the community as a 'doctor'. The smith and the 'doctor' of Pontamman reared a family of five sons and one daughter, who between them have left a brood of Griffiths in the valley of the Amman.

My mother was Margaret Morris, the daughter of a handloom weaver who taught his craft to his three sons. My uncles each had a loom in their garden and on holidays I would be taken to see them making Welsh flannel. This they would carry to the fairs at Carmarthen and Llandeilo, where the colliers' wives came to buy the flannel to make the shirts and pants which the colliers wore in the coal-mine. The old colliers would say that this flannel was the best because it absorbed the sweat and did not become clammy and cold or make one shiver, as did the shoddy stuff from the shops. My Uncle Sam developed a kind of flannel which was much prized by women for their costumes—even the ladies of the 'county' became his patrons. So it was that William Griffiths and Margaret Morris came from two families of craftsmen. How sad it is to relate that there is no longer a single smith or weaver in either of the families. The old crafts, with those of the bootmaker, saddler and dressmaker, have become lost arts, and with them has gone a way of life and its values.

Ten children were born to my parents—six sons and four daughters. Two of the sons died at birth and the eight of us who survived grew up in the cottage in Betws. I was the lucky one, *y cyw melyn olaf* ('the last yellow chick'), as the old saying goes. By the time I had arrived the older brothers and sisters were already at work, so that I was nurtured in the days of affluence. The *hen gownt* ('the old debt') which every large family incurred while the older children grew up to working age, was already repaid. Indeed it was during my childhood that my father ventured to buy the old cottage and to build a new house. This brought me into contact with the two 'L's'—landlords and leases, and their uses and misuses. The house was built out of the stones ('pobbles') which the River Amman brought down from the Black Mountains. The landlord was the riparian owner, so my father had to pay a shilling for every load of stones we gathered from the river bed. My father contracted with the stonemason to trim the stones and build the house. When all was done the new house had cost no less than £150, and it was a happy day when father announced to the assembled family that the last penny had been paid and that the new house was now our castle. Except—and this is where the riparian owner changed his role and became the landowner—the site was leased to my father on a ninety-nine years' lease with what the lawyers called a covenant, and which I came to call by other names, for it meant that at the end of the ninety-nine years the house would 'revert' to the landlord.[1] However, that time was not yet, and

[1] This system is explained on pages 181–3.

so we rejoiced in our castle. And, of course, the smithy remained.

The village of the 'Beads-house' had by now been merged with the bigger village across the river to become the township of Ammanford. The world was beginning to discover the value of anthracite coal and new mines were being opened. The smiths' old customers, the farmers, were getting fewer so that Father had to adapt his skill to new tasks—the sharpening and tempering of the colliers' mandrels and the making of hobnails for the colliers' pit boots. This meant changing the working hours at the smithy—for the colliers would bring their tools at the end of their shift, around five in the evening, and they had to be ready for the next morning. To enable the job to be done in the winter months the boys of the family were recruited in turn for duties at the smithy —holding the candle while father sharpened the tools on the anvil, and holding the sharpened tools in the 'bosh', a tub of water into which the red-hot mandrel would be plunged and held until it was 'tempered', fit to cut the 'stone coal' in the 'little vein'. On Saturdays we became the collectors, going around the cottages to gather in the money for the work done during the week.

The smithy was, of course, the village parliament, where the local politicians gathered and argued about religion and politics and the parish council and more distant institutions. My father ruled his parliament with the same iron grip with which he held the colliers' tools. I can see the 'Stalin' there. He was a dissenter (*Annibynwr*) by denomination and a Radical in politics. His heroes were Gladstone, Tom Ellis and David Lloyd George—in that order. By the time I came to hold the candle the order had changed, for it was the time of the Boer War and Lloyd George was fighting valiantly against the enemy on his own side as well as the ancient enemy, the Tories. The village parliamentarians were sustained by the two radical weeklies *Llais Llafur* ('Labour's Voice') and *Tarian y Gweithiwr* ('The Workers' Shield'). One of the backbenchers would read the editorials to the 'House' and then the debate would continue until the last tool had been tempered and the 'House' stood adjourned. I cannot recall a single division taking place in my time—the smith would sum up and that was that. My last recollection of the village parliament is of the burning indignation at Balfour's Education Act of 1902—with the injustice of asking dissenters to pay for the schools of the alien Church. This carried us out of the smithy to the road to march to the demonstration at Ammanford where the great man himself—David Lloyd George—was the orator. So it was that I began my training in politics, demonstrations and all that goes to the making of a politician—on the way from one 'parliament' to another.

Meantime, there was school to attend—indeed two schools, the Board School and the Sunday School. The Betws Board School is still there and nowadays it proudly boasts of the two M.P.s who once were among its pupils, Ifor Richards, the Member for Baron's Court, and myself. In my days the head-master was John Lewis—a kindly man from Cardiganshire. He had two ambitions for his pupils: to learn to read and to enjoy reading, and to write in the 'Cusack' style—thin strokes up and thick strokes down. He told my father that I was a 'good pupil'. I am afraid that if he came back he would be furious with my handwriting, but pleased that the love of books and reading abides. For this precious gift which he nurtured so tenderly I salute his memory. Was it H. G. Wells who said, through one of his characters, 'The wonderful world of books—the happy refuge from the cares of every day'? John Lewis spoke no Welsh, and the only two songs which he taught us were 'The Last Rose of Summer' and 'Home, Sweet Home'.

We formed two teams, the village boys and the farmer boys from the hills around. We had no playing grounds, but we had a rich variety of games and, of course, cricket and rugger. While we were at school fame came to our community, for Dr Lloyd's son Percy had won his Welsh cap as a wing three. From that day we all dreamed that we too would some day streak along the touch line, ball tucked under our arm, and plunge over the line to score the winning try against England.

That was one school. The other was the Sunday School at the Christian Temple, the Welsh chapel with the English name. Here the 'headmaster' was John Evans the stationmaster. He was a born teacher who had a remarkable way with children. We would gather in the chapel vestry, a rowdy lot; in would come John Evans, always in a rush, jump on to the rostrum and no sooner had he called us to order with his '*Nawr te mhlant i*' ('Now my children') than we were his to command. Always he began with a song in Welsh, '*Mae Iesu Grist yn Derbyn plant bychan fel nyni*', and would send us home with:

6

> Dare to be a Daniel,
> Dare to stand alone,
> Dare to have a purpose firm,
> And dare to make it known.

And as we sang we knew who our Daniel was—John Evans the stationmaster.

Every year we would learn a cantata with a lesson to impress 'our young minds' with the need for the boldness of a Daniel to face life's battles. And the giant evil to be fought was . . . drink, as in the cantata, 'Buy your own cherries'. So I grew up in the simple society of our village—home, schools and play, and soon I was of the age to be launched on the workaday world.

At the age of thirteen I had reached the top of the ladder at the Betws Board School—Standard X-7. Already some of my classmates had started work at pit or mill and on Saturdays would swank about their pocket-money. At home I had over-heard whispered conversations about my future. Should it be the mine, the tinplate mill, or another school? One of my classmates had found a place at the intermediate school at Llandeilo and we envied him his cap and blazer. My father had his own plan for me. To the coal-mine for a year or so, and then to the Gwynfryn, a school established by Watcyn Wyn, our poet-preacher, to prepare students for the nonconformist ministry. This was the road along which I was to travel from pit to pulpit. But first to the pit as a collier's boy.

Sixty years after, I recalled that first day in the mine in an article in the *Western Mail* which, by the courtesy of the editor, I include in these memoirs.

I was going on fourteen and had reached the top of the ladder—Standard X-7—at our village school at Betws.

Ever since this last year had begun the 'Old Master', John Lewis, had been striving ever so hard to initiate us into the mysteries of algebra and mensuration. It must have been a hard task for him; it was certainly hard going for us.

When he grew tired of his labours he would hand each one of us a copy of one of his two favourite books—Ballantyne's *Coral Island* or Marryat's *Mr Midshipman Easy*—and leave us alone to read. Meanwhile, he would turn his attention to those lower mortals who shared our room, the Sevens, and on one occasion he made me feel very proud when he called my name and asked me to show my exercise book to them as an example in the art of penmanship, Cusack style, thin lines up and thick lines down!

The 'New Master', Rhys Thomas [a Betws boy who had come back to his old school as a teacher],was a man of music. He was the leader of our village brass band and that put him on a high pinnacle. After the Christmas holidays he had enrolled the X-7s to sing in the school choir. We were needed: the girls as 'top sopranos', and the boys as 'lower altos' to sing 'Y Bwthyn ar y Bryn' at the Dewi Sant concert.

Easter followed, and when I came back to school after the holidays most of my school mates had gone. The boys from the mountain (*cryts y mynydd*) had stayed to help their fathers on the farm. The boys from the village (*cryts y pentre*), had gone to work at the coal-mine, or the tinplate mill.

I felt very lonely at school and even lonelier of an evening as we gathered for cricket on 'Cae'r Ynys' by the Amman river. My old mates now belonged to a different world to me. They wore long trousers and flashy cravats. They flourished their pink packets of 'Cinderella' fags before my eyes and blew the smoke curling up to the sky.

They would keep on chattering about their new world as they talked of how many trams they had filled. It was worst of all on Saturdays, when we wended our way over the river to the bright lights of Ammanford Square. They would display their silver sixpence which made the penny in my pocket shrink.

I could not bear it any longer—not even till July when school would be over anyhow. I had to join them at once, at mine or mill. Which was it to be? I had three older brothers at home; two at the coal-mine, and the oldest one of all was already a millman at the tinplate works. It was the brother next to me, Shoni, who decided my destiny. He was working as a 'senior colliers' boy' (*crwtyn tro*) with John Davies [a Cardi, or native of Cardiganshire] at the Betws Colliery, and there was a vacancy in his stall for a junior (*crwtyn bach*).

That settled it. I was to start next Monday. At once preparations began for the great day.My mother had been to Uncle Sam's [the weaver] to buy his special blue Welsh flannel to make shirts and drawers. A brand new pair of moleskin trousers had been bought and washed to get the smell out.

Two big pockets had been sewn to the insides of the coat, which belonged to my second best suit, to hold the box and jack. My father had nailed my heavy boots, and best of all there was a strong leather belt and a pair of yorks to tie under my knees.

So it was that one Monday in June I set out with Shoni at six in the morning up the road to Betws Colliery. I was taken to the office to see old Picton the gaffer, and there I signed the book of the contract between me and the Ammanford Colliery Co. Ltd.

Off then to the lamproom to 'raise my lamp' with a command from the Lampman to remember my number—317.

Holding the handle tight I went on to the 'spake' and down the slant to the double parting of the little vein. John Davies's stall was the third up the 'heading', and when we reached near to the coal face and put our coats and waistcoats safely on the nails on the arms of the *par dwbwl*, the day's work began.

My first job was to fill the coal into the 'curling box' and carry it to the tram and empty it all inside the tram. There was a 'pitch' in the seam. From the upper side it was not too bad—I soon learnt that the 'box' would slide down—but from the lower side it was hard pushing.

In the course of the long day—from seven to half-past four— Shoni explained to me what the various tools were for: the two mandrels, *Cam a Cwt*; the sledge and wedge; the hatchet and the bar; and last, because the most hated, the *Tro-wr* to bore holes in the coal but leave marks on the groin!

There can be no more joyful banquet than the miners' snap time. I joined the *cryts bach* from the other 'stalls' on the heading to enjoy the bread and butter and cheese—with a tomato for 'afters' —and swill it all down with pearl-barley water, which Shoni had found to be best for slaking a thirst.

At long, long last came the colliers' 'Who goes home?'— 'Tools on the bar and out'. The journey back to the double parting did not seem half as long and we were soon on the spake and in no time out to the top and the June sunshine. The first day was safely over.

Home to a feast prepared by Mam for her three colliers—*Cawl-Cig a Tatws*, *pwdin* rice and tea. For the once, as a special favour, the youngest was at the head of the queue for the 'tub' and I rushed down to join my mates on Cae'r Ynys. . . . Once again I was one of them. I could now talk of trams and all that. The penny mother gave me had been quickly turned into a pink packet of Cinderellas, and come Saturday I would have a silver sixpence, for I was now earning 1s 3d, plus percentage, a shift.

That was a lot of money when pay day came once a fortnight, and I knew from Shoni that John Davies-Cardi gave his boys extra for themselves if they were good boys and gave all their pay to their Mam.

And so it was that on that Monday in June a new collier joined the ranks.

The hard struggle to raise a family of eight was now over, for all of us were at work and Father and Mother would find life easier. My two eldest sisters were working at the tinplate mill as 'plate openers'. The 'box' of plate (about 112 separate sheets) had been through the furnace, rolled and doubled, and rolled again, then dipped in the 'pickling tub' and would then reach the bench where my sisters and their fellow 'openers' would wrench each separate sheet away from the 'box' and pass it on its way to become *sospan fach*. My youngest sister had been put out to service with a local tradesman who was a trusted deacon at our chapel, and the other sister stayed at home to help Mam. My eldest brother had started work at the mill and had advanced to the stage of a 'behinder' at the rolls, when he was struck by illness which was only cured by an operation at Guy's Hospital. On his return he changed to a 'healthier' job in the coal-mine. The other three of us were already in the mine on the way to become hewers of coal, and anthracite coal at that. We were now installed in our new house, Bryn Villa, with its commodious accommodation, kitchen, middle room and parlour, and four bedrooms, two big and two small. Of course there had to be some doubling up, two in a bed, by the younger ones. There was no bath or hot water; these were luxuries reserved for 'them'. So each day Mother, and the sister at home, had to boil water for the tub in which the colliers took turns, the youngest enjoying for a while the privilege of 'going first'. After the tub there would come the dinner. There would, first, be *cawl*, home-made broth, a kind of super version of what chefs call minestrone. On some weekdays (and always on Sundays) there would be butcher's meat; on other days Mother would draw upon the supply of bacon and hams which hung from the kitchen roof. The vegetables in their season would come from our garden, and there were always plenty of potatoes for, in addition to those we grew in our garden, there were the extras from the 'row in the farmer's field' which our family, like others, were allowed to plant under the reciprocal agreement by which the family helped the farmer with the harvest. Bread and cakes were home baked and there would be *teisen-lap*, a special kind of fruit cake baked on a flat iron 'bake stone'. Plain fare, but in plenty, and we all grew up strong and healthy. Two of my sisters lived to their eighties, the

other two lived out the allotted span. My eldest brother paid the
price of coal at twenty-nine, the next brother survived fearful
burns and lived to win fame as a bard and writer in Welsh. The
next to me, who sponsored me in the mine, went through the
battle of the Somme, and came back to the pit with his lungs full
of gas to work in the mine till he collapsed and died. Now I am
left alone in my seventies to turn the pages of our family album.

In the year in which I started work, 1904, came the 'Welsh
revival'. This was not one of those elaborately organized and
expensively advertised affairs we have seen in more recent times.
This was a homespun revival inspired by a young coal-miner who
had entered an academy to be trained for the nonconformist
ministry. Evan Roberts (for that was his name) came to one of
the chapels in our village and all our family went to hear him. I
do not remember a word of what he said, but I can still see him
standing up in the pulpit, tall, with dark hair falling over his
face, and the quiet voice reaching the gallery as if he were singing.
Why did it happen? That is a question beyond me. All that I
have are the memories of a boy who had just started work, of
how everything seemed to be suddenly different. There were
services down the mine, in which the gaffer took part, and our
home was turned into a chapel. For a year or two it transformed
life in the valleys, then it seemed to fade out, leaving behind a
void which was later filled by another kind of revival, as I shall
come to relate.

I count myself fortunate to have been nurtured in a home which
had its own world of books. Father had his Bible commentaries
and his radical journals. My eldest brother had religious books
by Henry Drummond, Jeremy Taylor and Thomas à Kempis. The
brother who became the bard had his tomes of Welsh poetry and
prose and his sheafs of manuscripts. The next to me had his own
world of boys' papers, three each week: *Marvel*, *Pluck* and *Union
Jack*. And in due time there was added my own collection of
pamphlets and periodicals. Most important of all in their
influence on me were the two journals which came to our home
because we were dissenters. These were the denominational
weekly *The Examiner* and its companion *The Christian Commonwealth*. Both had one feature in common, the weekly sermon by
the minister of the Congregational Cathedral (the City Temple),
the Rev. R. J. Campbell. These weekly sermons suddenly threw

two bombs into our family circle, the New Theology and Socialism. This set us all arguing at home, at chapel, and in the mine and mill. Four years after Evan Roberts, there came to our valley the new theologian from the City Temple, and from Merthyr the Socialist Scotsman who was causing a stir in the valleys. The journals and their sermons, and the visits of the preacher and politician, were to lead me to 'The Movement' which ever after was to be my life.

2

THE CAUSE

THE time was ripe for the coming of Campbell and Keir Hardie. The fires of the revival had died down. Individual lives had been changed but everything else remained unchanged. Work in the mine was as hard as ever, the struggle for a livelihood as stern as of old. What we needed was a religion which would change society, and a political faith with a vision of a new social order. We found the promise of both in those gatherings to which we travelled in May of 1908. Our first journey, a score of us, in the old horse-brake, was to Panteg Chapel, Ystalyfera, to hear R. J. Campbell. The chapel was crowded as the speaker mounted the pulpit. He was a striking figure in his black robe, with the boyish face, snow-white hair, and the quiet voice which seemed to pervade rather than fill the chapel. His address was a plea to all Christians to join in seeking to create a new social order founded on Christian ethics. There was a special plea to nonconformity to cut itself loose from the ties which bound it to the outworn philosophy of the Liberal Party, and a warning that unless the Free Churches found a new mission in the application of their principles to the social problems of the age, they would lose contact with the people and lose their hold upon the democratic forces which were emerging in the Labour and Socialist movements.

A few weeks later the same company were back in the same horse-brake on our way to the Miners' Hall at Gwaun Cae Gurwen to greet James Keir Hardie. If R. J. Campbell looked like a seer, Keir Hardie looked like a prophet. His address was a supplement to that we had heard at Panteg. The theme was a simple one:

The Labour movement is an attempt to enable the working class to realize itself, its thoughts and aspirations. At present the 'people' is a formless and shapeless and wiseless mass at best, an infant crying for the light, with no language but a cry. We will change all this by developing the self-respect and manhood of the workers and placing Labour so strongly on its feet that it will be able to stand alone without the aid of crutches, whether those be called Liberal or Conservative.

From those gatherings we returned with a new religion to inspire us—a cause to which we could dedicate our lives, and a call to action to 'change all this'. . . . Within a week we had formed a branch of the Independent Labour Party, and before the year was out I was to become the secretary. Now my life was firmly rooted—and the future beckoned.

Keir Hardie's call to 'change all this' found a ready and eager response from branches of the I.L.P. which sprang up like mushrooms in those last years of peace before 1914. The programme of the Independent Labour Party, which Keir Hardie had founded in 1893, made a stronger appeal to our religions idealism than the rival Social Democratic Federation, with its rigid Marxism and anti-religious bias. The I.L.P.'s socialist programme, which aimed at the collective ownership of the means of production through parliamentary action, was more in accord with our temperament than the S.D.F.'s class war. Moreover, the I.L.P. provided us with two immediate objectives as we launched our campaign in the South Wales valleys in 1908. First, the winning over of the trade unions to the Labour Party, and secondly, the conquest of the constituencies.

The key to the achievement of the first objective lay in the winning over of the Miners' Union. Two years before when the Miners' Federation of Great Britain had held a ballot of its members and rejected the proposal to affiliate the union to the Labour Party, the South Wales miners, as ever in the vanguard, had voted for affiliation by 41,843 votes to 31,577.

In the General Election of 1906 the older leaders, Mabon, Brace and Tom Richards, had clung to the alliance with the Liberals and had fought as Lib.-Labs. But a new generation of leaders was emerging, men like Vernon Hartshorn, George Barker and James Winstone—all members of the I.L.P. In our own valley we found a champion in Johnny James, who was all the more influential because he could talk to the miners in the

Welsh language. In every mine the members of the I.L.P. became the spearhead in the effort to better the result of the 1906 ballot in the new ballot then pending. This time we not only won in South Wales but were able to rejoice in winning a national majority and thus bringing the Miners' Union into the Labour fold.

This accomplished, we now turned our attention to the winning of our constituency. At that time my valley was included in the East Carmarthen constituency. It was cut off from our town, Llanelli, and linked up with the rural areas of the Upper Towy Valley. It was, of course, a Liberal stronghold and the Member was Abel Thomas, who was more influential in that he was the son of a nonconformist minister than for his prowess at the Bar or his oratory at Westminster.

Our first job was to create a constituency organization and to find a candidate. Now that we had won over the miners the first was made easier and we soon had a conference to establish a constituency organization. We found our candidate too—for in Burry Port there was a young doctor who had joined the I.L.P., and had already endeared himself to the miners by standing up to the coal-owners and the insurance companies in fighting the compensation claims of disabled miners.

Now we had our organization and our candidate and we were ready for the road—literally, for it was to highways and byways that we went for our meeting-places. Alas, even the village square has become too perilous and noisy today for the open-air meeting, to the impoverishment of our democracy. Every Saturday evening we would set our soapbox, and when we became more affluent, our portable rostrum, on the corner of the village square. We were all assigned our duties—chairman, collector, pamphlet seller, and the decoy to mix with the crowd and be ready to ask the first question. In my turn I performed each duty, graduating in time to be the regular chairman. We had a champion pamphlet seller, Harry Evans, a cobbler who came from Swansea and who, not only at our meetings, but at all times, would have a stock of pamphlets in his pockets. What an excellent selection of titles he was able to offer . . . 'An appeal to the Young', by Peter (Prince) Kropotkin, 'The Christ that is to be', by Philip Snowden, and 'Can a man be a Christian on a pound a week?', by Keir Hardie. I heard Hardie tell a story about this last one. When a pamphlet seller in Glasgow went around

Clydeside shouting the title, from somewhere came a voice: 'What a d—d silly question. What else can a man be on a quid a week?'

We were blessed with a rich supply of speakers: Dan Griffiths the teacher, and Farley Heft the dentist, both from Llanelli; Johnny James of the Miners' Union, and from the Swansea Valley a young journalist, W. H. Stevenson, who was later to become the editor of the *Daily Herald*. And there was the favourite with our congregations on the square, Johnny Jones from Pontardawe. Johnny had a lovely tenor voice—he was first tenor in the male voice choir—and his speech was composed of a series of poems from Shelley and Morris and Walt Whitman, all covered by the title of his address, 'Socialism—the Hope of the World'. When I asked him for a return visit and queried what his next subject would be, Johnny replied: 'You can call it what you like, comrade, the same it will be.' The same it was, to the delight of our regulars. Now and again we were honoured by a visit from one of our national star speakers, and in the autumn of 1908 we were thrilled to have a visit from the hero of Colne Valley, Victor Grayson. We had a crowded audience at the biggest hall, at Brynamman, and a wonderful address, and then a shock. We were all young, and all teetotallers. Judge, therefore, our dilemma when our orator at the end of the meeting asked one of us to take him to the nearest place where he could have a whisky. It speaks volumes for our devotion to the cause that a volunteer was found to do even this task. It took a visit from two brothers from the U.S.A., the Rev. Stitt Wilson and the Rev. Ben Wilson, and a stirring talk by Stitt on 'Moses—the first Labour leader' to restore our faith in 'stars'.

2

The spadework having been diligently done for two years, the time had come to go into battle to win East Carmarthen for Labour. By the time the second election came in 1910 we had as much as fifty pounds in the funds. The number of I.L.P. branches had doubled and we were all eager for the contest. We knew it would be a tough battle. The Liberals were as strongly entrenched as they were in most Welsh constituencies. Those were the days when, as someone remarked, every chapel vestry was a Liberal committee room. The old war cries still had their pull. The old

Church of the establishment had yet to be dethroned. And the bulwark of the Tories, the House of Lords, was challenging the Liberal Government of Asquith and Lloyd George. This, said the Liberals of the valley, was not the time to split the 'progressive vote', and when we declared our determination to fight we were charged with being financed by 'Tory gold'. We were not frightened by this cry; we had vowed to change all this, and that included Tories as well as Liberals. We had something that money could not buy—conviction and enthusiasm. Every evening our members were out on the streets, holding meetings at every street corner, distributing our literature and ready to argue all through the night. It was an exhilarating experience. Inspired by the response we were getting we began to feel that we might pull it off at the first go. But, alas, when the votes had been cast and counted this is the sad story they told:

> Abel Thomas (Lib.): 5,025
> Mervyn Peel (Con.): 2,515
> J. H. Williams (Lab.): 1,176

We soon recovered from our defeat, and now worked and waited for the next opportunity. It came unexpectedly two years later with the sudden death of the Member. Dr Williams was once more our valiant standard bearer. Our membership had increased and our enthusiasm was as buoyant as ever, but we were soon to realize that this time the struggle would be even harder. The Liberals had selected one of the most famous preacher-politicians, Towyn Jones, as candidate, and to add to his strength he was a minister of one of the largest chapels in our valley. We brought down upon us the wrath of the elders of nonconformity for daring to oppose Towyn. And something else happened in this 1912 by-election which lost rather than gained us votes. One day there stalked—yes, that is the right word, stalked—into our committee rooms at Ammanford a tall lady, dressed in an unorthodox style, trilby hat, short hair, collar and tie, and with a cigarette at the end of a long holder. She introduced herself as Miss Nina Boyle, of the militant suffragette movement. They had no members in the constituency so would be willing to join forces with us during the campaign, and if we would allow one of their speakers to address our meetings they would meet half the cost. The bargain was struck and for the rest of the campaign we shared our platform with such stalwarts as Mrs ('General') Drummond of the formidable physique and booming voice, and Annie Kenney with her piercing eyes and Irish lilt. We lost votes because of our youthful gallantry but were amply repaid by the experience. What a pity it is that none of those early campaigners for votes for women ever reached the House of Commons. The Mother of Parliaments would have been stirred by these daughters of the revolution.

This 1912 election was to be the last opportunity we had of fighting on the electoral front until 1918. Meantime, so much was to happen. There were, however, two immediate consequences of those two elections in our constituency and similar contests in other Welsh constituencies which were to have profound effects on the development of the political and industrial movement in the valleys.

I have related how the upsurge of the I.L.P. in the valleys was inspired by the complementary influence of R. J. Campbell's 'new theology' and Keir Hardie's call to action to establish an independent party, freed from dependence on the Liberal crutches. In combining the two we were presenting a dual challenge to Welsh nonconformity. The orthodox leaders became alarmed at this growth of 'heresy' and the Sunday sermon was increasingly devoted to attacking this new peril. The position of those of us who had embraced the new religion was made difficult. We felt that we were unwelcome at the chapel and many young men drifted away. The drift became even more evident when the elders of the chapels found that their political temples were also being assailed by this new force. This conflict between the old and the new reached its climax in a by-election which took place in 1910 in the Mid-Glamorgan constituency. The miners, having by this time become affiliated to the Labour Party, nominated one of the new men, a member of the I.L.P., Vernon Hartshorn, and he became the first miners' man to fight as Labour—without prefix or suffix. The Liberals chose a local industrialist as their candidate, a steel owner, F. W. Gibbins. From the outset of the campaign the Liberals turned the conflict into a fight for or against Socialism. A young nonconformist minister, the Rev. W. F. Phillips, who had already won notoriety for his bitter personal attacks upon Keir Hardie, virtually took over the campaign from the tongue-tied industrialist. Armed with quotations from the writings of some

European Socialists which expressed their anti-clerical attitude, Phillips roused the older nonconformists with the slogan: 'Choose —Christ or Socialism.' From that time an estrangement grew between the chapel and many of the younger members who had found in Socialism not an enemy but a fulfilment of their religion.

From this time dates the beginning of the decline of nonconformity as a political force in Wales. The older, and more orthodox, clung to the Liberal Party, and especially to David Lloyd George. And when in later years the bitter conflicts within the Liberal Party led to its downfall, the political power which nonconformity had enjoyed for nearly a century in Wales vanished with it. If only nonconformity had aligned itself with the new political forces which soon were to become all-powerful in the valleys the subsequent history of both Chapel and Socialism might have been different. Here is one of the 'ifs' in the recent history of Wales which I hope will some day attract the attention of one of our historians.

It was during this period of electoral conflict, and the consequent strain between Socialism and Chapel, that a new and powerful force began to emerge in the industrial and political life of South Wales. The Miners' Union had been among the first to provide scholarships for residential courses at Ruskin College, Oxford. When a conflict arose between the college authorities and the principal, Dennis Hird, out of the desire of the students to have courses in Marxist economics, the Welsh students, notably Frank Hodges and Noah Ablett, were among the leaders who followed the dismissed principal into the venture of a new 'Labour college'. The rebels came back like heroes from the battlefield and soon won over the South Wales Miners' Union to the support of the new college. Even more important was their emergence as tutors of classes which soon multiplied in the valleys. Noah Ablett wrote a book, *Easy Outline of Economics*, which was the pure gospel of Marxism. The book, and the classes, soon began to inspire a new movement towards industrial unionism and syndicalism.

The new ideas found fertile soil in the industrial turmoil of the Cambrian Combine strike; the 'riots' at Tonypandy and the intervention of the military, as we then believed, on the order of the then Home Secretary, Winston Churchill, and culminating in the national strike of the miners for a minimum wage and the passing of the Minimum Wage Act of 1912. The new leaders formed an 'unofficial reform movement' and outlined their programme for militant action in an explosive pamphlet, 'The Miners' Next Step'. The first step was to bring all workers in the industry into one union, to be followed by a series of demands leading eventually to the taking over of the industry by the miners. The simple boldness of the plan, and the fervent advocacy of its authors, notably Noah Ablett, W. H. Mainwaring and A. J. Cook, found a response in the ranks of the miners. Thus was born one of the forces which were to survive the war of 1914–1918 and to continue to influence the Miners' Union in the industrial conflicts of 1921 and 1926.

In our West Wales anthracite valleys the activity of two Labour college students, D. R. Owen and Jack Griffiths, was to lead to the establishment at Ammanford of an institution which, in its time, won some notoriety and, more important, came to exercise considerable influence on the industrial and political life of the area. Among the supporters which the Labour college had attracted was George Davison. Davison had been in the civil service in his early years. Through his hobby, photography, he had become associated with the establishment of the firm of Kodak in Britain. This had brought him considerable wealth and some of this he gave freely to the Labour college and to movements which the students formed after their return home. One evening he came to the economics class at Ammanford, of which D. R. Owen was the tutor and I was the secretary. The class was held in the dingy anteroom of the local Ivorites Hall. Whether it was because of the dinginess of the surroundings or the brightness of the students, or perhaps both, Davison told us he would provide us with a better meeting-place. The old vicarage in the High Street was on the market, and he acquired it and transformed it into 'the White House', so called because the old house was given a coat of white paint like his home on the Thames. Davison had come under the influence of what he used to describe as the 'philosophic anarchists', and when the White House was refurnished he provided the nucleus of a library, stocked with the works of Peter Kropotkin and Gustave Hervy. We formed an organization to which we gave the name the 'Workers' Forum', and for some years the old vicarage became the centre of socialist activity in the valley. There would be classes on most evenings, and Sunday evenings after chapel hours there would be lectures on a wide variety of topics. During the

war years of 1914–1918 it became the home of those who were
opposed to the war and there were times when the authorities
eyed it with suspicion. From its classes and gatherings emerged a
team of young men and women who became leaders in the
industrial and political life of the valleys in the post-war years
and their influence lasted beyond the time of the closing of the
White House.

3

We never thought it would come to war in Europe. To us
Germany was the country of the most powerful Socialist Party in
the world, led by the anti-militarist August Bebel. In France Jean
Jaurès was at the head of a Socialist Party which had already
become so influential that no Government could dare go to war
against its opposition. At home the Labour Party had grown
in Parliament, and in the country under the leadership of men
like Hardie, MacDonald and Snowden. The Socialist International had resolved that, if ever war became imminent, the
united force of European Socialism would be mobilized to prevent
it by declaring a general strike. To our dismay, when war was
declared on that day in August 1914 all was lost. In Germany
August Bebel had to confess that 'race and nationalism were
older and more powerful than class solidarity'. In France Jean
Jaurès was assassinated, and his once great party overwhelmed in
confusion and defeat. In Britain the Labour Party was divided, and
even in South Wales we learnt that Keir Hardie had been
shouted down in his constituency. In 1915, broken-hearted by
the tragedy, Keir Hardie passed away. At the by-election which
followed, a one-time militant miners' leader, C. B. Stanton,
stood as a war supporter against the official Labour candidate, the
miners' nominee James Winstone, and won an overwhelming
victory. We in our own valley were derided, and persecuted, as
the 'White House gang', the enemies of our country.

In this hostile atmosphere a few of us endeavoured to hold on
to our beliefs and convictions. Two years were to go by before,
in 1917, a series of events occurred which suddenly transformed
the scene. In March of that year came the dramatic news of the
revolution in Russia. This was followed by the re-emergence of
the Socialist International and the holding of the Leeds Convention. Arthur Henderson resigned from Lloyd George's

coalition and returned to leadership in the Labour Party. The split which from 1914 had threatened to destroy our party began to be healed. In our anthracite area the Miners' Union began to prepare for the challenge which the end of the war would bring, by organizing a chain of Trades and Labour Councils. One of these was established at Ammanford and I was elected secretary. The council became a force in the valley and soon turned its attention to the election which would follow the end of the war. In the redistribution of parliamentary seats in 1917 Carmarthenshire had been allotted only two seats where previously there had been three. Our valley was now linked with the town in the new Llanelli constituency. We proceeded to organize a party for the constituency and I was appointed to act as agent for the area covered by our trades council. Our old candidate, Dr Williams, was still available and with the industrial areas now linked together we felt confident that we could win. Our hopes were strengthened by the divisions which had become acute in the ranks of the Liberals. Llanelli had been represented by a Radical-Liberal, a man of great distinction in the literary as well as the political field, Llewellyn Williams. He had opposed Lloyd George since the formation of the coalition. Now he had to fight for the nomination against Towyn Jones, who had been a strong supporter of L. G. Llewellyn Williams lost and we were afterwards led to believe that, if approached, he would be prepared to stand as our candidate. It was an attractive proposition but we remembered how Dr Williams had stood faithfully by us and loyalty prevailed. Once Towyn Jones was selected by the Liberals, the local Tories announced that they would support him.

This alliance of the Liberals and the Tories was a turning-point in the political history of Wales. For a century the 'Tories' had been the enemy. In our earlier contests we had to fight against the charge of 'splitting the progressive vote'. Now we found the Liberals in radical Llanelli, with a famous nonconformist minister as candidate, fighting under the same banner as the ancient enemy. When eventually the election came in 1918, notwithstanding the influence of Lloyd George, and his coupon, we came within an ace of winning, the figures being:

J. Towyn Jones (Coalition):	16,344
J. H. Williams (Lab.):	14,409
Majority :	*1,935*

The writing on the wall was clear. The reign of the Liberals was nearing its close. We were on the road to victory.

4

The years which followed were to be turning-points in my life and career. A month before the 1918 election I had been married to Winnie Rutley, of Overton, Hampshire. The way of our meeting from our separate villages, so many miles apart and so different in their background, is a story which still remains fresh in our memories half a century after. One of my closest personal friends, Edgar Bassett, who was also a comrade, went to work from the Co-operative store at Ammanford to the Co-op at Basingstoke. He wrote asking if I would send some books to a young woman who was working in the same store as he was at Basingstoke. At that time Edgar and I and our two friends Tommy Thomas and Luther Isaac had discovered Zola's *Germinal*. Life was full of such discoveries—Wells and Shaw, Anatole France and Henri Barbusse, Jack London and now Zola. So in response to the call from Basingstoke I sent a copy of *Germinal* to Winnie Rutley, accompanied by a letter addressed to 'Dear Comrade' and signed 'Yours fraternally'. Letters were followed by mutual visits to Wales and Hampshire, and in October 1918 we were married at the Congregational Church, Overton.

My father-in-law had been employed all his life at the Portals Mill at Laverstoke, most of his working life engaged in preparing the wire moulds for the watermark in the special paper used for Bank of England notes. His wife was the daughter of a carpenter named David Treacher. For Grandfather the daily round at work was only incidental to the great mission of 'saving souls' by sermon and song at the village Methodist church. My father-in-law was a local preacher and Winnie played the organ—to a congregation in which, in both pulpit and pew, the family predominated. In Overton, as elsewhere, the Methodists were the radicals of the community, so that the advent of a Socialist son-in-law was not too heavy a burden to bear. At my end it was the language which worried my mother, but, after meeting Winnie she blessed me with the assurance that 'she was very good—considering'. Within a year of our marriage, living as young married couples had to even in those days, in apartments, life took another turn, which was to bring us both to London for two exciting years.

For most of my generation 'schooling' (formal education) began and ended at the village school, with the 'three R's', reading, reckoning and 'riting. If we were clever scholars we could pass the Labour exam at twelve and start to work as my older brothers had done. As the youngest I was more fortunate and stayed at school until I was thirteen. I was even luckier in that by the time I started work the era of the 'classes' had arrived. There were the 'evening classes', where we could learn the 'science and art of mining' and begin to climb the ladder that could take us to the top as a colliery manager. I joined this class soon after I started work. I was not one of the tutor's prize pupils. I was good at reading and writing but never at reckoning, and the boy who could not reckon would never become a manager. When at eighteen years of age I joined the I.L.P. the pamphlets introduced me to the world of industrial history and economics. One of our members had heard of the W.E.A. and succeeded in securing a class for us with one of their tutors, William King, to guide us through the mysteries of political economy with Henry Clay's *Economics for the General Reader* as our textbook. We were set the task of writing an essay each month. The tutor told me that he had been impressed by my essays and encouraged me to join the correspondence course provided by Ruskin College. I began to dream of the day when I would become a residential student at Ruskin. Then came the row at Ruskin, the founding of the Labour college and the textbooks changed from Clay to Marx. When the Labour college reopened after the war, the South Wales Miners' Union offered a number of scholarships for a two-year residential course. By this time I was married and it seemed as if my dream of college would never come true. But my wife was determined that I should sit for the exam and, if I won a scholarship, she would come to London with me and find her own livelihood. So it was that on a September day in 1919 I made my way to the mansion in Earl's Court which was the 'college', my wife found digs in the same neighbourhood, and a job at Bayswater with Davis the cleaners, and life began anew. When we assembled on that first day there were forty of us—all in our twenties, with years of work at mine, mill and railway behind us and two years of lectures, books, arguments and fellowship in store. There was a strong contingent from the valleys—Nye Bevan, Ness Edwards, Bill Coldrick and two Williamses who were later to be my colleagues in Parliament.

The founder-principal Dennis Hird was, by then, an old and ailing man, and his place was taken by one of his former pupils, W. W. Craik. W. H. Mainwaring, one of the authors of *The Miners' Next Step,* was our tutor in economics (Marxist), and a venerable old gentleman who had been a don at Oxford was to labour hard trying to persuade us to add another language to those we learnt at school. The curriculum was designed to equip us for the stern battle ahead—industrial history, economics, trade union law and practice, to which was added a course in philosophy as set out in the *Positive Outcome of Philosophy* by a German Marxist, Joseph Dietzgen. All of it hard stuff at which we laboured with varying degrees of success. Fortunately our life was made easier, and enriched, by the visiting tutors H. N. Brailsford and J. F. Horrabin (J.F.H. of the *Daily News* maps). J.F.H. not only instructed us by his courses on economic geography and English literature but turned us into actors to perform Shaw's *The Shewing Up of Blanco Posnet.* There were two other visitors who, in different ways, added to our pleasure. There was J. T. Walton Newbold (later to be the first Communist M.P.), and there was Clara Dunn, who would come once a week to instruct us in the art of public speaking. She deserves a niche in the story of those days—because she helped Nye Bevan to overcome his stutter and so gave us one of the great orators of our age. We owe much to our tutors and visiting lecturers, but most of all, I think, we are indebted to the extramural activities. There were the endless arguments by night and by day, the weekly debates, the open-air meetings in the parks and street corners at which we would often be brought down by the wit of the cockney, and the classes, which, after our first year, we were deemed to be qualified to serve as tutors. I was privileged to take three such classes, at Battersea, Luton and Mitcham. Those were the days of the great rallies at the Albert Hall, and we were there. There was the memorable afternoon when Frank Horrabin took us to see, and hear, Sybil Thorndike in *The Trojan Women.* For me there were also extras in the company of my wife. Saturday evenings at the theatre, in the great days at the Hammersmith Lyric to see Drinkwater's *Abraham Lincoln,* and Henry Ainley and Meggie Albenezi in Tolstoy's *Resurrection* at the Court; the Sunday evenings at Kings Weigh House to hear Dr Orchard— and on to Marble Arch to enjoy the double programme of the 'orators' and the singing of the Welsh exiles. Two years away from the 'hooter', free from hard toil, surrounded by books, engrossed in argument—and sharing the riches of life in the big city. The two years sped on and it was time to go home—back to the mine, the union, evening classes and politics. The apprenticeship was over. We were ready for the future.

3

MINERS' LEADER

I

THOSE were the days when coal was king and the valleys were the throne. For beneath the rugged mountains there was coal in abundance—steam coal for the navy, coking coal for the furnaces and anthracite for the hearth. And as the cry went out for coal and still more coal, the roads to the valleys were crowded with men in search of work, wages and 'life'. They came from the countryside in the north and west of the principality and the shires across the Severn. As they came they brought with them their way of life—the chapel and the choir; the Rechabite 'tent' and the pub; the rugger ball and the boxing booth—all mixed up together. And as they settled in the valleys the cottages climbed ever higher up the mountainside until the mining village looked like a giant grandstand. The life of the collier was hard and brittle. The day's toil was long and perilous. Every day someone would be maimed—and every year some valley would experience the agony of an explosion. Yet in spite of it all or, perhaps, because of it all, the men and women who came to the valley created a community throbbing with life. Thrown together in the narrow valley, cut off from the world outside, they clung together fiercely, sharing the fellowship of common danger. Life in the valleys has a magic all its own, and to us who grew up in the glow of its fires there comes a nostalgic longing—*hiraeth* as we say in our mother language—for the fellowship of long ago. Listen to us singing—and you will understand.

Transplanted from the quiet of the countryside into the turbulent world of industry, the worker needed a defence against the harsh realities of his new life and found it in the union—the 'Fed', as the South Wales Miners' Federation was called. The federation was not only a trade union; it was an all-embracing institution in the mining community. In the pits it kept daily watch over the conditions of work, protecting the men from the perils of the mine, caring for the maimed and the bereaved, and providing the community with its libraries and bands and hospitals and everything which helped to make life bearable and joyous. In the work and in the life of the community, the federation was the servant of all. When I was elected Miners' Agent to the Anthracite Miners' Association in 1925 my old chief John James called me to his 'den', the room in his house which was his office, and charged me to remember that 'people will come to you when they are in trouble. They will need your help and it will be your privilege to help them if you can. Remember always that what they will want most of all will be to share their trouble with you—so listen to their story patiently to the end; this will be the greatest service you can render them'. I have always tried to remember this advice.

I was responsible for the work of the union in twenty-nine collieries. Each day would bring its varied tasks: the settlement of piece-work rates for each seam of coal; the handling of disputes over allowances for 'abnormal conditions'; seeking the reinstatement of a man who was sacked; and ensuring that those maimed or bereaved by accident or disease received the meagre compensation to which the law entitled them. The word 'compo' is written in blood in the annals of the miners.

Strange as it may now seem, there was not at that time even the meagre 'compo' for the dreaded silicosis or its ugly twin pneumoconiosis. During the hours the miner spends underground he breathes polluted air—a frightful mixture of coal- and rock-dust together with the fumes of the explosives used to blast the coal and rock. Even the machines which now relieve the miner of some back-breaking tasks add to the peril as they churn up clouds of dust. When in 1928 silicosis was scheduled as an industrial disease the regulations were stupidly restrictive. Even when the medical board certified the workman to be disabled by the disease, he could claim compensation only if he could prove that he had been engaged at some time in drilling or handling rock containing 50 per cent of free silica. When a claim was disputed on these grounds I would visit the mine, accompanied by the pit leader, in search of silica rock. As the disease generally takes many years to develop to the disabling stage, the search sometimes involved more than one colliery, and would often mean a risky job in visiting abandoned workings. One day at the end of a long search, with only one more old working to explore, the colliery manager who was with us refused to venture into the abandoned workings because it was 'too dangerous'. My comrade said to me: 'Let's risk it.' We scrambled over the fallen rock, and when we reached the coal-face my companion turned to me and, holding a piece of rock with the quartz shining in the light of our colliers' lamps, whispered: 'I brought it with me.' We fought our way back and showed our discovery to the manager. He looked at it and asked, 'Did you really find this in these old workings?', and as we both said 'Yes' he winked and said: 'I will believe you.' The workman got his compo—and I pray that my good companion will have been forgiven the 'white' lie. He will be happy in the knowledge that the 50 per cent stupidity has been banished and that there is now no call upon any of our successors to risk their lives to ensure that the silicotic miner gets compensation.

In my days the miners' agent was a member of the executive council of the South Wales Miners' Federation by virtue of his office. At the first meeting I attended the crisis of 1926 loomed ahead. In the reports we gave to our colleagues every miners' agent had the same story to tell. The miners everywhere were in a bitter mood. They had never forgotten their betrayal in 1919 when the Sankey Commission's recommendation that the industry should be nationalized was rejected; they had fought like Trojans for three long months in 1921, only to be further burdened with the 'ascertainments system'[1] which held down their wages. In the summer of 1925 they had been saved only by the solidarity of their comrades—and the threat of a general strike. Now they heard of the preparations being made by the Baldwin Government to resist the trade unions when next they threatened a general strike. They were resolved to fight rather than give in. 'Not a penny off the pay—not a minute on the day.' That was the deep resolve of the miners in the early days of 1926. It was a grim baptism for a beginner as I joined my colleagues on the first of many journeys to London for our Miners' National Conference.

[1] *See* pages 39–40.

The story of 1926 has been told and retold a thousand times. To those of us who lived through those nine days of the General Strike the memory of the fellowship they kindled is precious. It was the finest manifestation of working-class solidarity in our history, a quiet revolution true to the character of our nation.

There was little or no violence; the strikers played rugger with the police in the valleys. The local organization improvised to conduct the strike was a revelation of the resources and the quality of democratic leadership within our ranks. Everyone felt that the miners had a just cause, that they were fighting the battle of every worker in the land, and realized that if the miners went down all would be defeated. What a tragedy it was that it ended as it did—with the T.U.C. calling off the General Strike and the miners left alone to face the cruel ordeal of long months of struggle. The argument as to who—or what—went wrong in those fateful hours before 12th May has been going on ever since and will go on for very many years yet.

In company with my Welsh colleagues I had left the headquarters of the Miners' Federation of Great Britain in London as soon as the General Strike had been called. Back at our posts in the valleys we were virtually cut off from communication with London. When the news came that the General Strike was called off but that the miners would stay out we were confused and angry. The next day my fellow miners' agent and I made our way to the Miners' Conference to hear the report of our leaders—Herbert Smith and Arthur Cook—on what had happened. We were told that in the last days of the General Strike the T.U.C. negotiating committee had accepted the offer of Sir Herbert Samuel—who had presided over the Royal Commission on the Coal Industry set up by Baldwin in 1925—to act as a liaison with the Government and to seek a settlement of the miners' dispute. Herbert Smith told us, in his own words: 'If anything was happening at Eccleston Square [the T.U.C. headquarters] we were not in it. We knew nothing of a definite character until 9th May. It then came out that there had been meetings with Herbert Samuel. We knew him well and did not want further dealings with him. The miners had had plenty of Herbert Samuel.'

So one of the most glorious episodes in the history of British trade unionism was to end in mutual distrust and bitterness which left scars that have not been fully healed even to our day.

We returned to our men in the valleys. In the anthracite coal-field we called our pit delegates to prepare our plans for the struggle which lay ahead. We had but a few hundred pounds in the kitty. We could not meet one week's strike pay. We sat down to consider how best to use what little we had to help sustain our men and their families. The children would be given a midday meal at school, the wives could get relief on loan from the guardians; the Co-op and the tradesmen promised credit to the limit of their resources. We decided to set up kitchens in the miners' halls and use our money to provide one meal a day for the miners and the womenfolk. The miners love their gardens and each one promised to bring his vegetables to the kitchen, the women would cook and serve, and even the poachers promised to devote their harvest of salmon and rabbits to the feast! When our money began to run out help from outside came along. Dr Marion Phillips organized women's committees all over the land to collect for the miners' cause, and the Russians earned the enduring gratitude of the miners by coming to our aid. The male voice choirs toured the land and helped to replenish the coffers. The kitchens stayed open through the long months of struggle and there was not one day without a meal at the miners' hall. If, to the miner in the valleys, the *world* seemed to be against him, the *weather* was on his side through those glorious days of sunshine and luminous evenings of the summer of 1926. Someone dis-covered the 'gazoot', a kind of trumpet, and overnight carnival bands, arrayed in all the colours of the rainbow, appeared on the scene to take part in the competitions which were destined to become a colourful feature of life in the valleys for many years. If the debts accumulated as the months went by, there were also the gains. I remember an aged miner saying to me towards the end of the struggle: 'I have counted that on the average rate of accidents in the mine, the strike has saved nearly a thousand men from an early death and scores of thousands from disease and mutilation.'

When the summer was over and the leaves began to fall the prospects became bleaker and the strain began to tell. We heard that nearly forty thousand had gone back to work in the mid-lands coalfield and that a man named Spencer had formed a break-away union. Even in South Wales seven hundred had capitulated and we heard with consternation that one pit in the anthracite field had been opened with blackleg labour. When winter came we had to give in—and return to work on the owners' terms. Alas, not all who came out could go back, for the managers took it out of the activists!

When we appealed to the coal owners to reinstate the men they had victimized our appeal fell on deaf ears. It was beyond them to be generous even in their hour of triumph.

3

When the 1926 conflict began I was a young apprentice beginning to learn my craft. Into the seven months of struggle and endurance had been crowded a lifetime of experience which was to have a profound effect upon my attitude to my work and responsibilities. My pride in our men had been deepened and strengthened. Their loyalty had been magnificent. They had answered every call. They had endured months of privation. Their savings had been exhausted and the future mortgaged with debts to the local traders and the boards of guardians, and at the end of it all they had to return to work for longer hours and lower wages and under conditions imposed by their hard taskmasters.

It was a terrible price to pay. There must be a better way than this, I was sure, to win for these brave men the security and living standards their toil and sacrifice deserved. To find this new way I felt was my responsibility as their leader. I had emerged from the testing time of the struggle with my prestige enhanced and my influence strengthened. I had shared with the men the ordeal of battle. Like theirs, my savings were exhausted and the future mortgaged. My wife had joined the womenfolk of the valley in their part in the struggle. Our home had become the 'surgery' where the maimed and afflicted came for help and sympathy. The miners looked to me for guidance and leadership, and I was resolved to give of my best in their service.

During the strike I had formed firm friendships with the miners' leaders, in South Wales and the other coalfields, who were of my generation. Throughout the long months of the struggle, when we had been 'back-benchers' in the union, we had spent many hours exchanging views and formulating plans for the day after the battle. In these discussions we were often joined by Vernon Hartshorn. He had a clearer view and sounder assessment of the problems confronting the coal-mining industry than any of the other leaders. The home demand for coal was bound to decline. The first great rival to coal, oil, was already displacing it from many industries; more efficient systems were reducing the amount of coal required in industries like that of steel; and the domestic coal fire was giving way to gas and electricity.

The export trade had been lost in the 1914–1918 war, and the new states established by the Versailles Treaty, such as Poland, were subsidizing their exports and keeping us out of former markets. The British coal industry was faced with the powerful challenge of rival sources of fuel and power and had entered upon a transition stage from a 'one-fuel' to a 'multiple-fuel' economy. These changes, coupled with our knowledge and experience of the coal owners, strengthened our conviction that it was only by and through public ownership that the industry would be able to adjust itself to the new situation. For the time being our hope of public ownership had been defeated by the rejection of the Sankey Commission's recommendations. Even the Samuel Commission's recommendations for the rationalization of the industry under private ownership had been cast aside by the owners after their victory, and we could not look to the Baldwin Government for any constructive approach to the industry's problems. The coal owners had only one solution to offer, lower wages and longer hours with lower prices, as the means of winning back the markets coal had lost at home and overseas.

When in the early months of 1927 the Miners' National Conference assembled to review the situation, following the return to work, the delegates from each coalfield had the same sad story to tell. Pits were closing, thousands of our men were on the road, those at work were feeling the lash of the triumphant coal owners, the stalwart union men had been victimized and the membership of the union had slumped disastrously.

We joined in a message to our members and to the country:

> The fight is not over. The conditions imposed by the owners cannot bring goodwill or the spirit of conciliation. Longer hours and lower wages cannot bring peace to the coalfields; nor will district agreements be allowed to shatter our strength and unity. Our organization is still intact and we are determined to recover the ground that has been lost.

To recover the ground that has been lost! We returned to our task to build again with worn-out tools. As we journeyed home my colleagues and I realized that the struggle to recover lost ground must lead to a search for other ways than that of subjecting our men to the burden and tragedy of conflict. And in this task we realized that we would need the assistance of our fellow trade unionists and the restoration of the unity which had been lost in those bitter days of May 1926. The air was still poisoned by recriminations. It would not be easy to overcome the feeling of bitterness which still prevailed.

It was with the resolve to restore the trust between the Miners' Union and the Trades Union Congress, and so to secure the help of our fellows in finding new ways to solve the coal industry's problems, that we went back to work in our union.

One of the leaders most anxious to heal the wounds of 1926 was the general secretary of the South Wales Miners' Federation, Tom Richards, who had been elected one of the miners' representatives on the T.U.C. General Council. One day in the early thirties he asked me to see him at his office in Cardiff. He began by telling me how anxious he was that the old wounds of 1926, which still festered and poisoned the relationship between the Miners' Union and the other unions, should be healed. And, to my surprise, he told me that he believed I could help and urged me to apply for the post then vacant of assistant secretary to Congress. I accepted his advice and in due time was notified that I was one of six on the short list, to be interviewed by the General Council. This was the first time I had entered the sanctuary of Transport House and it was all rather overwhelming.

I was not successful and the choice fell upon Vincent Tewson. However, the lodges of the federation began to press me to stand for the vice-presidency, and at the annual conference in 1932 I was elected to that office. At forty-two years of age I was, up to that time, one of the youngest ever to be elected to the post. The old guard who had served the federation from its formation in 1898 had almost all passed away. One of the few who remained was Enoch Morrell, who was then president.

It was a wonderful experience to work under him and when two years later he retired I was elected president by the unanimous vote of our conference. It was a great honour to be elected president of the South Wales Miners' Federation and to follow the old stalwarts who had occupied the chair—William Abrahom (better known under his bardic name of Mabon) the first Welsh miner to enter Parliament; William Brace, Vernon Hartshorn, James Winstone and Enoch Morrell. It was also a tremendous responsibility to lead the union when it was fighting for survival. I was immensely pleased when the conference elected my close friend Arthur Jenkins as vice-president. We had both been students at the Labour college, and in temperament and outlook we supplemented and complemented each other. At our side was the general secretary, Oliver Harris, to remind us of our limitations as well as our opportunities.

Within a month of my being elected president I called a special conference of the federation to set before our members the two immediate tasks upon which our energies were to be concentrated.

First, to rid the coalfield of the bogus Spencer Union and to win 100 per cent membership throughout the coalfield.

Second, to mobilize all our forces in an endeavour to raise the wages of our men from the scandalously low level to which they had fallen after 1926.

When I became president in 1934 there were 140,000 miners at work in the South Wales coalfield but only 76,000 were members of the federation. Our funds were almost exhausted. We had 20,000 unemployed members who paid a contribution of 1d. a week and for this we provided a complete service to them, including the heavy legal costs of fighting their compensation cases. The conference pledged itself to work for 100 per cent membership at all the pits and endorsed our plan to drive out the Spencer Union. I had decided upon the bold plan of attacking the rival union at the Taff Merthyr Colliery, in East Glamorgan, where membership of that union was a condition of employment, written into the contract the men were compelled to sign on starting work. Our plan was to recruit members to the federation at the colliery, then advise them to inform the management that they were withdrawing their consent to the contributions to the Spencer Union being deducted from their wages. If they were dismissed thereafter we would protect them. Our first step was to find if there was any recourse to the courts which we could invoke. I went to London to consult Mr Upjohn, who had been the friend and counsellor of all my predecessors. This was the first time I had met him, but I had been told what to expect—an eagle-eyed man with a sharp tongue who would treat me as a hostile witness.

I told him that what we contemplated was to sue the colliery company in the name of the first workman at Taff Merthyr to be sacked because he refused to allow deduction from his pay towards the Spencer Union, and seek an injunction on the ground that the closed shop agreement between the company and the rival union was contrary to the principle of natural justice. With that he turned to me and asked: 'What denomination do you belong to?' and on my replying, 'Congregationalist', he said: 'Look here, young man, suppose you sank a mine and decided that only Congregationalists would be employed at the mine. If you made that clear to them and they agreed to work for you on those conditions, then that would be within the laws of England. I want to help you, as I have helped all your predecessors since my dear friend Mabon. I agree that the contract you have described is wicked, but a lot of things are wicked without being illegal. You will have to find some other remedy—and if I know my Welsh miner you will find one. Goodbye and good luck.'

There was nothing for it but to put Plan No. 2 into operation with all its attendant risks! We set about to recruit members at Taff Merthyr Colliery. The management predictably sacked them as they joined—and I then appealed to our members all over South Wales to sign notices to terminate their contract with the coal owners, and to hold them until I made the call for action. The response to my appeal was immediate and overwhelming; the colliery company relented and in the end we secured an agreement that if we called off the threat of a strike and the men at Taff Merthyr returned to work the owners would agree to the men holding a secret ballot, under independent supervision, to decide which of the two unions they wanted. We had no fear of a ballot—the Welsh miner would never vote for a company union. The management at Taff Merthyr did their best to try to sabotage the settlement, and prevent the ballot being taken—but as it turned out the ballot became unnecessary for the miners found another way of getting rid of the Spencerites.

Miners are miners the world over, and one day the news reached South Wales that miners in Rumania had staged a novel strike by staying down the mine and refusing to come out until their demands were met. The unique character of this action, and its success, were hailed by us with delight. This was the answer to the problem of what to do to get rid of the Spencer Union—the 'non-pols', for it was when the federation men came out that they went down the mine: if we stayed down, they would stay out. Soon after the news from Rumania I was besieged by the leaders at the collieries where the 'non-pols' were entrenched for permission to emulate the example of our Rumanian comrades. This confronted me, and the executive council, with a dilemma. It was a breach of the Coal Mines Act to stay down the mine beyond the permitted hours. If we called upon our men to stay down we would be in breach of an Act of Parliament designed to protect our safety. To this some of the enthusiasts had an answer. 'You close your eyes—we will do it on our own.' They did just this at several collieries and, notably, at the Nine Mile Point colliery. The pit was situated in a glen, with the wooded hills rising steeply almost from the pit shaft. The colliery had been taken over by the Ocean Colliery Co., one of the sponsors of the Spencer Union. It was a strange alliance, for the general manager of the 'Ocean' was a leading nonconformist layman, W. P. Thomas. Like so many other Liberal traditionalists he had made friends with the ancient enemy, the Tories, and found new enemies in 'these Socialists'. When he heard that the miners at 'one of my' collieries had followed the example of the miners of Rumania he is said to have cried out: 'What are we coming to?'

The men at Nine Mile Point had been complaining to the manager for some time that those who belonged to the 'non-pols' had been favoured in the allocation of working places. A hundred of them decided to stage a 'stay-in' strike—and they stayed down for nine days. At first the management had refused permission to have food sent down to the strikers, but they soon yielded, and thereafter each day would witness a procession of wives and mothers to the pit-head bringing sandwiches and Welsh cakes and flasks of tea to sustain their husbands and sons. When I asked the manager to meet me to discuss the dispute, he at first refused, saying: 'Bring the men out, then I will meet you.' On the sixth day he relented, and when we met he at once said, 'The company have decided to close the colliery for a week or two and will undertake to meet you during that period and arrange with the federation for a resumption of work on terms to be agreed between us'—and not with the non-pols. I agreed to this offer and arranged that I would put it to the men, and recommend their acceptance. It was a fine Saturday morning when Arthur Jenkins and I made our way to the glen and when we reached the colliery thousands of men, women and children had assembled on the hillside, with hundreds of police to keep them company.

The scene at the pit bottom that day remains vivid in my memory. The nine days below had left their mark; the elderly looked weary—the young had grown beards. I was greeted by the 'patriarch' who had opened and closed each day with prayer, and in between had transformed the stay-down strikers into a choir. The leader escorted me to the platform—an upturned tub—and called for order. They listened to me intently as I explained the terms of the settlement, and plied me with questions. Then the leader announced that a vote would be taken for or against the acceptance of 'our president's recommendation'. 'Down with your lamps!' he cried. 'And now all in favour, lift your lamp up and hold it while I count.' It was one of the proudest moments of my life when every lamp was raised. We sang 'Bread of Heaven'. This was the bread they could not deny us. Then, in good order, the older men first, they ascended the shaft to the sunshine and home.

This was the beginning of the end of the Spencer Union in Wales. As one old miner told me that day, 'I was sure from the start that there was no abiding city for "them" in Wales.'

The miners have long memories. There are those who would say that memories of past injustices have been the curse of the industry, and there is some truth in this. But—fair play for the miner—he has a lot to remember. And there is one name that the Welsh miner remembers with bitterness and scorn, the name of Schiller. This is the story of Schiller. In 1930, Ramsay Mac-Donald's second Labour Government passed an Act of Parliament which provided for the reduction of the hours of work from eight to seven and a half. The coal owners insisted that there should be a corresponding reduction in wages. In South Wales the union refused the owners' proposals and, in accordance with the Conciliation Board agreement, the dispute was referred to a single arbitrator, and someone in authority at Westminster appointed Mr F. P. M. Schiller, K.C. We had never heard of him before and have never forgotten him since. On 6th March 1931 he made his award. He reduced the minimum percentage from 28 per cent to 20 per cent. This was bad enough, but it was his award on the rate of the subsistence wage which made his name a byword in the valleys. It was scandalously low before he came—7s. 10½d. for a day-wage man twenty-one years of age and over. He awarded a 'differential' subsistence wage of 7s. 6d. for a married man with children; 7s. 3d. for a married man without children and 7s. for the single man. Mr Schiller justified his award on the basis of the financial position of the industry in South Wales as revealed in the 'ascertainments', another word which evokes memories. In 1921 when the Government handed back the industry to the coal owners they immediately demanded a reduction in wages. The miners refused to budge and there followed the three months' national strike. When the strike was settled a new system was devised to determine the percentage to be added to the basic rates—piece-work and day-wage rates.

It was a complicated system; a full statement of its detailed provisions would take a score of pages. Its essential features can be summarized as follows.

It provided that the owners in each district, like South Wales, would submit each quarter an account showing on one side the proceeds from the sale of the coal, and on the other the total cost at the pit-head of producing a ton of coal. These accounts, for each colliery separately, would then be examined by two sets of auditors, one for each side, and they would then add up all the figures to present the ascertained results of the finances of the coalfield for each quarter. If these showed a surplus this would be divided as to 85 per cent to be devoted to increase wages and 15 per cent to add to the owners' profits. If there was a deficit this would be carried forward to the next quarter's account. When the ascertainment system was adopted it was hailed by some of the bright economists as a great discovery and by the profit-sharing devotees as a new dispensation. Introduced to an industry already on the slide down, it proved to be a calamitous innovation. It was the root cause of the 1926 strike and provided Schiller, with his lawyer's logic, a justification for his infamous award. The 1931 agreement under which the Schiller award was made expired in the first year of my presidency and I made up my mind to terminate it and to seek a new agreement. I was determined to destroy the 'ascertainment system' and to refuse to submit the wages of our men to the dictates of a single arbitrator. Having won the battle with the Spencer Union and increased our membership by more than twenty thousand, I felt confident that we could, if it became necessary, call our men out. We put forward demands for a new agreement with increases in the minimum percentage and the subsistence wage and, in addition, for a re-examination of the ascertainments system.

We submitted our case on the ground that this system was based on a false premise that the money received by the owners at the pit-head was a true criterion of what the owners received for the coal our men produced. By this time the entire coalfield was owned by a few large companies; one of them, the Powell Duffryn Co., controlled more than a third of the total output. These big combines had taken over the coal salesmen at the ports and by pocketing the distributors' profits were able to show a loss at the pit-head and a profit in their balance sheets. Having given notice to terminate the 1931 agreement, we had a dozen meetings with the owners, only to be met with the same answer —no. We took our case to the national board set up by the Labour Government, but the owners refused to attend. When we declared our intention to strike, the new Minister of Mines— Ernest Brown—intervened, and at the eleventh hour we reached a settlement to refer the dispute to a board of three arbitrators, with the proviso that the board would examine and pronounce upon our case for the revision of the ascertainments system. The board awarded us an increase of 2½ per cent in the minimum percentage and fixed the subsistence wage at 7s. 8d. a day. Modest as it was, it abolished the insulting differentials of the Schiller award. Small as it was, the increase in wages was hailed with delight by the miners. It was the first increase in wages they had won in ten years. And even more than the increase in wages we rejoiced that the board of arbitrators had pronounced in our favour on the ascertainments system when they declared:

> The figures obtainable from the ascertainment tables in their present form do not give any complete picture of the profits and losses in the coalfield under the conditions which now prevail, and we were glad to hear from both sides of a willingness to reconsider the form of these returns in the light of modern circumstances.

This pronouncement was of importance to every coalfield in the country, since every district had been bound to the ascertainment system since 1921. As president of the South Wales miners I was a member of the national executive of the national union; and I collaborated with the new president, Joseph Jones of Yorkshire, and the general secretary Ebby Edwards, who had brought his rich Geordie dialect and Northumbrian shrewdness to our counsels.

We decided to launch a public campaign for an increase of two bob a day for all the miners of Britain. We knew that no purpose would be served by appealing to the coal owners and that an appeal to the Baldwin Government would be in vain. We resolved to take our case to the public. In the autumn of that year the whole nation had been deeply disturbed by the explosion at the Gresford Colliery. The pit had to be closed and over two hundred miners left in an underground grave. When I visited the colliery the day following the explosion an old miner told me that many of the entombed miners had 'risen their pay' before they went down the mine that day and he said, sadly and bitterly, 'There will be few pay packets down there with more than £2 in them.' The revelation at the inquiry, at which the union was represented by Stafford Cripps and D. R. Grenfell, had created the uneasy feeling that the poverty of the miners was driving them to neglect the safety rules for fear of losing their jobs. The public were responsive to any move to help the miners, and our two-bob campaign met with the warm support of every section of the community except the owners and the Government. The owners went on saying 'no' and the Government passed by on the other side. Then a strange thing happened. Some of the industrialists who were large consumers of coal had been conscience-stricken by our revelations of the low wages paid to the men who risked their lives to provide the fuel and energy for their industry. They made a public declaration that they would be prepared to pay more for the coal they bought provided that the increase was used entirely to improve the miners' wages. Their example was emulated by a large number of private firms and public bodies. This shamed the owners, and even the Government felt moved to act by persuading the owners to meet the union and to offer an increase. In South Wales we secured another increase of 2½ per cent in the minimum percentage and raised the subsistence wage to 8s. 1d. a day—the highest it had been since 1924.

Back in my home in the valley I reflected on the work attempted and the progress achieved in the attainment of the two objectives I had set when I became president eighteen months before. The membership of the federation was nearing 100 per cent—the rival union was in full retreat and on the way out; we had secured two wage increases, and now saw the restoration of the men's confidence in the union. We had turned the tide for the men who were at work in the mine—but in our jubilation we were disturbed by the increasing number of our comrades on the road—workless, unwanted and almost forgotten. Then in 1935 the Tory Government instituted the 'household means test' and set the whole of Wales aflame.

4

For every two men at work in the mines there was one on the road. Many of those without work had been idle for five and some even for ten years. They would gather together in the village squares and mourn their lot, condemned to live out the rest of their lives in poverty and despair. They had long ago exhausted their right to unemployment benefit and were wholly dependent on public assistance. Even this was in danger of running out as the rate burden soared. In Merthyr Tydfil the rate required for public assistance alone was twenty shillings in the pound of rateable value—and the rateable value was going down with the closing of the collieries and with empty shops and deserted houses. If the burden of the unemployed failed to move the Government, they became alarmed at the burden of the rates. They decided to transfer the responsibility for assistance to the unemployed from the local authorities to the state. They set up an Unemployment Assistance Board to determine the rate of assistance and the conditions to govern its payment. The board was composed of eminent people, men and women whose names were known for their service to the state, with experienced civil servants to guide them. But—none of them had ever been unemployed. This was something beyond their experience. The board submitted scales of assistance, based on a 'household means test', to the Minister of Labour, Oliver Stanley: he in turn submitted them for the approval of Parliament. The Labour Members—and notably the Members from the mining areas—warned the Government of the consequences, but the scales were approved by the Tory majority.

When they were applied they evoked a storm of protest in South Wales. To give an example of how they affected our unemployed and their families (and it is by no means the worst case), that of a household consisting of a father, mother and one unemployed son. The father working at the coal-mine would have taken home wages of £2 4s. 0d. a week, while the son was receiving public assistance of 17s. 0d. per week. Under the regulations the father's wages of 44s. a week were regarded as a sufficient income for the family and in consequence the son's assistance was cut off altogether. There were many families in which the position was reversed—the son at work and the father's assistance cut off, leaving the father dependent for every penny upon his son. Of the 160,000 unemployed in South Wales at the time, 100,000 of them had exhausted their benefit and were subject to the inquisition and indignity of this household means test. When the full implications of the new regulations became clear there was a storm of protest. Ministers of religion denounced them from the pulpit; local authorities of all political alignments called for their withdrawal; and chambers of trade joined with trade unions in attacking the mean scales which would further deepen the poverty to which the people of the valleys had been condemned for a decade.

I felt that this universal condemnation should be canalized into joint action by every section of the community, and the union agreed to my proposal to convene a Welsh national conference at Cardiff. I have taken part in many conferences in our capital city, but the conference to protest against the means test in 1935 stands out in my memory. It was more akin to a religious gathering than a conference. The singing was even more expressive of our feeling than the speeches. The conference decided to send a deputation to London forthwith to meet the Minister of Labour. I was asked to lead the deputation, and in company with Mrs Rose Davies, one of the most respected women in our public life, to put our case to the minister. Oliver Stanley agreed to meet us within a few days of the conference. We decided to place before him a factual account of the effect of the new scales and regulations upon the unemployed and their families. He turned to the officers at his side and asked if they could dispute the accuracy of the facts in the cases we had cited, and was told that they could not—they were all strictly in accordance with the regulations. Then turning to me he thanked us for coming to see him and for stating our case so clearly. 'I will go into the whole matter immediately,' he said with a voice full of emotion, and, brushing his brief aside, walked out of the room.

The campaign against the household means test was the last I was to lead as president of the South Wales Miners' Federation. I was proud that, once again, the miners' union had spoken for the people of Wales.

Within a few months of that deputation being received by

Oliver Stanley, he had left the Ministry of Labour, to be succeeded by Ernest Brown; and when the new minister came to submit revised regulations to Parliament I had taken my seat as the Member for Llanelli.

5

Politics were in my blood. In my I.L.P. days trade union work had been an extension of political activity from the hustings to the colliery lodge. To win the miners for the Labour Party, to canvas for the new leaders who were my comrades in the I.L.P., to work for the public ownership of the industry, these were the objectives we sought to attain.

I had been a political agent before I became a miners' agent. During the ten years in which I served as a trade union officer I found time to do my share of work for the party. Ever since I joined the I.L.P. I had nurtured the ambition to become an M.P. When I gave up my post as agent to the Llanelli Constituency Labour Party I had promised my closest friends that when the opportunity came I would come back to stand as their candidate. However, when the opportunity did come in 1936, with the passing of Llanelli's Member, Dr J. H. Williams, it was to confront me with one of the most difficult decisions of my life. I was torn between the pull of politics and the deep satisfaction I was experiencing in my work as miners' leader. If it had been any other constituency than Llanelli my decision would have been different. The decision was all the more difficult because my wife was anxious for me to stay on in my work for the union. Thinking it all over I remembered that some of my predecessors as president of the South Wales miners had combined the presidency with membership of Parliament. I made up my mind to say 'yes' to Llanelli and at the same time offer to continue in my post as president.

At that time the post of president was not, as it subsequently became, a permanent full-time post. Like my predecessors I combined the presidency with the work of miners' agent, doing two jobs for one salary plus an honorarium of £50 a year. I placed the matter before the executive council and informed the members that I would accept whatever recommendation they decided to make to the coalfield conference, with whom the decision rested. The council considered the question in a frank and friendly atmosphere and finally resolved that the position of president could not adequately be filled by a Member of Parliament. The conference, after a debate during which generous tributes were paid to my service in the chair, accepted the recommendation.

Arthur Horner, the incorrigible rebel as he has described himself, was elected as my successor. As generally happens when rebels are appointed to positions of responsibility, Arthur proved himself a cautious leader, combining the roles of a skilful negotiator and a champion of moderate policies in the industrial field, whilst pursuing militant policies in the political sphere.

The ten years I spent in the service of the Welsh miners were some of the happiest of my life. For me the coal-miners are the salt of the earth. They are not angels—they would not be colliers if they were. They are like all the rest of the human race, a mixed bag of all sorts. As one of my old mates said when someone had referred to one of us as an odd fellow: 'We must have some odd fellows or we shan't have all sorts.'

There is something distinctive in the character of the man who goes down the mine. Each day as he tears away another layer of coal he ventures into the unknown, a pioneer every day of his life. This makes him an adventurer at work and at play, an individualist who is not self-centred, a man who knows that his every act involves the safety of his mates. His loyalties are fierce and his hatreds intense. Everyone is either 'one of us' or 'one of them'. If you are 'one of us' you will be enveloped in the warm friendship of comrades; if 'one of them' you will be for ever outside the pale.

The collier expects a great deal from the man he entrusts with the leadership of the union, and woe betide the leader who is unfaithful to his trust. He can understand and bear with a leader's human frailties; some of the best-loved leaders have had more than their share of human weaknesses. What will not be forgiven is swollen head: *'Who does he think he is?'* Yet he expects his leader to be someone he can look up to—without the leader looking down at him! It's a stiff test, yet if the leader comes out with credit the rewards in esteem and affection are rich beyond measure.

I believe that I just passed the test. I know that I have been rewarded with precious friendships and with memories that will abide to the end of life.

4

MEMBER FOR LLANELLI

I

LLANELLI. There is magic in the name. It is the symbol of all that is most precious in our Welsh way of life: the deep-rooted love of our native heath, and the intimate and warm-hearted fellowship of community life; the colourful Welsh vernacular with its bibilical 'thee' and 'thou'; the love of music which makes it the natural home of the *Eisteddfod*, and the oratorio, and the pride in the choir and its conductors from R. C. Jenkins to John Thomas; the tradition of pulpit oratory from Dafydd Rees, Capel Als to Jubilee Young, of Zion; the classic slopes of Stradey where the giants of rugger from Harry Bowen to Albert Jenkins, inspired by the strains of *Sospan Fach*, have conquered the invaders from the Maoris to the Wallabies; the radical spirit which has been inscribed in its civic motto *Ymlean Llanelli* ('Forward, Llanelli'); this is the village by the sea which grew to be an industrial town without losing the virtues of the village.

The story of the growth of Llanelli from the village of five thousand people in 1821 to a town of forty thousand in 1941 is typical of the transformation wrought by the first industrial revolution. It began with the discovery of coal in the hills around and in the valleys whose rivers run into the bay of Carmarthen. There was coal in abundance, 'ring' coal for forge and furnace and anthracite for the hearth. Across the channel in Cornwall there was tin and copper, but no coal. So the industrial venturers from the Celtic fringe of the south-west of England came to Llanelli to build their furnaces and mills. Their names are woven into the history of the town and are commemorated in the names of its streets—Raby, Neville and Tregonning. They were followed by the makers of tinplate from the shires beyond the

46

Severn—Trubshaw, Richard Thomas and Baldwin. Llanelli became 'Tinopolis' and has survived all the changes from the Old Castle pack mill to Trostre's strip mill. It has had its good times and bad times. The Mackinley tariff which closed the doors of its best market for tinplate, the U.S.A., nearly ruined the town. Its sturdy workers—the rollermen, doublers and behinders— crossed the Atlantic to teach the Americans the mysteries of their craft. They even went to Russia, for was not Timoshenko the descendant of Timothy Jenkins? In their turn the Americans exported their strip mill to Llanelli. Llanelli shared the fate of the rest of South Wales in the thirties, and in the years of rebuilding has attracted, and welcomed, industrialists from England, Germany and Switzerland. In the century and a half of its growth, Llanelli has welcomed a host of people, and has absorbed them all into its way of life, and made them proud of its heritage. It remains today what it has ever been—the strong fortress of our language and traditions, and of our radicalism.

In the early years of the change a young man came from the rural hinterland of West Wales to minister to the dissenters at Capel Als. He came in 1829 and for the next forty years he was the unchallenged leader in the religious and political life of Llanelli, and became one of the famous generation of nonconformists who nourished the radical tradition which we have inherited. In the eighteen-forties the south-west was the battle-field of Wales' peasants' revolt, with the rise of the Sons of Rebecca against their oppressors. The historian David Williams, in his moving story of the 'Rebecca Riots', has related how David Rees became one of the leaders of the revolt even though he deplored violence plotted in the midnight meetings at Mynydd Sylen. *The Times* vehemently attacked the nonconformists in general and singled out David Rees for its wrath, accusing him of inciting the revolutionaries by preaching in Welsh from the text, 'And they blessed Rebekah and said unto her . . . let thy seed possess the gates of those which hate them.' The famous magazine *Blackwood's* described David Rees as 'an illiterate fanatic . . . a little Pope within his little circle of the great unwashed, who would benefit greatly from a sojourn in Newgate or Cold Bath Fields'; and a writer in another periodical described his writings in the journal he founded—*Y Diwygiwr* ('The Reformer')—as 'vile trash published by a preacher at Llanelly, a sort of little bishop in his dirty diocese of colliers and

47

coppermen'. David Rees was not the kind of man to be brow-beaten by the scribes or pharisees. He not only preached and wrote—he practised his radicalism at the coal-mines which he opened and the schools he founded. In 1842 when the members of the Royal Commission on the Employment of Children visited South Wales, David Rees gave evidence before them and, when asked what he would do with the children who entered the mines at seven years of age, he firmly replied that he would keep them in school until they were fifteen years of age—thus anticipating the 1944 Education Act by a century.

The trade union movement has deep roots in Llanelli, and the name of one of the pioneers—Tom Phillips ('*Twm Phil*' to his contemporaries)—is revered to this day. The new unionism of the eighteen-nineties spread to the town. Will Thorne came to organize the workers at the new gasworks, and Ben Tillett, finding that the men at work in the finishing departments of the tinplate mills were unorganized, enrolled them into membership of the Dockers' Union—the forerunner of today's Transport and General Workers' Union.

The railwaymen at Llanelli have always been the advance guard in trade unionism and politics, and have produced succes-sive generations of local leaders, as well as national leaders like Dick Squance, who became the General Secretary of A.S.L.E.F. The 1911 railway strike gave the town its martyrs when two young men were shot by the soldiers brought in after the reading of the Riot Act. The citizens of the town and its neighbourhood have maintained David Rees's passion for education. One of the first intermediate schools established after the passing of the Welsh Intermediate Act of 1899 was at Llanelli, and half a century later one of the first 'all-Welsh' schools was founded there. The adult education movements have received strong support in the town and the W.E.A. and the Labour college classes have trained successive generations of leaders for the trade union and Labour movements. When in 1917 the two mining valleys of the Amman and the Gwendraeth became linked with the town in the new parliamentary constituency of Llanelli there began for me the close association with the constituency which in turn I have served as Labour agent and Member for more than half my life, and with the town which has honoured me with the freedom of the borough.

2

When I returned from my two years' sojourn at the Labour college to work at the mine in 1921, I resumed my association with the Labour Party in the constituency. The splendid result we had achieved in the difficult circumstances of the 1918 election had encouraged us to hope that the next time victory would be ours. The party decided in 1922 to employ a full-time agent and I was appointed to the post. When I took up my new duties at the beginning of September 1922, the Lloyd George Coalition seemed to be firmly entrenched and likely to go its full five years' term. I estimated that I should have a full year in which to work at improving the organization, but no sooner had I installed myself in the rooms above a boot stores in the town's main shopping street than the famous Carlton Club meeting of the Tory Party, led by Bonar Law and Stanley Baldwin, threw Lloyd George overboard and plunged the country into a general election. Fortunately our candidate, Dr Williams, was ready to fight his fourth election campaign in eight years, and by this time his name was well known throughout the constituency.

From the moment we kicked off we sensed that the wind was in our favour. Our meetings—and we held a dozen every evening —were joyful rehearsals in preparation for the festival of the eve of the poll at the market hall in Llanelli. I have warm memories of those meetings in the market hall with its crowd of five thousand in serried ranks cheering us on to victory. The memory of the 1922 eve-of-poll meeting remains vivid in my recollections. We were living in the aftermath of the 1914–1918 war with the disappointed hopes of 'a world fit for heroes to live in'. There was a sickness to be cured and we had a doctor as our candidate. My brother, the bard 'Amanwy', came to our aid with a slogan, in Welsh, which I rendered into English as 'the doctor who cures man's ills will help to cure the world's ills'. And Wales and the world were ill in that year of 1922; the depression which was to engulf the valleys was already arousing fears, and the Graeco-Turkish War had revealed how precarious was the peace made at Versailles. These were the themes of that memorable eve-of-poll rally at the market hall. Tomorrow was to be a new day for Llanelli! When the result

J. H. Williams (Lab.):   22,213

G. Clark Williams (Lib.):   15,947

Majority :   6,266

was declared from the balcony of the town hall the immense crowd that filled the square cried with joy: 'We've won!' The cry echoed through the town and re-echoed through the valleys on that memorable day in November of 1922.

Our task was now to consolidate our hard-won victory, and to ensure this we had to have a voice in the local press. At that time there were no fewer than four weekly papers published at Llanelli, but what we needed was our own weekly, and the party's head office came to our aid. They started to turn out a four-page paper, two sides filled with national coverage and two sides blank to be used for local news and comment. We decided to make use of this service and the *Llanelli Labour News* was born, with myself as editor, manager and salesman. I gathered around me a team of young men as members of the staff and for a time the paper flourished and reached a circulation, at its peak, of nearly ten thousand. At the time of the anthracite strike of 1925 the *Labour News*, with its exposure of the machinations—financial and industrial—of the coal combines of Mond and Szarvasy, attracted national attention and was accused of being the fomenter of industrial strife and violence. The Anti-Socialist Union sent down its emissaries to the anthracite coalfield to investigate the causes of the strike and reported that they had discovered a revolutionary plot to overthrow the established order—and gave pride of place among the plotters to the *Labour News*, in a lurid document under the title of 'The Red Peril':

> The *Llanelli Labour News*, in my opinion, is the most influential socialist newspaper in South Wales. The *Llanelli Labour News*, which is run by the local Labour Party, took a prominent part in the stirring of class feeling. Its method of propaganda is to publish full details of the anthracite and other companies and of the profits taken from industry. As a result, every miner in the anthracite field—this is my personal experience—is familiar with the shareholders, the directors and the full financial history of the local combine. . . .

We naturally made the fullest use of this tribute from the enemy, and were proud to be described as the most influential

Socialist newspaper in South Wales. Our difficulty was to secure advertisements, and the *Labour News* survived for only three years. Even so it was of immense service to us at a time when we had to fight three elections in successive years, with the debt of the last one unpaid when the next one came along. The second of the three, in 1923, was not difficult; we held the seat with an increased majority. The real test came in 1924—the 'Red Letter' election.

I was fortunate in being able to secure a visit from the Prime Minister on the Saturday before the poll. I had first met, and heard, Ramsay MacDonald in 1912 at the national conference of the I.L.P. at Merthyr Tydfil. His handsome presence, deep baritone voice and Celtic lilt captured us completely. His courageous stand during the 1914 war had deepened our admiration for him —and we were all proud when he came to Wales to fight and win Aberavon.

In the 1924 election the constituency was covered with his photograph—this was our answer to our political foes, Tory and Liberal alike, who had conspired to defeat our Prime Minister, using the Campbell case [1] (as we were convinced) as an excuse, and now, on the very eve of the poll, forging the Zinoviev Letter. We would answer them when Ramsay came to the market hall. On the afternoon of that Saturday, when my office was besieged with visitors who had come from far and wide in search of tickets, a group of journalists arrived hot from London to report the Prime Minister's speech. They told me that they had been sent down to Llanelli in the belief that Ramsay would be making an important pronouncement on the 'Red Letter', and they asked me to arrange for them to meet him before he spoke to our meeting so that they could send their story in time for the Sunday newspapers. I told them that this was impossible, and showed them the Prime Minister's programme for the day with our meeting the last of a dozen gatherings he would be addressing. They took copies of the programme and set off to try to catch him on his journey. When the time arrived for the meeting to begin the hall was packed to suffocation and the street outside was crowded with people, many with tickets, who had failed to get in. When Ramsay arrived the vast audience inside—and outside—

[1] An intended prosecution for sedition of J. R. Campbell, acting editor of a Communist journal, was withdrawn, and the Government defeated on a motion for an inquiry.

joined in the singing of one of their favourite hymns—the bard Watcyn Wyn's vision of the day when every continent 'neath the firmament would hail the Nazarene. The address was in tune with the hymn—with peace on the horizon if only we had the courage to reach out. The crowd was thrilled and after the Prime Minister had gone on his triumphant way to Aberavon the streets rang with shouts and songs till the early hours of Sunday. When the crowds had dispersed and I was left alone in my office a knock came on the door, and in walked one of the journalists who, in a voice full of emotion, told me: 'I belong to the party and I came here feeling sure that Ramsay would announce that he had suspended the Foreign Office official, a man named Gregory, who had issued the "Red Letter" to the press and denounce the letter as a forgery. It's too late now,' he added; 'he's let us down!', and then left without telling me his name.

In the years to come, 1931 and after, that conversation with the unknown journalist was often recalled as, with sadness and sometimes with bitterness, we remembered the leader to whom we had vouchsafed our trust and whom we had saluted as our hero. The sadness and the bitterness have remained and coloured so many of the controversies which have divided and often threatened the life of our party. But on that Saturday evening in 1924 I was full of gratitude for the service Ramsay MacDonald had rendered us at Llanelli, faced with such a strong challenge to our fortress. In the event we beat off the challenge and held the fort though with a majority reduced to two thousand. That was the last time that our political opponents came anywhere near to defeating us—in the years ahead the story was to be of ever greater triumphs for Labour and of lost deposits for our foes.

When in 1925 I was appointed miners' agent my closest friends at Llanelli, while they cheered me on my way to a new career, made me promise that I would some day come back to succeed the doctor as the Member for Llanelli. And when, in 1936, Dr Williams died, they called me back and I answered the call.

A by-election is regarded by the faithful as an opportunity for hearing the 'big guns' of the parties, and the campaign brought many of our leaders to speak in my support. Among them was George Lansbury, who had but recently resigned from the leadership of the Parliamentary Party and with whom I had formed a close friendship in my days as president of the South

Wales Miners' Union. The campaign was a comparatively quiet affair; the result was regarded as a foregone conclusion, and the opposing candidate fought a remarkably clean fight. The election took place on 26th March 1936 with the following result:

James Griffiths (Lab.):	32,188
William A. Jenkins (Lib.-Nat.):	15,967
Majority:	*16,221*

This was the first of eight elections which I was to fight as Labour candidate for Llanelli and from this start with a two-to-one vote I was to be returned with overwhelming majorities in the years to come.

3

I had many times looked down upon our rulers from the dizzy heights of the Strangers' Gallery, but in the close-up view from the third seat above the gangway they looked very different, some larger and some not so large.

I had nervously made my way along the Government front bench as, having taken the oath and signed the book, I shook hands with Mr Speaker. When I had taken my seat I looked across at that bench. Deep in his seat behind the dispatch-box was the Prime Minister, Stanley Baldwin. He seemed to be always there, or roaming around the corridors. Some said that he should have been working in his room, working and not wandering around. One day he came into the library and spoke to me. He had heard that I had been president of the Welsh miners and asked if I knew the general manager of the Baldwin Coal Mines. When I told him that I did, and not long before had settled a dispute with him at one of the family's collieries, he chuckled: 'Very good.'

Alongside of him on the front bench were familiar figures whom I was to see much of in the years ahead, in their days of triumph and disaster. Sitting among them was my old political hero Ramsay MacDonald. I had not seen him for years, and he seemed but a ghost of the Ramsay I had cheered in bygone days. The handsome face was careworn and sad, the voice but a faint echo of the deep organ tones which once had thrilled me. He seemed out of place in that company.

Below me on the Opposition front bench were the colleagues with whom I was to work in the counsels of the party and Government, led by Clem Attlee, then at the beginning of his long reign as Labour's leader.

On the back benches I was surrounded by the old 'cloth-cap' M.P.s. They were good companions, those horny-handed sons of toil. I delighted in hearing them tell their life stories, each one a history book in itself. Will Thorne, who started his working life in a barber's shop at six years of age, and founded a trade union when he was thirty (the Municipal and General Workers'), had just completed thirty years as West Ham's Member. Billy Banfield, once an operative baker, had dedicated his life to the abolition of the 'slavery of night baking', and Jack Jones, of Silvertown, brought the vocabulary, and the grievances, of dockland to Westminster. Then there were my mates who had made the pilgrimage from pit to Parliament: sturdy, down-to-earth characters like Gordon Macdonald, and romantics like Jimmy Welsh, whose 'Songs of a Miner' expressed in poetry the joy and anguish of the miner's life. To make me feel at home there were my compatriots, down on the Opposition front bench George Hall and Dai Grenfell, and around me on the back benches my fellow students from the Labour college, Arthur Jenkins, Bill Mainwaring and Nye Bevan.

Nowadays the 'cloth cap' is giving way on the Labour benches to the 'cap and gown'. The Labour benches of the sixties are rich in academic talent, but those of the thirties were richer in the character moulded in life's struggles.

Life as a back-bencher had its frustrations as well as its thrills. As president of my union each day was filled with its multifarious tasks, every moment occupied by the calls on my services, and at the end of the day back to my home in the valley. My week's work now began with the long train journey on the Monday morning, leaving my wife to care alone for the family until my return on Friday. The salary of an M.P., £400 a year, supplemented by the £100 my union allowed to meet extra expenses, was not enough to run two homes. I had to find digs. Hotels and clubs were far beyond my means. I was lucky to find an old pal of my union days on the benches, Edward Dunn, Rother Valley, and he arranged for me to stay with him at a boarding house in Bloomsbury, sharing a room for five shillings per night, bed and breakfast. I soon got into the routine of the daily round. I would

Home and smithy, Betws village.

Betws colliery, where the author started his working life.

At the time of the stay-in strike at Nine-Mile Point Colliery, Monmouthshire, 1935. James Griffiths, then President of the South Wales Miners' Federation, with the Vice-President, Arthur Jenkins, and a local union officer.

Addressing a miners' demonstration in the Forest of Dean, 1936.

...nvassing tinplate millmen in the by-election of 1936, when the ...hor was first elected M.P. for Llanelli.

As Minister of National Insurance, with East End mothers collecting the first payments of family allowances in 1946.

At the home of a retired miner and his wife in County Durham, in 1948.

About to descend the shaft of the Great Mountain Colliery, Tumble, Llanelli, in 1948. The author is in the right-hand front seat in the leading wagon.

Launching the 1959 General Election series of television programmes. Left to right: Harold Wilson, Anthony Greenwood, Hugh Gaitskell, Aneurin Bevan, James Griffiths, Richard Crossman.

As Secretary of State for the Colonies, 1950. At a school in Singapore.

In Kenya, 1951. Saying goodbye to Mr Kenyatta, centre, and Mr Hamiti Watihuo.

At Accra, 1953, with Kwame Nkrumah, then Prime Minister, seated on author's left, and other members of the Ghana government.

With Hugh Gaitskell and Julius Nyerere, Prime Minister of Tanganyika, afterwards President of Tanzania, at the Labour Rally in 1957.

First Secretary of State for Wales, 1964.

set out from the digs as soon as breakfast was over, walking to Westminster when it was fine, and taking the twopenny tram ride, via the tunnel to the Embankment, when the weather was unkind.

On arrival at the House, the first call would be at the Members' post office to collect my mail, and then straight to the library to bag a place at one of the tables. The salary did not run to a secretary; my letters to constituents and, on their behalf, to ministers, were all my own work. The librarians then, as since, were always ready to help, and I was able to enjoy the riches of the bookshelves. The mornings were divided between letters and literature. The meals in the dining-room were too expensive but, fortunately, we could have snacks at 'Annie's Bar' in the Members' lobby, and other meals in the tea room. It was a day to be remembered when the Kitchen Committee provided a cheap high tea in the Members' dining-room at six o'clock; this was more like home. The sittings began in those days at 2.45 p.m., and I would be in my place for prayers. I confess that the attraction was to hear the chaplain, Canon Don. He had a deep bass voice, and it was a joy to hear him read the prayers. If he had been on the benches he could have been one of our best orators.

From the first day question time fascinated me, and it still retains its fascination. I soon joined the ranks of the regular questioners and in my second year was runner-up in the number of questions asked. The undisputed champion was Colonel Harry Day. Harry was by profession a theatrical impresario, and it was rumoured that he employed an expert to prepare his questions, three each day. As soon as his questions were answered Harry would be away to his theatres until the Whip brought him back to vote at ten. My first questions were directed to the Lord President of the Council, to whom I appealed to set up a medical research council investigation into silicosis. The Lord President of the time was Ramsay MacDonald, and he invited me to see him in his room in the House. He welcomed me cordially and listened eagerly as I told him of the ravages of silicosis in the South Wales coalfield. He promised to put my request, with his support, to the council, and in due time a team of experts, headed by Dr D'Arcy Hall, came down to Wales. From their report came the scheduling of pneumoconiosis as an industrial disease.

There were fewer committee meetings then than there are

now to take Members out of the Chamber as soon as question time was over. The benches were full for the debates. There were more impromptu and fewer set speeches than today. I admired those Members who could intervene in debate on the spur of the moment. On the Tory side the best was Lord Winterton, and on our side Chuter Ede and Billy Kelly of Rochdale. When they were in their places there would be no fear of the debate petering out.

Having served my apprenticeship at question time I now faced the ordeal of making my maiden speech.

I was, as is every new Member, overwhelmed by the conflicting advice tendered to me on when to launch into this important venture. Some counselled waiting a while, and others urged me to plunge in and get it over quickly, whilst everybody said: 'Don't let it worry you.' Being something of a worrying sort, I made up my mind to make it sooner rather than later. The occasion came in the debate when Neville Chamberlain introduced his fifth budget. He had given his budgets Dickensian names, beginning with 'Hard Times' and on to the fifth, 'Great Expectations'. Among the expectations which he held out was a Special Areas Reconstruction Association, a high-sounding title to which he had characteristically added 'Limited'. One million pounds was to be provided to enable the association to establish new industries in the Special Areas, with a proviso that not more than £100,000 was to be spent on any one project.

This proposal enabled me to make my maiden speech on a familiar theme—coal and tinplate. My speech had what is described as a 'good press' and the Chancellor, in winding up the debate, referred to it in generous terms:

> There was another speech, a rather remarkable maiden speech, which was made by the Member for Llanelli dealing with the Special Areas. I am sorry I did not have the advantage of hearing that speech, but I heard it exceedingly well spoken of as a vigorous and forceful presentation of a particular case.

The success of my first venture into parliamentary debates led to calls for my services from the constituencies, and so began the pilgrimages which over the years were to take me at week-ends and recesses to conferences and meetings all over the country. It also won for me the confidence of my colleagues, and within three years of my election to Parliament I was elected as one of

Labour's front-bench speakers. My election has an interest beyond that of my personal career. The General Election of 1931 had been disastrous for our party, reducing the number of Labour Members to fifty-two, and depriving the party of the services of many of our ablest speakers. The year 1935 had brought a modest recovery in our fortunes and increased our number to 136. Even so, we were short of Members with ministerial experience and Clem Attlee decided that our front bench needed new recruits. In these matters of parliamentary protocol precedent is all-important, and Clem Attlee found one to come to his aid. In the General Election of 1906 the Tories had suffered a crushing defeat and many of their former ministers had lost their seats. The leader, Arthur Balfour, anxious to improve the debating strength of his front bench, had secured the approval of the Speaker to bring on to it one of the rising Tory stars, F. E. Smith, who had made an outstanding maiden speech. Armed with this precedent, Clem Attlee secured approval of his proposal to bring twelve back-benchers to Labour's front bench. The press, sacrificing mathematical accuracy for a catch phrase, immediately christened the new team 'Labour's second eleven'. The new front-bench men were, in accordance with party custom, chosen by ballot and I was one of them. Commenting on the result of the ballot the *News Chronicle* said: 'Labour's front bench has notably gained by the inclusion of Mr James Griffiths, a Welshman who has already made his mark on the back benches as a thoughtful and fluent speaker. Mr Griffiths's promotion is rapid; he had been in the House for only two years.'

I was now confronted with the ordeal of a second maiden speech—this time from the dispatch-box. The test was all the more severe as I had to make the winding-up speech from our side. I had already been long enough in the House to realize that this was a difficult task for even the most experienced parliamentarian. In that last hour of a debate, especially when it is followed by a division as was the case that evening, the winding-up speeches have to be made against the background of noise from tramping feet and wagging tongues. More reputations have been destroyed than made in that hour.

Fortunately, as in my first maiden speech, this was also on familiar themes, unemployment and poverty in the distressed areas. My Labour colleagues were generous in their support, and my effort was voted a satisfactory beginning for a new recruit.

From this day, 23rd November 1938, I was to occupy a place on one or other of the front benches for more than twenty years, and it is interesting to recall that the minister who replied to me that evening—Alan Lennox-Boyd—was in later years to be my opposite number in debates on colonial affairs.

5

THE PACIFIST DILEMMA

WHEN I entered Parliament in 1936 the Labour Party was deeply disturbed by the worsening international situation. The rise of Fascism and Nazism confronted us with a cruel dilemma. The trade union and socialist movements had been the first victims of the evil forces which had triumphed in Italy and Germany. We were tormented by our impotence, as our comrades in these countries were persecuted and the movements to which they had given their lives utterly destroyed. Yet we dreaded the possibility of waging war even against the enemies of all we treasured. The tradition of anti-militarism and pacifism was deeply rooted in our British Socialist movement. I was nurtured in this tradition. I had grown up in a nonconformist home where war was condemned as one of the greatest of evils. When as a youth I joined the I.L.P. socialism and peace were one and indivisible, and James Keir Hardie was our apostle. With what enthusiasm and certainty we had hailed the resolve of the Socialist International to mobilize the forces of the working class, to use their industrial strength to stop any war the capitalists and imperialists might unleash! In 1914 the I.L.P. had stood firm in opposition to war and Ramsay MacDonald became our political hero. In 1917, when hope seemed to be lost, our hearts were uplifted by the international conference at Stockholm, and Arthur Henderson's resignation from Lloyd George's coalition. These events rekindled our faith that the movement would return to the tradition of anti-militarism and peace.

In the twenties and thirties a new leader had emerged who personified the Socialism which had won our minds and stirred our hearts. George Lansbury's life of dedicated service had made him the best-loved leader of our movement. We all looked forward to the days of recovery and triumph under his leadership. Then the controversy broke out which was to lead to his resignation. Fascism was abhorrent to him—and Mussolini's brutal attack on Abyssinia confronted him with a cruel choice. His pacifism was so deeply ingrained that he could not support military sanctions even against Fascist aggression. I was a delegate from my union at the 1935 conference at Brighton when Ernest Bevin led the onslaught which caused George Lansbury's resignation. In that conflict I supported Lansbury, and was saddened by the personal attack which Bevin made on him. Here were leaders who represented the two traditions which had made our movement. Ernest Bevin was the greatest leader our trade union movement had produced in my time. As a young union officer I had learned to admire his massive personality and immense courage. George Lansbury represented the religious idealism and compassion which made our movement a cause. Together they would have been a formidable partnership which could have made the Labour Party a mighty force in the land. There were few who did not leave that Brighton conference with sad hearts and forebodings about the future of the party. It was the kind of crisis, with its personal overtones, which could have broken the party for a generation. That it did not do so was due to George Lansbury's magnanimity and Clem Attlee's wisdom.

When I took my seat in the House of Commons for the first time George Lansbury was one of the first to greet me. He then occupied the corner seat traditionally reserved for ministers who had resigned. I was to have ample evidence of his loyalty to his successor Clem Attlee, and of the affectionate regard Clem had for George. During my period as president of the South Wales Miners' Federation, George as editor of the *Daily Herald* had given me staunch support, and he came to Llanelli to speak for me at the by-election. He was to experience the agony of the pacifist dilemma when faced with the challenge of Fascism. As the threat of war became imminent he visited the U.S.A. and Russia to appeal to their leaders to take urgent action to halt the drift to war. Then he sought an interview with Hitler and, to his surprise, was invited to meet the German Führer.

On his return from Berlin he related his experience at this interview to a group of us in the House. When he had been granted the interview, he was asked to submit beforehand the questions he proposed to put. On arrival at the chancellery he was met by Hitler's official interpreter, Herr Schmidt, who handed to him a document containing a list of the questions he had forwarded, set out in both German and English, together with the replies the Führer would make in German, with the official English translation. He had been warned at the British Embassy in Berlin that the Führer would greet him with the Nazi salute, and so he did, but George just walked up to the table where Hitler stood and, extending his hand, said: 'Good morning, thank you for seeing me.' 'Then,' said George, 'the rigmarole began. I would read out a question in English—Schmidt would read out the same question in German, and Hitler in turn read out the reply in German. It was all so futile and I decided on the spur of the moment to try and break through all this charade.' When the prepared questions had all been asked and answered, George turned to Schmidt and said: 'Will you please thank His Excellency and say that there is one further question that I feel I must put to him. Please explain to him that I represent in Parliament a constituency in the East End of London, and that a number of my constituents are Jewish people—please ask His Excellency if he can give me a message I can take back to them which will offer some hope that the treatment of their people in Germany will be changed.' Schmidt was reluctant, even afraid, so George thought, to put the question to Hitler, but George insisted. When Schmidt came to the word 'Jud', Hitler jumped to his feet and, giving the Nazi salute, poured out a torrent of words. Whereupon George said to Schmidt: 'You need not trouble to translate—I know what the answer means.' The world was soon to know the meaning of that answer!

I came face to face with the challenge, and its cruel choice, in my first year as a Member when I visited Czechoslovakia and the Free State of Danzig. I attended the Miners' International Conference at Prague in August 1936. The Polish miners' president brought a number of Sudeten miners to meet us. The Nazi, Henlein, was then waging his campaign for union with Germany among the Sudeten people. Our Sudeten comrades described to us the reign of Nazi violence in their coalfield, and sadly confessed that even the miners were falling under the terror. They felt themselves powerless to resist, and over and over again they pleaded, 'Our only hope is in you, the British working class. We depend on you.' On my way home from Prague, and for months afterwards, I could not forget those poignant words: 'We depend on you.'

Later that same month Arthur Jenkins and I were asked by Stafford Cripps and Ellen Wilkinson if we would visit Danzig. The Free State of Danzig had been established after the First World War by the League of Nations, and the League was still represented in the country by a High Commissioner. In the February of that year the Nazis had gained a majority of one in their Parliament, the Volkstadt, and the Nazi leader Greiser was ruthlessly suppressing the trade unions and the Socialist and Liberal parties. When we arrived at Danzig we were met by Mr Hofka, the president of the free Trade Union Association, and Mr Brost, the brilliant young editor of the Socialist daily which had just been suppressed by Greiser. Our first call was upon the British representative, to whom we gave the address at which we were to stay during our ten days' visit. We then called upon the High Commissioner for the League of Nations, in his office overlooking the square, and within sight of the Volkstadt buildings. We were greeted with Celtic warmth by the commissioner, Sean Lester, an Irishman who had taken part in the 'troubles' and was an enthusiastic Sinn Feiner. We talked about Ireland and Wales—mixing politics with rugger as Welsh and Irish do when they meet. Then he said: 'Before I tell you what is happening here, let me look out of the window to confirm my suspicions. . . .' He walked over slowly to the big bay window overlooking the square, and then came back to his desk and said: 'Go over to the window one at a time, and look down and you will see two hulking fellows, one by each portal; have a good look at them; they are Greiser's spies, who are to watch you every moment you are in Danzig.' We looked and saw the two men. Lester was right, for they were at our hotel door every morning, and saw us to the door every evening of our stay, always near, without ever saying a word to us. The commissioner took a copy of our itinerary and before we left told us he was sure that we would receive an invitation to meet some of Greiser's men. 'My advice', he said, 'is to accept, and listen, and come and tell me all about it.'

Sure enough the invitation came to dine with Greiser's men at the Casino at Zoppot, and along we went—our spies trailing behind. We were greeted by an old German Army officer, who had been a prisoner of war in England during the First World War, and could speak English. With him was Herr Dr

Hapfelkorn, who greeted us in Welsh, and at once asked, 'How is Aberystwyth?' It transpired that he had been a lecturer at the college, and began by telling us of his pleasure in introducing his students at the University of Danzig to the riches of English literature, especially to John Galsworthy's *Forsyte Saga*. All this led gradually on to his real mission—to extol the wonderful work the Führer was doing for the Fatherland; and how Herr Greiser was carrying on the work in Danzig. He was sure we had already learned during our stay that Danzig was a proud German city . . . and so he went on for an hour or more until the time came to leave. We assured Herr Doktor that we would report back faithfully what we saw and heard in Danzig.

We visited the home of the leader of the Liberal Party, Dr Lazarus, who was experiencing all the hate of the Nazis for his race. His wife, an Englishwoman, was breaking down under the strain. She told us of the Nazis' latest cruelty. Every other day for the past few weeks the telephone would ring, just before the time her husband was due home for lunch. On answering it she would be asked if Dr Lazarus had reached home. On her replying that he had not yet come but would soon be home, the voice at the other end would say, 'Oh yes, you can expect him soon today, but some other day . . .' and then the receiver would be slammed down. When the time came for us to leave, she broke down completely and cried: 'Take me home with you!' Some time later Arthur and I were able to help them to find an escape route to the U.S.A., and they called to see us at the House of Commons on their way to start life afresh after the months of terror.

On the day before we began our journey home Hofka, Brost and three of their friends joined us on a trip up the River Vistula. They had hired a launch and one of the friends had been included in the party because he could navigate the boat. We spent the whole day on the river and having thrown off the spies we felt free to talk about plans for the future. Once again we faced the cruel dilemma. Was it to be dumb submission to Nazism or to meet force with force? They were considering a resort to arms, but Greiser's grip on the country made it impossible to procure arms in Danzig. Day after day they would have news that another of their stalwarts had been arrested and taken they knew not where. They lived in daily dread that it would be their turn next.

When the time came to say farewell their last word to us was: 'We depend on you and your country.' Later we learnt that one of the men who had accompanied us on our sail up the Vistula was one of Greiser's spies!

When we returned to Parliament after the summer recess of 1936 the civil war in Spain became our major preoccupation. I joined with other Labour members in forming a group to organize support for the Republican Government. In January 1938 I was one of a delegation, led by Bill Dobbie, former president of the N.U.R., which visited Spain. We travelled by train from Paris to Perpignan and by road over the Pyrenees to the Spanish frontier, where we were met by representatives of the Republican Government. Together with Jock Davidson, one of the young Scottish M.P.s, I travelled in a car driven by a Catalonian metal worker named Oliviero, who was to be our guide. When we reached the town of Figueras, in the fold of the Pyrenees, we saw two aeroplanes flying low towards us. Oliviero stopped the car and gestured to us to get out and, following his example, we threw ourselves flat down on the road. This was Franco's welcome, but fortunately the planes overshot their target and the bombs dropped beyond us on the mountainside. Late that evening we arrived at Barcelona to be greeted by the Prime Minister, Prieto, who had come to that city in an endeavour to reconcile the factions whose bitter controversies had nearly wrecked the unity of the Republican forces in Catalonia. He was afraid that the internal divisions in the ranks of the Republicans, and the terror of the dive bombers, would destroy morale and result in the loss of Barcelona, upon whose industries they depended so heavily.

When Jock Davidson and I reached our room at the hotel suddenly and without any warning the lights went out, and the room was shaken violently by a bomb explosion. The next day we were to learn a lesson which we duly conveyed to our own A.R.P. experts. The bombers came again as we were on our way by car to visit some factories. The people caught in the streets rushed for the Metro, and the safety of the underground. This experience at Barcelona convinced us that if bombs fell on London our people would seek the shelter of the tube stations.

It was when leaving Valencia for Madrid that our party had the frightening experience of travelling through the town while bombs were falling, some of them perilously near our cars. On reaching Madrid we were told that the B.B.C.'s nine o'clock news referred to a broadcast on Franco's radio, announcing that: 'The British Socialists' cars had been bombed, as a warning to them to go home.' We rang up the *Daily Herald* and arranged for messages to be sent to assure our families that we were alive and well. It was an eerie experience travelling into Madrid, and to our lodgings in the basement of a tenement, through the pitch darkness of the blackout.

The next day was spent in the company of General Miaja. In the darkest hour of the war, when the Government had been compelled to leave the capital, Miaja had rallied soldiers and citizens with La Pasionaria's cry of '*No pasarán*' ('They shall not pass'). He was a colourful personality, and as we drove with him through the streets he stood up in his car and saluted the people with clenched fist, as they cried '*Miaja-Miaja—No Pasarán, No Pasarán*'. There had been some talk about abandoning Madrid, and moving Miaja's army to another sector, and he was anxious to convince us that this would be disastrous for the Republican cause.

My last memory of Madrid is of a young officer who sat next to me at dinner on our last night in the capital. Following a brilliant university career he had begun what promised to be an equally brilliant career in the legal profession. He told me that his grandfather had been a supporter of the famous revolutionary Enrico Ferri, and how proud he was to be following in his grandfather's footsteps. Soon after this a soldier came and handed him a letter. He glanced at it, then turned to me and with a '*Buenas noches*' hurried out of the room. The next day I was informed that the letter contained instruction for a specially dangerous assignment, which he carried out alone, and from which he did not return.

On our journey home we called to meet the survivors of a company of the International Brigade which had fought savagely, and sustained heavy casualties, in the battle of Teruel. At Tarragona we attended the funeral of five British sailors who had been killed when their ship had been bombed. We laid wreaths on their graves, and Bill Dobbie and I paid tribute to their memory. As we left Spain we were once again reminded, as at Prague and Danzig: 'It all depends on you in Britain.'

It was after my return from Spain that I ventured, for the first time, to intervene in a debate on foreign affairs, opened by Neville Chamberlain on 24th March 1938, and my speech reflected the experience of my visits to Prague, Danzig and Spain when I said:

> Since 1931 the democratic countries in Europe have been on the retreat and the Fascist forces have been marching on. Every year, and now almost every month, witnesses a new defeat for the forces of democracy and a new win for the powers of Fascism—Austria, Czechoslovakia and now the Nazi triumph which is today reported from Danzig. The Prime Minister, in his speech, held out no hope for the Spanish people but only a direct encouragement to Italy and Germany to go on to the final conquest of Spain. Democracy and freedom have no frontiers. Wherever the fight for them takes place that is also our struggle.

In a speech later that year I confessed: 'I am by temperament a pacifist but I must realize that there is a problem to which we must continually come back however one may attempt to run away from it that, sometime, somewhere, some aggressor may cut across all conventions and break the peace of the world.'

Even at this eleventh hour, like most of my colleagues, I clung to the hope that the League of Nations, fully supported by the democracies, could save the peace. There were others, notably Hugh Dalton, who believed that it was too late to rely on the League, and that we should concentrate our energies on rearming and building up an alliance with France and the Soviet Union. Stafford Cripps, who at this time was outside the party, continued his efforts to form a Popular Front Government to replace the Chamberlain regime. In June 1939 he asked Bill Dobbie, Ben Smith and me to meet him. He told us that a Colonel Count Schwerin, a member of Hitler's General Staff, was in London. Stafford was anxious that before the Count returned to report to the Führer, we should meet him and tell him that, if Britain went to war with Germany, the trade union and Labour movement would be solid in support of war against Nazism. He arranged for us to meet the Count in a private residence in Mayfair at which only the Count, his aide and ourselves would be present. From the Count we heard the now familiar story which was a repetition of the one I had heard a year before from the professor at Danzig. I told him so and reminded him of what the Nazis had done in Danzig. We left the Count in no doubt as to our attitude and asked him to convey to the Führer our view that Britain would be united in the struggle to rid the world of Nazism and Fascism.

Whether Count Schwerin did so we were never to know. A year after we heard that he had been killed in the first bombing raid on Berlin.

About the same time Edgar Mowrer, whose book *Germany Puts the Clock Back* had created a deep impression, came to address a meeting of Members. He described Mussolini as an unscrupulous adventurer with whom France and Britain could make a bargain, if they were prepared to pay the price, but that Hitler was an insane fanatic with whom no bargain was worth while—we either had to crush him or be crushed by him.

For me the dilemma was resolved.

6

LABOUR AND COALITION

I

THE Labour Party Conference at Southport in 1939 was dominated by the debate about the proposal for a Popular Front, the expulsion of Cripps, Bevan and Strauss, and the emergence of a new figure, a young trade union delegate who swayed the conference against the rebels—his name, George Brown. For me the conference was notable for another reason. I was nominated for a seat on the national executive and succeeded in getting the seventh place in the constituency party section. This was the beginning of a long period on the executive, and as I had been elected to sit on the front bench in that same year I was destined to be at the centre of politics for the next twenty years.

When the executive met for its first meeting following the conference in June 1939, the agenda reflected the hopes and the fears of that fateful year.

If even at the eleventh hour war could be averted the Parliament elected in 1935 would have run its course in 1940—and we should have to prepare for another General Election. In the hope that this would happen the executive set up a committee to begin preparations for the electoral battle. But when we turned our attention to the international situation this hope seemed unreal as we contemplated the scene. The Spanish Republicans had been overwhelmed by Franco and his Fascist allies, and Munich had spelt the doom of Czechoslovakia. The League of Nations had been undermined by the cowardice of its creators, and within three months of our meeting Britain was at war with Hitler's Germany. Instead of preparing for an election and, as we had hoped, the return of a Labour Government, the party had to decide whether to join a war-time coalition.

'Labour must stand on its own feet—without the aid of political crutches, be they Liberal or Conservative.' This declaration of independence by the founding father, Keir Hardie, had become one of the deep-rooted traditions of the party. The fate of the Liberal Party following the First World War, and the experience of our own party in 1931, had deepened the resolve to maintain our independence and to have no truck with coalitions. When Neville Chamberlain invited Clem Attlee to join a National Government on the outbreak of war in September 1939 the proposal was unanimously rejected. However, the situation changed dramatically when, in May 1940, the distrust of the Chamberlain Government rose to bitter anger at the failure of the Norwegian campaign. In the debate which followed, the party decided to turn the motion for the adjournment into a vote of censure, and the vote in the division lobby marked the end of the Chamberlain regime.

On the day following the debate the members of the party's national executive made their way to Bournemouth, where our annual conference was to assemble the following week. When the executive met that evening Clem Attlee reported that Neville Chamberlain had again invited Labour to join a National Government under his leadership. Clem had made it clear to him that the party would not join any government of which he was the head. It appeared that there had been a suggestion that Lord Halifax might take over, but that found no favour in our ranks. When the executive learnt that Churchill was willing to form a war-time coalition the executive was unanimous in its decision to join, and the conference, when it met on Whit-Monday 1940, was equally unanimous in support and resolved that 'the Labour Party should take its full share of responsibility as a full partner in the new Government, which, under a new Prime Minister, commands the confidence of the nation'.

The entry of the party into a coalition confronted the Parliamentary Labour Party with a difficult task, that of sustaining our leaders in the administration and, at the same time, preserving the identity and maintaining the unity of the party. When the Parliamentary Labour Party met we made two decisions designed to ensure the fulfilment of both these requirements. First, we decided that M.P.s who were not members of the Government should continue to sit on the Opposition benches, and, secondly, to appoint by ballot an administrative committee whose members would sit on the front Opposition bench. I was elected a member of the administrative committee and served on it throughout the period of the Churchill coalition. We were fortunate to have two Privy Councillors on it, Lees-Smith and Pethick Lawrence, and we appointed them as our principal spokesmen from the front bench. When we took our places, our right to be there at all was challenged by one of the Tory M.P.s, Sir Herbert Williams, and also by Jimmy Maxton, who claimed that as the leader of the four I.L.P. M.P.s, the only Members opposed to the war, he was entitled to take the place of the Leader of the Opposition. The Speaker, when asked to guide the House, ruled:

> The custom of the House is described by Erskine May as follows: 'The Front Bench on the Opposition side, though other Members sit there, is reserved for leading Members of the Opposition who have served in the offices of State.' The present circumstances are, as far as I know, unprecedented. It cannot be said that there is now an Opposition in Parliament in the hitherto accepted meaning of the words; namely, a party in Opposition from which an alternative Government could be formed. It will be noted, in the passage which I quoted from May as regards the Opposition front bench, that other Members occasionally sit there. In recent years it has been the practice of the Opposition to invite a few prominent backbenchers to sit on the Opposition front bench, and I see no objection to the practice being continued as regards those who have already been invited to fill those positions.

Once again Erskine May had come to the rescue, and this time, let it be confessed, to the rescue of the Labour Party, enabling us to retain our identity throughout the whole of the period our leaders served in the coalition.

The Parliamentary Party was able to meet regularly, and the administrative committee maintained a close link with our colleagues in Government, and enabled us to keep the party together through all the strains and stresses of the war-time controversies. There was only one occasion in which the party divided the House against the Government, and in the light of subsequent events that single vote had its special significance for both the party and the country.

In one of the darkest hours of the war, at the end of 1942, the Beveridge Report fell like manna from heaven. The Welfare State has by now become so generally accepted as an essential part of a civilized society that it is difficult for the present generation to appreciate the impact the publication of the Beveridge Report made on our people in 1942. It was one of the few Blue Books which overnight became a best seller, a symbol of the determination of our people to build a new Britain, and a test by which politicians and parties were judged. As soon as the report was published the Trade Union Congress, the Co-operative Congress and the Labour Party declared their support for the Beveridge Plan and called for its early implementation.

When arrangements were made for a three-day debate on the Beveridge Plan in February 1943 it was at first agreed that it should take place on a motion supported by all parties in the coalition, as it was made known that Churchill was anxious that there should be no division on Beveridge. He had appointed a Cabinet committee to consider the proposals and deputed the chairman, Sir John Anderson, to open the debate from the Government benches. It turned out to be of Churchill's errors of judgment. John Anderson (later Lord Waverley) had enjoyed an immense reputation as one of the ablest of top civil servants. Later he served as Governor of Bengal, and on his retirement from that post entered Parliament. Within a year he joined the Government under Neville Chamberlain. He was known as a man who counted every penny twice and so was the worst possible choice as chairman of the Government's committee on post-war reconstruction. His speech in the debate was so full of 'ifs' and 'buts' that it caused obvious embarrassment to his colleagues on the Government benches, and infuriated ours. To add to our mis-givings another civil servant turned minister, Sir James Grigg, Secretary of State for War, refused to allow a summary of the Beveridge Plan to be circulated to the forces on the ground that to do so would have 'conveyed the impression that the scheme was settled Government policy, whereas in fact no decision of any kind had been taken'. The speech by Anderson, and the veto by Grigg, confirmed our fears that the reactionaries within the Government had carried the day. At a meeting of the party during the seond day of the debate it was resolved, notwithstanding impassioned appeals by Ernest Bevin and Herbert Morrison, to table a motion expressing dissatisfaction with the Government's attitude to the Beveridge Plan, and to carry our motion to a division. I was entrusted with the task of moving our resolution and, though it was defeated by 325 votes to 119, the long-term effects of the division were important.

Sir William Beveridge has recorded how, at the end of the division, I said to him: 'This debate, and the division, makes the return of a Labour Government to power at the next election a certainty.'

2

The publication of the Beveridge Report and the debate in Parliament aroused intense interest on the problems of post-war reconstruction and I was frequently invited to speak on these topics.

I was honoured in being invited to deliver one of the Fabian Autumn Lectures in 1943 and 1944. The two series were devoted to the problems of post-war reconstruction and among my fellow lecturers were R. H. Tawney, G. D. H. Cole, Harold Laski, Sir William Beveridge and Aneurin Bevan. In the first lecture, under the title 'Industry—the Servant of the People', I spoke of the opportunity which the public ownership of industry would provide to establish a new relationship within the nationalized industries. I had experienced within my old industry how, while the machine relieved the miner of much of the heavy soul-destroying toil of the old days, it also deprived him of the personal satisfaction which he derived from the old skills. With the development of modern machines the daily round becomes more boring and less satisfying to so many workers. We must find within our publicly owned industries a new purpose which would give meaning to the lowliest tasks. I returned to this theme in an address I delivered to the annual conference of my union, when I spoke of the opportunity that nationalization of the coal-mines gave the industry to develop and build a new system of industrial democracy, a combination of miner, technician and management. I went on to say: 'Our forefathers built this union to fight the boss. We have to make it the instrument through which the men we represent exercise effective control, in partnership with management, in the running of the industry.' The conference gave a cordial welcome to my address and decided to publish it and distribute copies to the miners in the coalfields.

The Beveridge Report aroused interest not only at home but also overseas, notably in the U.S.A. Brendan Bracken, then Minister of Information, invited me to undertake a speaking tour in the U.S.A., and in August of 1943 I set off for the States.

My four months' tour took me to twenty-eight states, and the meetings I addressed varied from the ten thousand workers at the Boeing plant at Renton, Seattle, to the students of Marx at the Tom Mooney Labor College at San Francisco; and from the thousand G.I.s at the State University at Columbus, Ohio, to gatherings of Welsh people who were eager for news of the land of their fathers.

My visit to the Tom Mooney College evoked memories of the famous 'Mooney case'. During a strike parade at San Francisco in 1916 a bomb was thrown into the ranks of the demonstrators and killed some of them. Tom Mooney, who had the reputation of a militant trade union agitator, was arrested and charged with having participated in the bomb-throwing. The trial aroused world-wide interest and was widely publicized in the British press. As the trial proceeded the opinion strengthened that Mooney had been 'framed' and that his conviction was secured by perjured evidence. When Mooney was sentenced to death a wave of indignation arose and petitions were organized calling for his release. I had organized a petition in our valley and meetings to protest against what we were convinced was a false charge. We rejoiced when we heard that the death sentence had been commuted to one of life imprisonment and then we joined in the demand for Mooney's release. For many years our pleas were unsuccessful, but in 1939 the then Governor of California granted him an unconditional pardon. Tom Mooney died in 1943 at the age of fifty-nine. When I visited the college in 1943 I began my address with a tribute to his memory and told my audience of the efforts we had made in my far-away valley in South Wales at the time of his trial. The gathering stood in silent tribute to his memory. The students I addressed were all of the 'left' and most of the questions centred upon two issues which were then being hotly canvassed in the U.S.A. The first was 'the failure of the British imperialists to launch a "second front" because of their fear and hatred of Communism', and the second, without any realization of the contradiction, was that 'Roosevelt had been outmanœuvred by Churchill to send American forces to Europe, and so leave China to meet the full blast of the Japanese onslaught'. This alleged 'betrayal' of China was hurled at me in all my meetings on the Pacific coast, a charge fomented by a campaign conducted by the famous novelist Pearl Buck. I remember the meeting at the Tom Mooney College for another reason. I had put my watch on the table to time my speech, and shortly after I had begun speaking I noticed the watch moving away, whereupon I pulled it back; but it moved again—and the chairman whispered to me: 'Go on, it's only a tremor.' I carried on, and the earth tremor was forgotten in the turmoil of the argument about China and the second front in Europe!

When I got back to my hotel I found that my fellow residents, remembering the earthquake of 1906, were far from eager to retire to their rooms, and waited up until the assurance came that there had been a tremor some hundred miles south of San Francisco, but that no serious damage had been caused, and that all was now over.

I attended the New York State Convention of the American Federation of Labor at Rochester, to describe the role of the British trade unions in the war and, in particular, the work of Ernest Bevin at the Ministry of Labour. The president of the convention was an Irishman named O'Donovan. On our way to the meeting he took me on one side and warned me that 'he had no time for the English' and as there would be many Irishmen in the audience I had better be prepared! I replied that I understood how the Irish felt—that we also had our troubles with the English—at which he asked: 'What are you, brother?' and I confessed that I was a Welshman. When O'Donovan came to introduce me he began by relating this conversation, with the result that I was heard with rapt attention and given a standing ovation, ending with the president giving notice that at the next session he would move that I be made an honorary life member. In due course I received a certificate recording the honour bestowed upon me.

From the Irish to the Welsh and this time to meet the best loved, and most hated, American union leader of the time, John L. Lewis. I had a long interview with him in the sanctuary of his office in Washington. The massive frame, the bushy eyebrows and the deep bass voice combined to make him look, as well as sound, formidable. His father had left the coal-mines in West Wales to work in the American mines, taking with him his wife from a mining village in Monmouthshire. Our talk began with an exchange of experiences as miners' leaders. In building up the United Mineworkers Union of America John L. was compelled to face the guns of the thugs employed by the coal owners to keep him away from the mines. His unyielding courage had earned him the deep affection of the miners. He told me of how his father had brought with him the old miners' Luddite attitude to the machine, and of the early strikes against the introduction of mechanized mining. In contrast he himself had called the men out on strike because the mine owners refused to adopt the most modern machines available! The power of his union was now being weakened by the rapid development of 'strip mining' (opencast). The accident rate at their mines was even worse than at ours, and his reaction to this was to increase his efforts still further to mechanize the mines, and so reduce the number of men condemned to work in them. We shared the hope that we would live to see the day when the last men would come safely out of the last mine. At the close of our talk he asked me whether my schedule would take me to Springfield, Illinois, and, on learning that it would, asked me if I would call upon his aged mother, who lived there. I called to see the mother and talked to her, at her desire, in Welsh, and sang one of the songs she still remembered, *Myfi sy'n magu'r baban*, a mother's lullaby. Many years later I was one of a company of miners' leaders who entertained John L. Lewis to dinner, on one of his rare visits to this country. In the course of a reply to the toast of his health he referred to the great kindness I had shown to his mother. John L. had many enemies, but they mattered little compared to his three loves—his mother, his motherless daughter and the miners.

3

I returned to England in January 1944 and found that events had begun to move to the closing stages of the war. Mussolini had gone, Italy was out of the war, and the invasion of Europe was imminent. When I attended a meeting of the National Executive at Transport House our attention was beginning to focus on the election which we were certain would follow quickly after the end of the war in Europe. Under Herbert Morrison's chairmanship a committee, of which I was a member, began the preparation of our election programme, 'Let us Face the Future'. Within the party opinion had already crystallized in favour of holding an election as soon as victory was won in Europe. It was felt that the continuation of the war in the Far East would be no sufficient reason for further prolongation of a Parliament elected

in the distant past of 1935. The emergence of the Commonwealth Party, led by Richard Acland, and the defeat of Government candidates at by-elections, provided clear evidence that the
country wanted a change. Of our leaders it was Herbert Morrison
who, more than any of the others, sensed this mood for change.
He was convinced that in addition to our traditional voters large
sections of the middle class could be won over to the support of
Labour. In the programme 'Let us Face the Future' this view was
set out: 'We appeal to all men and women of progressive outlook
to support the Labour Party, and urge all progressives to see to it
that the next Government is not a Conservative but a Labour
Government which will act on the principles of policy set out in
the present declaration.'

When the new programme was submitted to our annual conference in May 1945 the war in Europe was over. On the day on
which the executive assembled at Blackpool for the conference
Clem Attlee had received a letter from Winston Churchill. In
this letter Churchill referred to talks he had had with Attlee and
'your principal colleagues' from which he had gathered that 'the
Labour Party, instead of leaving the Government on the defeat of
Germany, would be willing to continue the coalition until the
autumn'. On our rejecting this proposal Churchill came back
with another, to continue the coalition until the war against
Japan had been won, and, in his own words: 'If you should
decide to stand in with us, all united until the Japanese surrender
is compelled, let us discuss means of taking the nation's opinion,
for example, by a referendum, on the issue whether, in these
conditions, the life of Parliament should be further prolonged.'
When the executive came to consider Churchill's proposals both
were rejected. There had been more support for the proposal—
to continue the coalition until the autumn—by those members
who thought that this would upset the plans of the Tory Central
Office for a repeat of the 1918 'Vote for the man who won the
War' election. There were a number of us who would have
agreed to this, but only on the understanding that there would be
no committal on post-war policy, which in any respect would be
contrary to that set out in 'Let us Face the Future'. Herbert
Morrison, as the architect of the programme, came down on our
side and this was decisive. Before the conference ended Labour
was out of the coalition, and we were on our way to the triumph
of July 1945.

After all this—*what?* This was the theme which dominated the election campaign. I had taken part in every election since 1910. This was the first in which I was to venture outside my native Wales, though my itinerary included a tour of the Principality. I was one of those chosen to broadcast for the party and my message was expressed in these words: 'Labour does not offer ease and comfort. What we shall offer is the opportunity for every man and woman to use their capacities to the full.' I found in the letters I received following the broadcast, as well as at the meetings I addressed, that the theme suited the mood of the people. The party had agreed that we would not descend to personal attacks, and how right we were was demonstrated by the boomerang effects of Churchill's 'Gestapo' broadcasts. Churchill shocked the most thoughtful electors by his attacks upon the men who had helped to sustain him through five years of blood, sweat and tears. The very idea that the men who had been his comrades had suddenly become sinister plotters evoked as much hilarity as indignation. It is generally believed that Churchill made the 'Gestapo' broadcasts on the advice of the Conservative Central Office. It turned out to be the worst error in election tactics that I remember. Instead of winning the election for the Tories it only made their defeat more certain and decisive.

In my own constituency I enjoyed my greatest electoral victory, polling 44,514 votes against 10,397 for my opponent, fighting as a 'National' candidate. My majority was the second largest in the country.

The day after the count I received a message to come to London at once, and arrange to be on call during the week-end. I was naturally delighted, for this could only mean that I was being considered for a place in the Government. I was summoned to No. 10, and ushered into the Cabinet Room. Clem Attlee sat in the Prime Minister's chair, with the Chief Whip, William Whiteley, by his side. Then, as always, Clem wasted no words but came straight to the point, and invited me to join his Government in the post of Secretary of State for the Commonwealth. When he noticed that I hesitated to reply, he asked me if I would prefer another post. I at once replied: 'Yes, I would like to serve as Minister of National Insurance,' to which he answered: 'That's a good idea—that settles it—good day and good luck.'

I returned home happy that I had got the job I wanted, even

though I was disappointed to find later that I was not in the Cabinet, and that the Commonwealth Secretary was.

When I reached my home in the garden suburb at Burry Port, just outside Llanelli, I found the press and photographers assembled in force, and that they were intrigued to find a minister living in a small suburban house, and even more to find my wife busy with the housework and doing her own cooking.

On Monday I was off again to London, this time on my way to 6 Carlton House Terrace, to begin my ministerial life.

7

MINISTER OF NATIONAL INSURANCE

I

'A REVOLUTIONARY moment in the world's history is a time for revolution—not for patching.'

This call for revolution came not from Moscow or Peking but from the one-time director of the London School of Economics, Sir William Beveridge, when he presented his plan for social security in 1942.

It was symbolic of the new revolution that the Minister of National Insurance, charged with the task of implementing the plan, and creating the Welfare State, should find himself installed at Carlton House Terrace, once the citadel of aristocratic power. The minister was allocated what was described as the *Salon*, elaborately furnished in the Italian style. I was the third minister to occupy the *Salon* since the ministry was established in 1944. My immediate predecessor, who had served during the 'caretaker' period between the break-up of the coalition and the 1945 election, was Leslie Hore-Belisha. In accordance with tradition, as the outgoing minister, he called upon me to wish me well as his successor. He was a familiar figure, for I had sat in the Commons when, as Minister of Transport, he became famous for his 'beacons'. I also remembered him as the one-time War Minister who had been dismissed from office by Neville Chamberlain for some obscure reason which, if lobby gossip was to be believed, reflected no credit upon Chamberlain or the military establishment. Winston Churchill had brought him back from the political wilderness, and he told me with what pleasure he had looked forward to resuming his work at the ministry. His

79

defeat in the election had come as a shock, and as he bid me goodbye there were tears in his eyes as he said: 'This is the end of my career.' Politics can be cruel as well as tough.

A minister is fortunate, especially in his first office, if he is assisted by able and loyal colleagues. During my four years at National Insurance I had two parliamentary secretaries, George (now Lord) Lindgren, and Tom Steel. Both were the products of that nursery which has provided so many leaders for the party, the Transport Salaried Staff Association. The post of Parliamentary Private Secretary—P.P.S.—has always been, and remains, a mystery to those outside the precincts of Westminster. I described the P.P.S. to my mining friends as the minister's 'butty', and mine was certainly a 'butty', for Bernard (now Lord) Taylor, had been my closest friend ever since our mining days. I was equally fortunate to find an understanding compatriot in the Permanent Secretary, Tom Phillips, who had made his way from the village school in rural Wales to Oxford (the same college as Harold Wilson), and on to the higher ranks of the civil service. He was that rare phenomenon—the quiet Welshman whose pen was mightier than his voice. His minutes were a model of compressed lucidity, and his draft replies to parliamentary questions were designed to make supplementaries easy to answer. In a ministry which had to build up a nation-wide administration, and draw its staff from outside as well as inside the civil service, his shrewd judgment of men was an invaluable asset. This was proved in his choice of the Director of Establishments, H. V. Rhodes, who has put on record the task of creating the new administration in a pamphlet, 'Setting up a new Government Department', published by the British Institute of Management. One of our achievements was to establish the central office of the ministry at Newcastle-upon-Tyne, far away from Whitehall. Other departments have since followed our example, including the Treasury, by the transfer of the Royal Mint to Wales.

2

The Webbs, who lived in a world of Blue Books, once lamented that it took as long as thirty years before the recommendations of a royal commission were translated into legislation. The 1945 Labour Government boldly aimed to implement the Beveridge

Plan in full within three years, and bring it into operation on the third anniversary of the great electoral victory—5th July 1948.

This was a formidable task. It would necessitate five Acts of Parliament, scores of regulations and the creation of a nation-wide organization. Fortunately one of the five, the Family Allowances Act, was already on the statute book. The Americans have a custom of giving their legislation the names of sponsors in Congress, and it would have been appropriate to give the Family Allowances Act the name 'Eleanor Rathbone Act'. She had fought valiantly, against opposition from many quarters, for family endowment, and I had been one of her supporters in the many debates she initiated in the thirties.

Beveridge recommended allowances in cash at five shillings a week for every child in a family except the eldest, or only, child, and that this should be supplemented by services in kind to the value of three shillings per week.

I decided to bring family allowances into payment as soon as possible. My first job was to find the money, and I made the first of many visits to the Treasury. The Chancellor, Hugh Dalton, gave me the money, 'with a song in his heart', as he told our conference to the delight of our supporters and the fury of his critics.

I fixed the first family allowances pay-day for August Bank Holiday Tuesday, 1946, and on that day allowances were paid to $2\frac{1}{2}$ million families. By 5th July 1948 the number had increased to over three million. The cost to the nation was £59 million, surely one of the best investments the state ever made. It was a modest enough beginning in the endowment of the family, and it is sad to relate that we have never since found it possible to maintain the allowances, in cash and kind, at the same value as they had over twenty years ago.

We live in a world which is alarmed, and not without cause, by the population explosion. We may have a mini-explosion in Britain, but ours will be due to increased longevity rather than an explosive birth rate.

In 1948 I arranged for a survey to be made of the composition of the families receiving family allowances. This revealed that only two of every hundred families had more than six children, and sixty of every hundred had only two children. I am interested to find, from the ministry's latest report, that the composition of the familier receiving the allowances has changed but little since

81

1948. Therefore we should be able to maintain the allowances and services at the value equivalent to those provided in 1946.

3

To someone like myself, without previous ministerial experience, piloting two major measures through Parliament in one session was a severe test. That I survived the ordeal, and emerged with reasonable success, was due largely to the advantage of legislating in a field which my trade union experience had made familiar. This was especially so of the first measure, the National Insurance (Industrial Injuries) Bill. As I said in introducing the Bill, on its second reading: 'I know from my experience as a worker, and as a trade union officer, the tragedy of the "compo" man. In my village there are pathetic cases of industrial casualties left to limp their way through life.' I had bitter memories of the injustices of the law relating to compensation for the disabled.

Under common law the workman was entitled to claim damages from his employer for disability where the accident could be proved to be due to the employer's negligence. But, like so many of the ancient rights which we inherited from our forbears, this had been so qualified by the dictum of the courts as to be of little value to the workmen. In a judgment in 1837 the courts had enunciated what became known as the 'doctrine of common employment'. This decreed that 'a master is not bound to indemnify one servant for injuries caused by the negligence of another servant in the same employment, unless the negligent servant was the master's representative'. The number of cases in which the workman could overcome this obstacle were so rare that in practice the ancient right was of little value, especially as the workman had to choose between the alternative rights of 'claiming damages under common law' or 'benefit under the Workmen's Compensation Act'. The basic principles embodied in Joseph Chamberlain's Act of 1897 had been preserved in all the subsequent compensation legislation. The totally disabled workman was entitled to weekly compensation equal to half his average weekly earnings in the twelve months preceding the accident, subject to a maximum. The partially disabled workman was entitled to weekly compensation payment equal to half the difference between his actual pre-accident earnings and what he was earning or deemed to be able to earn at light employment.

An investigation in the South Wales coalfield in 1939 revealed that the average weekly amount of compensation paid to totally disabled men was twenty-four shillings. Hundreds of partially disabled were deprived of compensation under the 'half-difference rule'. Many, driven to desperation, had settled off for lump sums which would just clear off the debts incurred following the accident, leaving them to carry the handicap of the disability for the rest of their life, without a penny more compensation.

It was a proud moment for me when in 1948 the Labour Government abolished the unjust doctrine of common employment, and replaced the old system of compensation with a new service. The new Industrial Injuries Act was a clean break with the past. The responsibility for the payment and administration of benefits was taken out of the hands of the employers and insurance companies, and vested in the Ministry of National Insurance. The new scheme was financed by contributions from employers, workmen and the state. Weekly benefits and disablement pensions were based on the principle of the 'loss of faculty' that is 'in proportion to the loss of health, strength and the power to enjoy life attributable to industrial accident or prescribed industrial disease'.

When I became minister I found a Bill on the stocks embodying this new scheme which had been prepared by the Coalition Government. On examining its provisions closely I found one major defect which had to be removed. This was the case in which the new criterion of 'loss of faculty' did not adequately cover the loss due to the accident as, for example, the case of a railway engine driver who, having lost an eye, would be prohibited from again driving an engine. To meet this and similar contingencies I made provision for a special hardship allowance. Subsequent experience has shown how beneficial this provision has been. Under this new scheme, its benefits can be linked with those provided under the National Insurance Act—one of the many advantages gained from a co-ordinated system of social insurance.

Another advantage was the setting up of judicial tribunals to determine disputes, so removing one of the evils of the old system: the waste of vast sums of money in litigation.

On second reading in October 1945 I commended the Industrial Injuries Bill to the House of Commons 'not only because of its cash benefits, but also because it provides the foundation upon which a great, constructive human service can be built, to restore the injured workman to his old job or, if that is not possible, to train him for a new job or, if that is impossible, to care for him and his dependants. I am confident that we shall be able to make this scheme a real, living contribution to the social services of our country, and I shall be proud to help in that task'.

Looking back over the years, whilst recognizing that all the hopes I then expressed have not been fully realized, I still believe that the pride I then felt has been justified.

4

When the news of my appointment as Minister of National Insurance reached my native village one of my old neighbours asked another: 'What is this job Jim Griffiths has got?', to which came the prompt reply, 'Why man, boss of the Prudential.' I came near to agreeing with him when I saw the draft of the National Insurance Bill and read the first clause: 'Every person who, on and after the appointed day, being over school-leaving age and under pensionable age, is in Great Britain and fulfils such conditions as may be prescribed as to residence in Great Britain, shall become insured under this Act and thereafter continue to be insured throughout his life under this Act.' In plain English it was to be all in: women from sixteen to sixty and men to sixty-five. This established the principle of universality in our system of social insurance. The old system, beginning with Lloyd George's Act of 1911, had been selective. It covered only those employed under a contract of service and only those whose earnings were below £420 a year. The new scheme brought in everybody from the barrow boy to the field-marshal. The new Act went even further in breaking new ground. It was the first insurance Act in any country to bring under its cover the 'self-employed' and those who, in official language, were described as 'not gainfully employed'. My advisers estimated that we should have about twenty-four million contributors, of whom some two million would be self-employed, such as shopkeepers and farmers, and up to a million not gainfully employed.

Bringing them all in was easy—classifying some of them proved difficult, especially parsons and politicians. In which category should I put them? The clergymen of the Church of England had been held, by a legal decision under Lloyd George's Act, not to be 'under a contract of service'—but what about the nonconformist ministers? My good friend Dr Sydney Berry and I agreed that it would be contrary to our principles as Congregationalists to classify the ministers as 'under a contract of service' to their congregations. I was in no doubt that the politician's service could not be confined within the legal definition of a contract, so he became a self-employed contributor.

It was not only in its cover that the scheme broke new ground but also in the scope and variety of the benefits provided 'from the cradle to the grave'. It provided twice as many separate benefits as the old scheme and incorporated Beveridge's recommendation of a uniform standard for the principal benefits. Under the old dispensation, sick benefit was 18s. a week for the first six months and thereafter 10s. 6d., with no provision for dependants; the unemployed received 24s. a week with supplementary benefits for wife and children, and the old age pensioner ten shillings a week.

The 1946 Act provided uniform benefits for sickness, unemployment and retirement, with dependants' benefits in each case. In addition it embodied Beveridge's recommendation that the amount of the major benefits should be such as would provide for basic needs, on a subsistence basis. He calculated the amount required to provide a subsistence income in normal cases, on the basis of the cost of living in 1939, added 25 per cent to cover the subsequent increase in the cost of living index, and fixed the subsistence rate in 1942 at 24s. for a single person and 40s. for a married couple, with additional benefits for dependants. I accepted this basis, and to maintain the Beveridge level brought the rates up to 26s. and 42s. The next question was how to ensure that the level would be maintained. This was, and has remained, an unsolved problem. One of the practical difficulties is inherent in the insurance principle on which the scheme is based. I shared to the full Beveridge's view that benefits should be paid as of right on the basis of contributions and without any means test. My aim was to provide security with dignity. I considered the possibility of providing benefits on a sliding scale linked to the cost of living. This had practical difficulties in that it would require changes in contributions each time benefits were changed. I was reminded that when after 1918 war pensions had been tied to a cost of living scale it had worked well while the cost of living was rising and was abandoned the first time it fell. In the end, I provided in the Act that the minister should review the scale of benefits every five years with a view to adjusting them to changes in the cost of living and in the standard of life.

The provision of an adequate pension for the aged, in the context of the changes in the age-composition of the population, raised important industrial and social problems. In 1901 of the total population 32·5 per cent were under fifteen, and only 6·2 per cent were of pensionable age. By 1942 these proportions had changed to 16·5 per cent and 20·8 per cent respectively. Faced with these facts Beveridge had recommended that pensions for those who had already retired should be increased from 10s. to the new rate by instalments spread over twenty years. I found this unacceptable. The men and women who had already retired had experienced a tough life. In their youth they had been caught by the 1914 war, in middle age they had experienced the indignities of the depression, and in 1940 had stood firm as a rock in the nation's hour of trial. They deserved well of the nation, and should not wait for twenty years. I decided to raise the ten shillings to the new rate and they received their new pensions within three months of the 1946 Act receiving the Royal Assent.

The new pensions were paid conditional on retirement with an earnings rule. In accepting this provision I confess that I, like many of my trade union friends, was influenced by the experience that under the old scheme some employers, including local authorities in some rural areas, deducted the ten shillings pension from the wages of their employees. Moreover, I felt that the age-composition made it essential to encourage old people who could to remain at work. For them we provided an annual increment for every year at which they remained at work up to the age of seventy, and thereafter the pension to be paid irrespective of earnings.

In the sphere of the social services the spirit of the administration is as important as the provisions of the legislation. I recognized that the ministry would be dealing with people in adversity, and that the qualities required of the staff were courtesy and dignity. We should have a thousand local offices and I wished that we could have provided new buildings worthy of the service. The ravages of war made this impossible, and we had to make do with whatever building we could lay our hands on. From the moment I arrived at the ministry I had a daily reminder that we would have to deal with an immense volume of correspondence. To the man and woman in distress there can be no more infuriating experience than to receive a letter couched in official jargon. I therefore arranged with the Director of Establishments that a letter be sent to the staff at all offices urging each one of them to remember that 'the keynote is informality in writing to individual members of the public. Civil service jargon must give way to a style of expression that will convince correspondents that the department is making efforts to help them. Many of our correspondents will find difficulty in expressing themselves clearly, and it would be futile for us to reply to such letters in ''officialese'''. The staff responded magnificently and from the first day the ministry gained a reputation for courtesy, helpfulness and efficiency.

5

While I was engaged in piloting the Insurance Bill through Parliament, Nye Bevan was triumphantly carrying through his bold and imaginative National Health Service Bill.

In the second session we joined forces in promoting the Bill to establish national assistance. The Bill aimed 'to terminate the existing poor law and to provide in lieu thereof for the assistance of persons in need by the National Assistance Board and by local authorities'. Responsibility for providing assistance in cash was transferred from the public assistance committees to a national board. The responsibility for welfare services for those who by 'age, infirmity or any other circumstances are in need' was to be entrusted to councils' welfare committees. We aimed to provide monetary payments and welfare services which would be different not only in their scope and provision, but also in the spirit in which they were administered. Our colleagues helped with their suggestions, and one deserves a mention. One of our older trade union colleagues told me of the burden which he and his wife had carried for most of their lives. They had been blessed with only one child, and the blessing had turned into tragedy when they found that their boy would never grow up. Not once had they left him on his own, and were resolved never to part with him. My friend told me: 'I have been lucky to have earned good money all my life in a regular job. The financial burden of maintaining our boy has, fortunately, never worried us, but we know others for whom tragedy has been embittered by poverty. Please, Jim, do something for them in your new scheme.' The 1948 Assistance Act not only did this but ensured that a claim can be made on behalf of people like this irrespective of the family's income.

One of the most welcome changes in the new service has been the replacement of the workhouse by the new homes for the aged. Some of these, especially those smaller ones where the old feel really at home, fill me with pride, and I would give high priority to the provision of more of them.

Many old people still find it difficult to regard national assistance as different from the 'parish'. The findings of recent surveys of the number of old people who try to eke out an existence on an income less than that provided by assistance brought to light one of our most urgent social problems. I warmly welcomed the steps taken by Margaret Herbison to change the name of the ministry merging the assistance service into the Ministry of Social Security.

6

Beveridge called for a crusade to slay the five giant evils which afflicted our society—poverty, ignorance, disease, squalor and idleness. Within three years of our electoral victory, the Labour Government had provided the legislative framework and created the organization designed to rid our country of all five. To the Family Allowances Act we added four others—Industrial Injuries, National Insurance, National Health and National Assistance. During those same years Ellen Wilkinson and George Tomlinson, at the Ministry of Education, began to implement the 1944 Education Act. The school-leaving age was raised to fifteen, and it was planned eventually to raise it to sixteen.

Together these six Acts of Parliament provide the foundation of Britain's Welfare State. To those of us who were privileged to take part in this work, the Welfare State was not a luxury dependent on what was left over in the national Treasury but the first call upon our resources. To those others who, at that time and now, persist in deriding the security of the Welfare State, I would say as I did to the House of Commons in 1946:

> For a generation I have lived with the consequences of insecurity. To those who profess to fear that security will weaken the moral fibre and destroy self respect, let me say this. It is insecurity that

destroys. It is fear of tomorrow that paralyses the will. It is the frustration of human hopes that corrodes the soul. Security will release our people from the haunting fears of yesterday, and their gifts to the service of the nation.

In his report Beveridge warned us that 'freedom from want cannot be forced on a democracy, it must be won by them'.

In the nineteen-forties we fought and won a battle for the cause of social security. We rejoice that the present generation knows not the poverty and distress of the thirties.

Eternal vigilance is the price of freedom from want as of liberty. It is therefore all the more important that voices should continue to be heard calling the attention of the nation to poverty which still persists in our modern society—the poverty of the large family, the aged, the crippled and the lonely.

Until we have taken action to deal with these we shall not have completed the task of ridding our country of the five evils— poverty, ignorance, disease, squalor and idleness.

8

COLONIAL SECRETARY

I

WHEN, after Labour had just scraped back to office in the 1950 election, I was called to No. 10, I made my way hopefully and expectantly to the Prime Minister's room. Hopefully, for having completed my task of launching the national insurance and assistance schemes, I was anxious for a change. Expectantly, because I had won recognition as a competent minister, and had been tipped for promotion. My hope had centred on being offered one of the senior posts in home affairs, with a seat in the Cabinet. Clem Attlee came straight to the point, and said that he wanted me in his Cabinet. I was very pleased and thanked him for his confidence in me. When he followed this invitation with an offer of the Colonial Office I was taken aback. Hitherto the whole of my public activities, in the trade union and in Parliament, had been devoted to domestic problems. My constituency, in common with all the industrial areas of Wales, had been grievously affected by the economic depression of the thirties. The pressure of these afflictions—mass unemployment with its poverty, distress, the means test and all the other indignities and frustrations which had overwhelmed our towns and valleys—was so great and urgent that little time or energy was left to devote to other issues. When the Prime Minister asked me to become Secretary of State for the Colonies my first inclination was to decline. Clem Attlee seemed to sense my reluctance and told me that he was confident that my proven capacity as an administrator, and ability as a parliamentarian, would be equal to the challenge of the new office. Fortified by this expression of confidence, I accepted and have never ceased to be grateful for the opportunity of serving in the Colonial Office.

In my early days in Parliament I had greatly admired the group of Labour M.P.s who dedicated their lives to the people of the Colonial Empire. Among the ablest of these was Arthur Creech Jones. He was recognized in the House as a master of his subject, and was listened to with respect. He was of a studious nature and his speeches were always thoughtful and constructive. He had been one of the founders of the Fabian Colonial Bureau, and with Dr Rita Hinden had encouraged members of our party to interest themselves in colonial affairs, and to do some constructive thinking about the problems of the colonies. The four years in which he served at the head of the Colonial Office gave him an opportunity of implementing some of the policies he had so tenaciously advocated over the years. He was a hard worker, an able administrator and utterly devoted to his work. He was one of the outstanding Colonial Secretaries of the twentieth century. I was greatly honoured in being asked to follow a minister of his calibre and was under no illusion that this would be a test as well as an opportunity.

I realized that the challenge would be all the tougher because I was taking over when the tide of anti-colonialism was riding high in all the colonial countries. The six years of war had released powerful forces in the world. The European colonial powers had exhausted themselves in the conflict. The 'white man' had first been driven out of South-East Asia by Japan, which became the dominating power in the Far East. The eventual surrender of Japan after Hiroshima left a power vacuum which was rapidly filled by new revolutionary forces inspired by Mao Tse Tung's China. The war had come to Africa, and there too the people were on the march. The emergence of Russia as a world power was having repercussions amongst the colonial peoples in every continent. New political parties were springing up overnight, new leaders were emerging to fan the flames of revolt against the colonial masters. One writer describing the African scene in 1950 had likened the British colonial countries in that continent to a 'mass of explosive yeast'. Clem Attlee's historic decision to grant independence to India, Pakistan and Burma had given a tremendous impetus to the movement for self-government in every British colony.

When I first entered the portals of the Colonial Office I felt that I was entering a new and strange world, a world in tumult. The nineteen months I was to serve in my new office were to be the most exciting in my life—full of endeavour and adventure, a mingled yarn of happiness and frustration.

2

In 1950 Britain was still responsible for fifty-three colonies. It was customary for each Colonial Secretary, on assuming office, to set out the aims of Britain's colonial policy. In conformity with the custom I declared: 'The central purpose of our colonial policy is to guide the people of the colonial territories to responsible self-government within the Commonwealth, and in partnership with them to seek to establish the conditions upon which self-government can be firmly built.' Six months later I ventured, in a talk to a conference convened by the Fabian Colonial Bureau, to point the way forward to this objective. In the course of the address I said:

> We have undertaken the task of transforming the Empire into a partnership of self-governing nations within a British Common-wealth, to transform an Empire into a Commonwealth. I do not think it has ever been attempted before; it has certainly not been accomplished before. And we are endeavouring to accomplish this truly revolutionary change by seeking to replace the relationship of metropolitan power and colony by one of partnership. That is the road on which we are now well set, and along which we are advancing. Is it the best way forward? I believe that the true answer is that there is no real alternative. Theoretically, of course, there is the possibility that the partnership could be dissolved by one or both of the partners, that on our part we should abandon the responsibilities we have undertaken and are shouldering. To trans-late this into the current jargon—that we should get out and give the colonial peoples what is called independence. And I say 'what is called independence' advisedly, for what kind of independence would they achieve if we get out now? What, for example, would happen in Malaya if we got out today? I can tell you. It would not be independence, it would be the subjugation of the Malayan people by a ruthless minority, and the subjugation of their country into a docile satellite. And what would follow in Africa if we aban-doned now the partnership we have built and are developing? Does anyone think it would be independence for their people? What kind of independence? I am sure that I carry you with me when I say that ours is the better way—the better way for the people in Malaya and Africa and all over the far-flung colonial ter-ritories. It is a difficult task that we have undertaken—to guide the

colonial territories to responsible self-government. Democratic self-government cannot be given to a people, it must be won by them. And winning democracy means much more, and is more difficult, than overcoming oppression from outside. It means winning the battle against internal enemies—ignorance, poverty, disease and squalor. That is why we have emphasized that we regard our trust not only as that of guides to self-government, but also as partners in the task of establishing those conditions, economic, social and political, which are the prerequisites of a virile and successful democracy. The justification for our partnership is that these can best be established by our joint efforts.

It was a difficult task we had undertaken and its fulfilment depended upon the co-operation of the Colonial Office, the colonial service and the people within each of the territories.

3

The Colonial Office has now worked itself out of its job, and what remains of its once immense responsibilities has been transferred to the Foreign and Commonwealth Office. Now that it has passed into history it will be of interest to recall how it was organized and equipped for its task when it was still responsible for fifty-three countries and their seventy million people. The Colonial Office of 1950 was a miniature Whitehall in itself, with the Secretary of State holding all the portfolios. Its structure and organization had been adapted to the new task of transforming the Empire into a Commonwealth. For the work of day-to-day administration the permanent secretary and his two deputies had the assistance of seven officers, of the rank of assistant under-secretaries. Each of these had charge of a number of territories grouped in geographical regions. These were: East and Central Africa, Eastern Asia, Mediterranean, the West Indies, Western Pacific, the Atlantic and Indian Ocean.

The colonial service, at home and overseas, always attracted to its ranks men and woman of distinctive gifts and character, and I developed an immense admiration for them. In addition to the administrative staff the ministers were assisted by a number of specialist advisers on the multitude of problems with which they had to deal, including agriculture, animal health, co-operation, education, fisheries, forestry, inland transport, labour, social welfare, legal, together with a chief medical officer, an inspector-general of colonial police, and directors of geodetic, topographic and geological surveys.

The wide scope and variety of the work were even more interesting and exciting when one had the opportunity of visiting those at work in the territories and of meeting the people they served. To my regret, the opportunities of visiting the colonies were limited by my short tenure of office and by the difficulties imposed by the tiny majority of the Government in the House of Commons. I was able to make only three visits. The first, even though it gave me the distinction of being the first Secretary of State to visit the country during his year of office, was necessitated for other and grimmer reasons. Within two months of my taking office the situation in Malaya had reached crisis point and, accompanied by John Strachey, then Secretary of State for War, I set out for a month's visit to Singapore and Malaya.

4

From my first day at the Colonial Office I was bombarded with questions, demands and protests about Malaya. In Parliament the extreme right demanded to know when the Government was going to wage ruthless war to stamp out banditry and terrorism, while from the left came demands for the immediate grant of freedom to the Malayan people. From Malaya came reports of increasing tension. Rubber planters, in their lonely outposts, were being killed, their homes wrecked and the rubber trees slashed. Malays in their *kampongs* (villages), and the Chinese in their 'squatter settlements' alongside the jungle, were being forced at the point of the gun to deliver food and supplies to the terrorists. British soldiers were undergoing the hazards and perils of the jungle patrol. Faced with this grim situation the civil administration was strained almost to breaking point. During 1949 and the early months of 1950 the military and police forces had been reinforced from Britain, and the Australian Government had sent a military contingent. Immediately on taking office I had consultations with the Prime Minister and the Minister of Defence, Manny Shinwell, and our first action was to appoint a director to co-ordinate the military, police and civilian operations. This task was entrusted to Lieutenant-General Sir Harold Briggs, who had won renown for his leadership in the Burma campaign. He worked out a plan, the 'Briggs plan', the implementation of which was to bring ultimate success to the efforts to end the terror, and to set Malaya on the road to unity and independence.

In May of 1950, accompanied by John Strachey, I set out on my first visit to Asia. On our way to Singapore the B.O.A.C. Constellation came down at Cairo, Karachi and Calcutta. Even though our stay at these places on our journey was but a few hours, it was long enough to enable us to make a brief excursion into each of the cities, and to note the stark contrast of luxury and squalor. The road journey from the airport to the centre of Calcutta has ever since remained a vivid, and troubled, memory. The stark poverty which showed in the gaunt faces, the emaciated bodies of the people, and the indescribable squalor of the hutches which were their homes gave me my first glimpse of that 'other world' which we called the 'undeveloped' and which troubles our conscience and threatens the peace of the world.

My experience of this journey was enriched by the companionship of John Strachey. John was endowed with extraordinary gifts of intellect, character and temperament which in turn were inspired or depressed by a troubled soul. In his political career he had travelled a tortuous road from Mosley's New Party, through the Left Book Club, and finally to the conviction that the answers to the evils of our social order and to the ills of the world were to be found only in socialism and democracy. Since he came to Parliament in 1945 he had been the subject of venomous attacks which some of our political opponents reserve for those who have shared their background of public school and Oxbridge. They were furious at his appointment to the War Office.

At Singapore we were met by Malcolm MacDonald and the Governor, Sir Franklin Gimson. Malcolm was then serving as the Commissioner-General for the British territories in South-East Asia, and was already set on the career of Commonwealth diplomat in which he has been such an outstanding success. We immediately got down to discussions with them on the situation in Malaya. They confirmed our conviction that the country's pacification had to be sought in a combination of military action and plans for the social and political progress of the country. This would have been a herculean task in peacetime; it was an even tougher one in times of guerrilla warfare and political uncertainty within a country in which the different communities mistrusted each other. Malaya's population then totalled 5¼ million, of whom just over half were Malays, nearly two million Chinese, 400,000 Indians, with small groups of Eurasians, British traders, planters and administrators. When on my arrival I broadcast a message to the people I found it was necessary to translate it into Malay, two Chinese and two Indian languages, and even then there would be many whose dialect was beyond the resources of the broadcasting service. I immediately made a note that I must find someone from our B.B.C. to take over this vital service and I was fortunate to secure Hugh Carleton Greene, who went out and did a first-class job.

The Press on our arrival told us that, like all other V.I.P.s, we would be shown, and allowed to meet, only those places and people 'they' wanted us to see. But at the end of our visit they were generous enough to admit that their fears had been groundless. The editorial in the Kuala Lumpur *Sunday Mail* of 4th June 1950 told its readers that we had 'covered many hundreds of miles in a crowded and tiring programme, which has taken them into those areas in which the war is being fought in real earnest, and they have taken every opportunity to acquaint themselves with the views of people in every stratum of society'. The High Commissioner, Sir Henry Gurney, a man whose gentle manner concealed an iron will, made sure that we saw all the rough as well as the smooth.

I received an invitation—it was more like a challenge—to visit the rubber planters at Mentakab, in Pahang, one of the areas which had suffered most from the terrorists. I flew from Kuala Lumpur in an Auster plane, strapped in my seat next to the pilot. He was determined that I should see what the jungle was like, and we flew at tree-top height, coming down at every clearing. I stayed at the bungalow of the manager of the Sementan Rubber Estate, Mr M. B. Treble, and his wife. The bungalow was on a hill sheltered by trees, and within sound of the guns in a battle taking place near by. The next day Mr Treble took me into the town to meet some fellow planters, who had gathered from miles around to give me a piece of their mind. I found myself surrounded by fifty angry men—and they had a lot to be angry about, for they carried their life in their hands at work and at home. They wanted more soldiers, guns, police and more of everything. They did not believe that there was no money for this and, in any case, the rubber they produced and paid for in blood and terror earned the dollars which helped to keep us going back home.

I went on to visit tin-mines with exotic names like Petaling, Ho Min and Yap Fab Komagi. The miners were amused when I informed them that I represented a constituency in Wales, in which the tin they mined was turned into little saucepans! I talked to the Malays, and shared their meals in their tiny homes in the *kampongs*. I saw some of the 400,000 Chinese squatters' plots, which they had wrested from the jungle, and on which, by plodding on during all the hours of daylight, they were able to grow four crops a year. I sat with Tamil Indians in the clearings of their jungle village and listened to their mournful songs. I spent a whole day at a conference of the newly formed Malayan Trade Union Council—modelled on our own T.U.C. The president, a young Indian named P. S. Narayan, had built up Malaya's strongest union, the Rubber Workers' Union. The council was already setting an example in the promotion of unity among Malays, Chinese and Indians.

I had long discussions with the leaders of the three communal organizations, representing Malays, Chinese and Indians. The United Malayan National Organization (U.M.N.O.) was then led by Dato Onn bin Ja'afar, who had the advantage of being a kinsman of one of the sultans. Dato Onn had led the Malays' opposition to the British proposal to form a unitary Malayan state in 1945 which had compelled its withdrawal and replacement by a looser federation within which the Malay States retained their sovereignty. The Malayan Chinese Association (M.C.A.) was led by the veteran Cheng Lock. He was the first Chinese political leader I met. It was a fascinating experience. He told me the story of his early years of political activity in China as one of Sun Yat Sen's supporters. He was proud of his homeland and of its ancient civilization, and was sure that some day China would be one of the greatest nations in the world.

The Indian leaders were conscious of their difficult position, feeling encircled by the two other powerful communal organizations, and subordinate to both. Nehru had urged them to look to Malaya as their home, and to work with the other communities towards a unified democratic Malaya.

Before I left for Malaya I had been advised not to refer to the operations as a 'war' but as 'the emergency', and to the Malayan Liberation Army as 'bandits'.

It did not take John Strachey and me long to find out that the so-called bandits were a well-trained, highly disciplined and skilfully led force. Their field commander, known as General Peng, was as clever a military tactician as he was an astute political leader. It was estimated that he had about ten thousand men at his command, but he seldom committed more than a hundred of them in any single operation, so that his casualties were never heavy, and his recruitment more than made up for his losses. Many of them had fought with the partisans against the Japanese when they invaded Malaya. They were thoroughly trained in the tactics of the ambush, and had a remarkable capacity for lying still in the undergrowth on the edge of the jungle and then pouncing upon their victim, and quickly escaping back into cover as soon as the deed was done.

The strategy of the campaign was directed by the central committee of the Malayan Communist Party, whose headquarters was beyond the border, in Thailand. John Strachey and I were shown some captured documents which included a series of dispatches from Peng to headquarters. From these it appeared that there had been disagreement between Peng and the committee.

When the rebellion was launched in 1948 the strategy had been determined by what the dispatches referred to as 'the Eighty Days Thesis'; what the Japanese had accomplished in eighty ays the Malayan Liberation Army could also achieve. This had led to the dispersal of their forces over the length and breadth of the federation. Peng had urged that the time had come for a change, and that their operations should be concentrated on winning one state, preferably Pahang or Johore, and then proclaiming the Malayan People's Republic. It was the menace of this new strategy that led to the appointment of a director of operations.

My visits to our soldiers brought home to me the strain which the campaign imposed on them. A night spent in the jungle is an eerie experience. Night falls suddenly in Malaya and with the darkness comes the shrill chorus which reverberates through the jungle. The men on patrol never knew from where the attack would come and often it would come from behind. The skill, courage and good humour of our soldiers were beyond praise. I remember one day talking to a young soldier from a village in Kent. He was writing to his mother and explained to me how worried she was because the only thing she knew about Malaya was that when she was a girl she had seen Malayan tigers at a menagerie! 'Dear Mum,' he said; 'if she only knew it is not tigers but leeches which bother me.'

The last days of our stay were devoted to consultation with the director of operations, General Briggs. We gave approval to his plan, the major provisions of which were:

(1) The establishment of a war executive organization, composed of persons drawn from the military, police and civilian authorities at federal level, with corresponding organizations at state and local levels. These to have powers to act and adequate resources in manpower and finance to carry through the agreed operations.

(2) The federal executive to have power to conscript men and direct them to meet the needs of the police and civilian services.

(3) The setting up of home guards in each *kampong* (village) and town, and in the rubber plantations and mines to give protection to the workers and communities.

(4) And, as an essential step towards the cutting off of supplies to the insurgents, a plan for the resettlement of the 400,000 Chinese squatters in new villages, which would provide sufficient land for each family to support itself in food, and with adequate protection by police and the home guard to protect them against attack.

We forwarded an immediate dispatch to the Government at home for their approval to the plan being put into effect at once. It was clear to us that the situation had reached a critical stage and that, short of an all-out effort, there was a danger that Peng might gain control of one or two states.

On receiving the approval of London the plan was put into operation on 1st June 1950. The resettlement of the 'squatters' was the linch-pin of the plan and we were fortunate in that we had the full co-operation of the Malayan, Chinese and Indian communal organizations, so that by the end of 1950 more than 200,000 'squatters' had been resettled in new areas. It was planned to resettle the remainder by the end of 1951.

Our next task was to find ways and means by which to associate the communal organizations with Government administration at every level. This was not easy. The proposal for a war executive had aroused the fears of the Malays that this would lead to the re-imposition of a unified state which they had resisted in 1945, and that they would be swamped by the rapid increase in the population of the Chinese and Indians. However, common danger had brought them together into a communities liaison committee.

At our suggestion they agreed to consider steps to extend Malayan citizenship to the immigrant peoples. It was also agreed that responsibility for nine departments of administration should be entrusted to leaders of the communal organizations. This 'member system' was introduced in April 1951. It was accompanied by a local authority ordinance providing for elections to councils in the towns, and rural boards in the countryside. As in all underdeveloped countries, one of the major problems was the contrast between the prosperity of the towns and the poverty of the villages. I had visited many of the Malayan *kampongs* and seen the squalor in the rural areas. The Malay peasant is a gentle—some would say indolent—person; to me the indolence seemed the inevitable consequence of a never-ending and unavailing struggle against poverty. To promote economic and social development we established a rural development board, and I was successful in persuading Dato Onn bin Ja'afar to become its chairman. I arranged for a grant from the Colonial Development and Welfare Fund to be made available to the board. When we came home to report to the Government, we were confident that, with the full implementation of the 'Briggs plan', and of the measures adopted to promote economic development, and political progress, we could in time win the war and set Malaya on the road to independence.

In October 1951, during my last days at the Colonial Office, the sad news came that the High Commissioner, Sir Henry Gurney, had been killed in an ambush. To fill the vacancy my successor appointed General Sir Gerald Templar, who played a notable part in winning the war. He would be the first to acknowledge that his success was made possible by the work of his colleague General Briggs. The trouble in Malaya lasted for ten years. There is no easy victory in guerrilla conflict anywhere in Asia.

5

It was a frustrating experience serving as Colonial Secretary in a Government whose very survival was threatened at every division. So much was happening in all the colonies in that year, 1950, that I longed to be free to visit the countries and meet their people. I was particularly anxious to visit the African territories, but had to wait until the May of 1951 before I was able to gratify my desire. Even before then the first decisive step had been taken which was to lead to the establishment of a black African state and the emergence of the first African prime minister.

In 1949 a new leader had emerged in the Gold Coast. Kwame Nkrumah was then forty years of age. Born into a family of one of the minor tribes, from an elementary school he had proceeded to a teachers' training college and then on to Lincoln University in Pennsylvania. After a stay in London he had returned to his native country and straightway plunged into politics. He soon came to prominence in the African's political organization—the United Gold Coast Convention—but he fell out with the older leaders. He wanted 'positive action to enforce the immediate grant of dominion status'. In 1949 he formed a new party—the Convention People's Party (C.P.P.). The policy of 'positive action' brought him into conflict with the authorities and, with other members of the C.P.P., he was sentenced to a term of imprisonment.

My predecessor, Arthur Creech Jones, had set up a committee on constitutional reform, a committee notable for the fact that it was composed entirely of Africans, and presided over by a distinguished African judge—Mr Justice J. H. Coussey. The report of the Coussey Committee was published in August of 1949, and its recommendations for constitutional advancement aroused intense interest. It recommended that a new legislature should be established consisting of eighty-four members almost wholly elected by popular vote in a ballot on an adult franchise. The executive council was still to be presided over by the Governor but eight of its members were to be Africans, drawn from the members elected to the legislative council; and six of these would hold portfolios.

In December 1949 the Secretary of State accepted the Coussey proposals, and steps were taken to prepare for the elections to the new legislature. At first the C.P.P. rejected the Coussey plan, and in January 1950 organized a strike and a boycott of imported goods in protest against its implementation. When the elections came in February 1951 Nkrumah and some of his C.P.P. colleagues were in prison! However, the C.P.P. decided to nominate candidates including Kwame Nkrumah and the other leaders who were with him in prison. The election attracted world-wide interest. It was the first election to be held in a British African colony on the basis of adult suffrage, and the fact that half the electorate was illiterate gave rise to cynical comment. I recognized that the election would be a crucial test of our policy of exporting our Westminster model to tropical Africa. We were fortunate that in the Governor, Sir Charles Arden-Clarke, we had a first-class administrator and one of the wisest statesmen in the colonial service. Special care was taken in the preparation of the ballot papers to take account of the illiteracy of half the voters. Each party was allocated a visual emblem such as the picture of an animal with a ballot box embellished with a corresponding picture. The polling booths were manned by members of the administration and careful measures taken to make sure that there was no molestation of the electors. Observers who came from all over the world to watch and report on this risky experiment in democracy were at one in their testimony to the efficiency and fairness with which the election was conducted.

As the campaign got under way it soon became apparent that the C.P.P. would win the day. Kwame Nkrumah had, before his imprisonment, gained an undoubted ascendancy over the older leaders like Dr Danquah, and the fact that he was leading his party from jail made him a legendary figure. When the results were declared they showed that the C.P.P. had won a decisive victory and that their members would hold a commanding majority in the new legislative council. I immediately consulted with the Governor and we agreed that Kwame and his fellow prisoners should be set free and that, as the leader of the majority party, Nkrumah should be invited to join the Government with the title of 'Leader of Government Business', and that his colleagues should be asked to take over portfolios. We were not sure whether they would agree to serve, for the C.P.P. had threatened to boycott the new constitution and to use the majority they were confident of winning to undermine it and to demand immediate dominion status. However, when Arden-Clarke saw Nkrumah and appealed to him to seize this opportunity of serving his people, and I added my appeal to his, Kwame accepted and nominated the other leaders of the C.P.P. to take over the other portfolios. The first democratically elected government in British Africa was established.

The new Government entered upon its task with real advantages on its side. It had an overall majority in the legislative council, and effective control of the executive council. It had the fullest co-operation of the Governor and the administrative officers. The economy, profiting from the high prices for cocoa and other commodities, was in a flourishing state and the reserves in the Treasury would enable progress to be made with big projects for development such as the Volta Dam. When, shortly after he had taken over the reins, Nkrumah and his principal colleagues came to London, I was deeply impressed by their ability and enthusiasm. Kwame had immense charm and this, allied to his fluency on the platform, and his dynamic energy, augured well for the success of his administration.

In his 'inner cabinet' he had three colleagues who, in their different ways, made up a good team. The minister in charge of the department of trade and economic development, Gbedemah, was an able business man who had a good grip on his job. Botsio, in charge of education and the social services, was a younger man, with ideas and drive. Caseley-Hayford had the advantage of being the bearer of an honoured name—his father having been one of the founders of the African political movement in the Gold Coast. And there was Joe Appiah, reading at the Bar and soon to return home with his wife, the daughter of Stafford Cripps. I felt sure that if these leaders could hold together, and work together, all would be well.

For a time, all did go well, almost to that day in 1957 when the Gold Coast was transformed into the independent country of Ghana. When I attended the independence celebrations in Accra, I detected even amidst the jubilant fervour and the colourful pageantry signs that all was not well. Dissension among the leaders, the bitter hostility of the opposition leaders, and the misuse of power by the ruling party were all becoming increasingly evident. In the course of the years these were to bring about the downfall of Kwame Nkrumah. Nkrumah himself fell a victim to illusions of grandeur. He conferred on himself the title of Osagefo and assumed the powers of a kind of king-president. He dismissed from office and exiled his two ablest ministers, Gbedemah and Botsio, and made Joe Appiah into a bitter enemy. He imprisoned the old leader whom he had deposed, Dr Danquah, and aroused the hostility of the leaders of other African countries by his claims to be the leader of all the Africans. The story of Ghana which began with so much promise in that first triumph of 1951 has ended in tragedy. Kwame Nkrumah, who exiled so many of his best friends and replaced them with sycophants, is himself exiled from his country, and the once-welcomed new democracy has been supplanted by a military dictatorship.

The cynical critic will say, 'This is what comes of the foolish, if sincere, belief that we can transplant our democracy to the arid soil of tropical Africa.' I still cherish the hope that some of the democratic seeds sown in Ghana will survive and some day will grow again.

6

When in 1951 the opportunity came to pay my first visits as Colonial Secretary to Africa, it was to the lands of the lakes and mountains, the highlands and copper belts and the multi-racial societies of East and Central Africa that I journeyed. Taking advantage of the Whitsun recess of that year I spent three weeks in Uganda and Kenya. My wife came with me, and with us were Andrew Cohen, then African adviser to the Secretary of State, and my private secretary, Angus Mackintosh. We travelled in a Hermes plane which flew slowly enough to make the journey pleasant, and low enough to enable us to see the wonders of the pyramids and the Nile. *En route* to Entebbe we landed at Khartoum and then flew on along the White Nile towards its beginnings in the great Lake Victoria, where the torrents of Owen's Falls were being harnessed to produce 'white coal', as old colliers call hydro-power.

Uganda is a pleasant country. There is the town of Entebbe by the lakeside; the ancient capital of Buganda, Kampala, with its palace, cathedral and university standing like beacons on the surrounding hills; Murchison Falls with herds of elephants; the Ruwenzori Mountains (the 'Mountains of the Moon'); and the Queen Elizabeth National Park where the wildlife of Africa is preserved from the guns of the hunters and the traps of the poacher. The day after our arrival at Entebbe we set out in a Dove plane for Arua and Guru in the north to meet the chiefs of the Acholi, a magnificent body of tall men—the shortest being six foot five. Their story was the familiar one: the conquerors in drawing their boundaries had divided them from their brothers across the frontier in Sudan.

The journey north had its excitement for our party. Our pilot had flown low to give us a look at the Murchison Falls when we ran into a tropical storm. The fragile Dove was tossed about like a kite in the wind—but our pilot was equal to the hazard and brought us safely out of the storm to the sunshine below. There was a sequel to this adventurous journey. One night at home we heard on the nine o'clock news that in making this trip in a Dove, with Ernest Hemingway on board, the same pilot had run into a similar storm and had crash-landed near the falls, everyone emerging alive but shaken.

One of the outstanding memories of that first visit to Uganda is of the meeting with the members of the Cotton Growers' Co-operative at Namungalwe, in the eastern province. The African farmers had fought a hard battle with pests and had at last made a success of their venture into cotton-growing. The dedicated research workers at Serowe had grown a disease-resistant cotton seed which had boosted their harvest. The Growers' Co-operative had built up an efficient system of marketing, until they ran into trouble with the owners of the ginneries (factories) to which they sold the cotton. Every one of the ginneries was owned by a non-African, some British but most of them Indian. For some time the growers had been suspicious that they were being cheated in the weight of the cotton they delivered and that they were not receiving a fair price. The grievances had developed racial overtones, and during the previous year there had been disturbances leading to violence. The co-operative had asked me to meet their members, and so on a lovely African afternoon they gathered on what was their village green at Namungalwe.

It was a wonderful setting for a gathering, in an open space enclosed by tall coconut trees. The cotton-growers had come from miles around, most of them on their bicycles which ringed the circle of the meeting-place. I sat, with my advisers, on a bench by a table, while the leaders of the co-operative came, one after another, to tell the story of their grievances and to explain their demands. There had been a suggestion that a public board be set up to acquire the ginneries, but the growers were suspicious that this was a white man's trick. What they wanted was for their co-op to own the ginneries so that they could be sure that their bales would be honestly weighed, and paid for at a fair price. They put their case so clearly and convincingly that I arranged for the acquisition by the Government of twenty-five ginneries and the provision of a loan to enable the Growers Co-operative to buy their own ginneries on a hire-purchase system. I left the meeting at Namungalwe convinced that here was one of our institutions which we had transplanted all the way from Rochdale, to flourish among the cotton-growers of Africa.

Before moving on to Kenya I went back to Kampala to address two gatherings, one the symbol of the old deeply rooted tribal Africa and the other the symbol of the new Africa on the march to independence. First, to the Lukiko, the 'parliament' of Buganda and of their king Mutessa (the Kabaka). The Kabaka was absent from the throne at the Lukiko that day, being on a visit to London. I was introduced to the assembly by the Katikura, the leader appointed by the Kabaka. From the questions put to me it appeared there were already fears that, as Uganda was moving towards independence, the ancient privileges of the Kabaka and the Lukiko were being threatened. At the university college at Makerere the fears were of a different kind: that the colonial power would be reluctant to hand over the reins to the new leaders who were emerging from the classrooms and the debating societies of the college. These two visits, on the same day, provided clear evidence that the major problem of Uganda was to find a way by which the old and the new could be reconciled, and learn to co-operate in the building of a unified state. This did not prove to be easy in the years which lay ahead, and there were many clashes before the new Africa triumphed finally over the old under the leadership of one of the former students of Makerere.

7

When at the end of my first visit to Kenya in the May of 1951 I was asked for my impressions, I replied: 'Kenya was God's own country—with the devil's own problems.' Mother Nature has showered her gifts upon this fair land, but man, in his ruthless pursuit of power and his restless quest for adventure, had come near to turning it into a devil's brew. With its endless variety of scene, beautiful vistas and riches of tropical fauna and flora Kenya, like Uganda, is a tourist's paradise. During our ten days' visit, travelling between meetings on affairs of state, we enjoyed seeing the country and its beauties. Standing guard over the land, like two sentinels, are Mount Kilimanjaro and Mount Kenya. Early one morning we took off from Nairobi on our way to Mombasa. Below, thick cloud hung over the land, and the old Dakota shook like a leaf in the wind as it climbed up through the cloud. When at long last it emerged, we saw the two sentinels, a hundred miles apart, with their snow-capped peaks glistening in the sunshine. Our pilot told us that we had been fortunate for it was a chance in a million to get this breath-taking view of the great mountains. From the snows of Kilimanjaro we descended to the old town of Mombasa, with its busy port and the picturesque harbour full of dhows and sailing vessels. Towering over it was a massive relic of the Portuguese occupation—Fort Jesus. Built in 1592, it had served as a fort, a prison and finally as a museum. The main object of our visit was to see the new Muslim Institute built by the Aga Khan to provide technical education for young Arab and Indian Muslims. Built in red stone, in Arabian style, it had an enchanting look in the hazy atmosphere of this old town whose history dated back to an Arab settlement in the eleventh century.

The Governor of Kenya was provided with his own train to enable him to tour the country, and he arranged that we should travel in it, stopping overnight at key points and taking to the road in the day time to visit the villages and *shambas* of the Africans, and the towns and farms of the white settlers. We climbed (in a car) up the escarpment to look down on the Rift Valley below, and across the forty miles to the highlands beyond. Someone told me that the rift was part of a prehistoric upheaval which shook the earth from Lake Nyasa to Galilee. On the way back, in the cool of the evening as the sun was setting, we enjoyed one of Kenya's glories—the vast concourse of flamingos resting on Lake Naivasha. Then back to Nairobi and politics.

It was difficult to believe that fifty years earlier the site of this busy capital had been only a water-hole. When the railway was built in the eighteen-nineties it had provided a suitable site as a depot for the contractors. The depot had grown into a town and in 1950 it had been raised to the status of a city. In Nairobi I had a feeling (which I was later to experience on the copper belt of Rhodesia) of apprehension and unease. Some years before, on a visit to the U.S.A., I had experienced the same feeling in some of the towns in the mid-West. Notwithstanding their main streets and avenues, with their palatial offices and smart houses, there was a brashness about them and an undertone of suppressed violence. The people did not mingle in the streets, they just rushed past as if they were all strangers to each other. Towns can be built almost overnight; it takes time to transform them into communities.

The railway which had made a depot into a city also bequeathed to the old colonial and afterwards the new African rulers the problems and the headaches of a multiracial society. Indian workers had been brought to build the railway and stayed to become the traders of Kenya. The highlands, with their equable climate, had attracted white settlers from Britain and from South Africa who had fought, and overcome, the hazards of the tropics and turned the highlands into shires. When I visited the settlers' homesteads I had the feeling that the farms of East Anglia had been transplanted to Africa. Down on the coastal strip around Mombasa there was the Arab community which had survived the chances of time and the changes of history. Spread throughout the country in their own *shambas*, on the settlers' farms, and in the towns, were the five million Africans, resentful of the intruders who had taken their land and turned thousands of them into rootless proletarians. Though they lived in the same country the different communities seemed to exist in different worlds, speaking different languages, and cherishing different customs. The advent of African rule in the Gold Coast had excited the hopes of the Africans, aroused the fears of the white settlers, and made the Indians and Arabs apprehensive. I had received petitions and met representatives in London from each of the communities, and in December 1950 I had made a statement of the Government's policy for the three countries of East Africa—Uganda, Tanganyika and Kenya. In Uganda the African representation in the legislative council had been increased and the first steps taken towards an electoral system. In Tanganyika a committee had been set up to consult with the people of all races on the next steps in constitutional progress.

In Kenya the white settlers had been given, by pre-1945 Governments, what was described as 'parity of representation' on the legislative council, which provided that the 'Europeans', as they described themselves, had the same number of members as all the other communities put together. It remained a colony with the ultimate power held by the British Government, and in my statement I had made it clear that 'His Majesty's Government would continue to exercise their ultimate control over the East African territories including Kenya'. I reaffirmed in the statement that 'our objective is self-government within the Commonwealth. Self-government must include proper provision for all the main communities which had made their home in East Africa, but in the long run their security and wellbeing must rest on their good relations with each other. Good relations cannot flourish while there are fear and suspicion between the communities; it must therefore be our task to create conditions where that fear and suspicion disappear'. And I added that 'future policy must be worked out in consultation with those who belong to the territories. . . .' It was to consult on future constitutional changes that I had come to Kenya, and during my stay I had met the representatives of all the people. At that time the leader of the African representatives on the legislative council was Elihud Mathu, one of the Kikuyu people. Mathu had been among the first of the Kenya Africans to find his way to the university at Oxford, where he had graduated, and then returned home to serve his people. With him I made a visit to the district headquarters of the Kikuyu reserves at Kiambu. There to meet us was Chief Waruhiu (later to be one of the first victims of Mau Mau) and the District Officer. The D.O. had brought along an aged African, Kamiti Watihuo, who was believed to be in his ninetieth year and to be the only African still surviving who remembered the first white man to visit the land of the Kikuyu. Soon after our arrival came Jomo Kenyatta, and the rest of the day was spent in discussion with him.

It is a far cry from that day when Jomo Kenyatta was idolized by the Africans and feared by the other races to the present when he has become the father figure trusted alike by white, brown and black. This was the first time I met Jomo and I immediately felt the impact of his formidable presence, with his tall figure, head bent forward, bearded face and piercing eyes, bass voice and chuckle, half laugh and half cry, which seemed to come from deep within. My wife was later to describe him as a mixture of Bloomsbury intellectual and African chief. This fitted the impression I had derived from his writings, and was confirmed by the impact of his personality and our long talk that day on the farm; I felt that he was torn between the attraction of our Western ways, their virtues and vices, and his deeply rooted attachment to the values and customs of his own people—the Kikuyu. He was proud of the success of the school for Kikuyu boys and girls that he had established and was himself directing. He was the president of the Kenya African Union, and presented me with a statement of their aims and objectives. We spent most of the day discussing the political situation in Kenya. I told him that the ultimate objective of our policy was democratic self-government for Kenya, but that my immediate concern was to endeavour to secure the co-operation of the leaders of all communities in working out the next stage in constitutional advancement. He left me with the impression that there was little chance of my succeeding in my quest. From my meeting with Kenyatta, I went to meet the leader of the Indian community, A. B. Patel.

From the moment I met him I developed a deep regard for Patel. He was a handsome man, with sad eyes and a beautiful voice. He had built a large and successful practice as a lawyer. He had come under the influence of Gandhi, and had immense admiration for Nehru. The divisions in the Indian community were causing him great pain and he confessed that he was, for this reason, becoming disenchanted with politics. In the end this was to lead him to abandon both his legal practice and political life in Kenya, and to return to India to enter a monastery. But during my visit he took a constructive and helpful part in the efforts to promote racial co-operation.

These meetings with the Africans and Indians were followed by meetings with the European members of the legislative council. Their old leader, Albert Keyser, had recently retired through illness, and his place had been taken by one of the younger members—Michael Blundell. In his book *So Rough a Wind* Blundell has described this meeting, and as it is good for all of us to see ourselves as others see us, I venture to quote what he says:

> At our first formal meeting one of my colleagues took him to task for the decision of the Labour Government to give rapid advance to self-government to what was then the Gold Coast. This decision undoubtedly fired the imagination of the Africans everywhere, and accelerated enormously the forces behind the dismantling of the white man's control throughout the continent. Griffiths reacted rather sharply, banged the table with his fist, and in his strong Welsh voice said: 'And what was the alternative, man? Bloody revolution, that's what it was.'

At the close of this meeting Michael invited me to visit his farm to meet some of his rank and file who had been threatening rebellion. His farm was in Subokia, one of the loveliest areas in the highlands, and there I met some of the white extremists and repeated my warning—that the choice was between racial unity and co-operation, or revolution. Blundell and some of the other younger men among the white settlers shared my view that the wise course for them was to work with the leaders of the other communities. This encouraged me to make an effort to secure joint action by the leaders of all the racial groups to work out an agreed policy for constitutional change. On the last day of my stay I called them to a meeting at Nairobi. The Governor of Kenya at this time was Sir Philip Mitchell, and he has given an account of this meeting and of my proposals in his published diary, where he writes:

> *28th May 1951.* At 10.45 with Andrew Cohen and me, he saw Blundell, Havelock, Cooke, Patel, Rans, Mathu and Sheriff Abdulla. First he read a general proposition that within twelve months of the election of the next Council [May 1952] there be set up an inter-racial consultative body under an independent chairman from outside Kenya and with [Kenya] Government and Colonial Office representation, to examine the whole constitutional set-up and to make representations. If that were agreed he would not now disturb parity and would only make interim adjustments—an African seat for Africans in the executive council and two more Members in the legislative council, an additional Indian seat, and always two Muslims in the council, an Arab on the official side and three more European seats. These proposals to be regarded as totally withdrawn if the first [consultative body] is not accepted. After a brief adjournment everyone accepted all the proposals and the proceedings ended with a graceful tribute by Blundell to the Secretary of State and a very charming reply by him. So it is all settled in an atmosphere of sober responsibility and goodwill in the manner I had hoped, and by the personal influence of this remarkable man who has spread goodwill wherever he has been.

Alas, had we but known it in that May of 1951, it was already too late. Within eighteen months Kenya was to experience the grim ordeal of the Mau Mau rebellion. There have been many attempts since the rebellion to seek out its causes, and many people, including the Governor, Sir Philip Mitchell, have been blamed for their failure to discover the Mau Mau conspiracy before the rebellion. Whether these criticisms are justified or not is a matter on which people at the time, and since, have differed. What I do know is that during my visit not a single person of all those I met—African, Indian, Arab, European—or any of the colonial officers, ever even mentioned the word Mau Mau to me. I believe that the truth of the matter is that each of the racial communities was so completely locked up within its own separate world that none of them knew what was happening in the closed world of its neighbour. This was the tragedy of the multiracial communities not only in Kenya but also in those countries in the centre of Africa which I was to visit in the autumn of 1951.

In these first years of the nineteen-fifties few would have thought that it was the land I had described as 'God's own country with the devil's own problems', which was to be the first of Africa's multiracial countries to attain independence with the goodwill of all its communities. This it owes to the emergence of Jomo Kenyatta as one of Africa's greatest statesmen and to the wisdom of white men like Michael Blundell.

8

I have generally been regarded, by political foes as well as friends, as a person easy to get on with, and not too difficult to work with, but a contrary view was expressed in the memoirs of Lord Chandos and the writings of Sir Roy Welensky.

Lord Chandos (then Oliver Lyttelton) succeeded me as Colonial Secretary following the 1951 election. In his memoirs he wrote, on his taking office: 'Jim Griffiths, the outgoing Colonial Secretary, came to see me. I had always liked him in the old days, but his emotional approach to public affairs was to drive me first to boredom, and finally to exasperation.' And Sir Roy Welensky, in his *4,000 Days—The Life and Death of the Federation of Rhodesia and Nyasaland*, confessed that 'it is a sad fact but true that Jim Griffiths and I grated on one another from the outset'. It is interesting to reflect why these two men, so different in their origins and backgrounds, found me to be 'exasperating' and 'grating': Oliver Lyttelton, the Old Etonian and guardsman, politician-cum-business tycoon; and Roy Welensky, the railway-man who became a trade union leader and eventually the Prime Minister of the Federation. It was the controversy surrounding the birth and life of the ill-fated federation that was to bring me into conflict with them. From the scramble by the European imperial powers in the nineteenth century Britain had, by conquest or treaty, gained control of the lands which lie at the heart of the African continent. These eventually emerged as the colony of Southern Rhodesia, and the protectorates of Northern Rhodesia and of Nyasaland. Though the map-makers and the imperial administrators had divided them into three separate territories, their subsequent economic development had made them into a kind of African 'common market'. In Northern Rhodesia there was the copper belt, one of the richest sources of copper in the world, but to melt the ore coal had to be brought from the Wankie Colliery three hundred miles away in Southern Rhodesia, and thereafter the copper had to be carried through that country and beyond, to the ports on the Indian Ocean.

Nyasaland, the loveliest of the three countries, and the most thickly populated as well as the poorest in material resources, provided the man-power for the development of the industries of the two Rhodesias. This interrelated economic development had, over the years, led to the creation of common services and of a Central African Council to promote and administer them. The economic arguments for their closer political association were then, and still remain, powerful.

In 1950 it was urged upon me, and my colleague Patrick Gordon-Walker (who as Commonwealth Secretary was responsible for Southern Rhodesia), that there were new and urgent reasons for promoting the closer political association of the three countries. Representations to this effect were made by our advisers in Whitehall and many people from the Rhodesias, including the then Prime Minister of Southern Rhodesia, Sir Godfrey Huggins (now Lord Malvern), and Sir Roy Welensky. These political considerations have historical interest as part of the story of the federation, and for their relevance to the more recent crisis in Rhodesia. In 1950 the political arguments for federation were based on these considerations. From the end of the Second World War immigration to the Rhodesias had rapidly increased, especially from the south. Between 1945 and 1950 for every 100 immigrants from the United Kingdom to Northern Rhodesia, there had been 174 from South Africa, a large proportion of them Afrikaners. By this time the Nationalist Government was firmly in control in South Africa and was imposing its policy of apartheid on that country.

It was known that branches of the 'Broederbond'—the Afrikaners' secret society—were being established in Rhodesia. Equally disquieting was the announcement of the formation of a party in Southern Rhodesia under the name of 'Democratic Party'. The name deceived no one: it was made up of the extreme white racialists pledged to the policy of apartheid. It was for these reasons—that the desirability of promoting common action in the economic development of the three countries, and of ensuring that their political progress was in accordance with British principles and traditions—that Patrick Gordon-Walker and I agreed that the officials of our two departments, together with officials from the territories, should prepare a draft constitution for a Central African Federation. It was clearly understood from the outset that the proposal to amalgamate the three countries into a unitary state was ruled out, that the protectorate status of Northern Rhodesia and of Nyasaland would be maintained, and that all the people in the three countries would be consulted before a final decision was made.

The officials produced a draft constitution which provided for a white majority in the federal parliament, with special provisions for the maintenance of the protectorate status of Northern Rhodesia and of Nyasaland; the safeguarding of African rights and interests, and the preservation of the ultimate authority of the British Government and Parliament. The rights and interests of the Africans were to be safeguarded by the division of functions between the federal and territorial governments. All matters which most intimately affect the daily lives of the Africans would remain within the prerogative and absolute sovereignty of the territorial governments. In the federal government would be included a Minister for African Interests appointed by the United Kingdom Secretary of State. In addition to holding his seat in the Cabinet, the minister was to preside over an African Affairs Board, which would have the power to hold up any federal legislation which it judged might injuriously affect African interests, and submit it to His Majesty's Government for approval or disapproval.

The officials' proposals were published and commended for consideration without any commitment, and it was arranged that Patrick Gordon-Walker and I would visit the three countries for consultation with all the people, and would attend a conference of their representatives at Victoria Falls. Prior to attending the conference I visited the two protectorates while Patrick Gordon-Walker visited Southern Rhodesia. In Northern Rhodesia and Nyasaland I attended over a hundred meetings, most of them with the Africans, their paramount chiefs, their representatives in the legislative council, and the African Congress parties. I also had consultations with the European representatives and with the colonial officers in both countries.

I was again to discover, as I had in Kenya, that at the heart of the problems of multiracial communities were land and colour. Land was the African's life-blood and colour the exposed nerve. I remember how the deep and suppressed resentment at the colour discrimination came out during my first visit to Africa. My wife and I had been shown to our room and in a while a young African came along with our luggage. My wife asked him what his name was, but could get no reply, only a startled look, and when I asked him he hesitated, and then replied, 'Sir, I am called "boy".' I felt as embarrassed as he was, and was to experience the same feeling at hearing the way in which some white people would refer to the Africans as 'natives', in a tone which gave the word a sinister meaning. These two words 'boy' and 'native' were minor examples of the colour discrimination prevalent in these countries, and they seemed to me to cut even deeper than many of the others. The worst sin against a fellow human being is to hurt his dignity.

Before I went out to Central Africa some of my critics had derided the idea of consulting the African people on such a complicated matter as federation. 'They will not understand a word of what you say to them,' was their cry. My experience proved how false, and even dangerous, this assessment was. At all the meetings I attended they put their case clearly, they asked penetrating questions and held their own in argument. This was particularly true of the meetings I had with the miners on the copper belt. I met representatives of the two miners' trade unions, the white and black. I talked with former coal-miners from the British coalfields, amongst them one from my own valley, and regretted to find that they too had fallen for the 'boy' and 'native' arrogance. They felt, and behaved, like members of a superior race. This was especially noticeable in their homes with their 'boys' to wait on them. It was a far cry from the pitman's cottage. However, it was encouraging to find some who were disturbed and unhappy at the disparities between their standard of life and that of their black fellow-miners who shared the perils of the mines without the joy of the fellowship which once enriched their life in the valleys. As one of them said to me: 'This is like the old butty system, with its boss and hirelings which our forefathers fought against in the bad old days back home. We should be fighting it out here.'

At the end of three weeks of an arduous tour we reached Victoria Falls for the conference. It was held in the palatial hotel which stands beside the falls—'the Voice of Thunder' as the Africans call this majestic cascade of waters of the Zambesi. We began by breaking new ground, for this was the first time that black Africans had been allowed to enter the upper floors of the hotel.

The conference nearly broke up at its first session. In my opening statement I had given an account of the consultations I had held. I intimated that the Africans in Nyasaland were opposed in principle to federation; and that their representatives had come to the conference to give their reasons for the rejection of the proposals. Sir Godfrey Huggins immediately proposed that, in view of their rejection of the whole idea of federation, the Nyasaland Africans should leave. I intervened at once to say that they were at the conference at my invitation and that if they left I would leave with them. Sir Godfrey hastily retreated, but the rebuff rankled, and he was later to lament that I had turned the conference into a 'natives' tea party'.

Our discussion revealed, as the communiqué published at the close makes clear, that there were differences in principle, as well as detail, on the proposals for a federation. These would call for further consideration before any binding decisions could be made. Moreover, the conference agreed that in any further consideration of the proposed federation it would be essential to embody in its constitution provisions that would preserve the protectorate status of Nyasaland and Northern Rhodesia; ensure that, within their territory, land and land settlement questions would remain under the absolute authority of their territorial governments; and that the political advancement of the two protectorates would continue to be determined by H.M.G. in association with their own governments. The conference also recorded its apprehension at the spread of the propaganda for apartheid in the two Rhodesias, though this was expressed in officialese terms in the communiqué. To quote: 'The conference was gravely concerned at the dangers which would flow from any weakening or dilution of the British connection and British traditions and principles in the three territories, and agreed that they be so strengthened as to ensure that they should continue to prevail. . . .'

It was agreed that the issues raised at the conference should be further considered by all concerned before it was recalled. In the light of subsequent events the proposals made by the two African representatives from Northern Rhodesia—P. Sokota and D. Yamba—was of special importance. As recorded in the communiqué they declared that they would be willing to consider the question of federation, 'after the policy of partnership in Northern Rhodesia had been defined and, as so defined, put into progressive operation'.

Patrick Gordon-Walker and I returned home to find ourselves plunged into a general election campaign and, as a result of our party's defeat, replaced by two Conservative ministers—Oliver Lyttelton at the Colonial Office and Lord Ismay at the Commonwealth Office. Within a few weeks of taking office, Oliver Lyttelton made his first statement on the proposed federation. He announced that the Conservative Government was in favour of federation among the three territories on the general lines recommended in the official report; endorsed the safeguards for the two protectorates agreed to at the Victoria Falls Conference, and stated that he would ensure that these would be formally embodied in the constitution. He further stated that his Government was 'most anxious that there should be no delay in reaching final conclusions', and that the conference would be recalled in the middle of 1952, and that the 'intervening period is used to the best advantage for the necessary discussions in Central Africa. . . .'

It was clear to me from the discussions at the Victoria Falls Conference that the most important of these consultations would be those with the African representatives. These were bungled from the moment Lyttelton made his statement in November 1951. A month later the African Representative Council of Northern Rhodesia met to consider the proposal put forward by their representatives at Victoria Falls on the definition and implementation of partnership. They asked that the Government should prepare a definition for their consideration, and at the same time expressed 'their great concern at the statement made by the Secretary of State on 21st November 1951 and considered that it was too early for him to have made an open statement on the matter'. Their suspicions that the affair was being rushed without consultation with them were deepened when in January 1952 Sir Godfrey Huggins and the governors of Northern Rhodesia and Nyasaland came to London to discuss federation. No African was invited to be present. The consequence was that, when the full conference was convened later that year, the African representatives refused to attend.

Notwithstanding pleas from my colleagues and myself not to proceed with the conference in the absence of the Africans, Lyttelton and the European leaders from Central Africa proceeded to prepare a constitution for the federation. They made changes in the scheme prepared by the officials, the most important of which was to drop the proposal for an African minister, and the conversion of the African Affairs Board into a Standing Committee of the Federal Legislature—thus weakening the safeguards for Africans. From that moment they destroyed any chance of securing African agreement to federation. However, this did not deter them from carrying their plans through Parliament against the opposition of Labour and Liberal parties, and of imposing it on the protectorates, against the unanimous opposition of the Africans.

The federation lasted for only four thousand days. It was doomed from the moment when the British Government imposed it against the unanimous opposition of the African people. Sir Roy Welensky hastened its end when he joined with the Colonial Secretary in overruling the African Affairs Board the first time its members declared a federal Bill to be disadvantageous to the Africans, thus destroying the very safeguard for the Africans unanimously agreed to by all the representatives, including Sir Roy himself, at the Victoria Falls Conference. The federation was killed by its creators in Central Africa and Westminster. In the end Sir Roy, who had confessed that I grated upon him, spared me from the charge he made against the Conservatives of having betrayed him.

The story could have been so different, and the man who could have made it different was Welensky. He was by far the ablest of the European leaders in Central Africa. He had tremendous drive and energy and had fought his way to the top against the white establishment in the Rhodesias. As I discovered in my talks with him, he recognized that there was no future for the white man in Africa unless he learned to live and work with the Africans towards a multiracial society in which all would enjoy equality of status and dignity. If he had allied himself with the progressive Europeans like Sir John Moffat (a kinsman of David Livingstone) in Northern Rhodesia, and Garfield Todd in Southern Rhodesia, instead of the racialists, he could have been a great benefactor to his country. If only he had sought the friendship of African leaders, like Kenneth Kaunda, instead of persecuting them, he might have been the founder of a federation which would have developed into a democracy. Unfortunately he chose his friends among the racialists, who not only killed the federation but were later to reject, and humiliate, him and put in his place men of lesser ability like Ian Smith. In our discussions in the early fifties he had seemed aware of the danger that the country of his birth—Southern Rhodesia—might fall into the hands of the racialists and had considered federation the surest way of preventing this happening. He might even yet rediscover the ideas and the ideals which inspired his work for his trade union, and help to rescue his country from the apartheid which at one time he both feared and hated.

9

In March 1950 I had entered upon my work as Colonial Secretary with trepidation. I felt like a traveller entering a strange world. Twenty months later I was to leave with the deepest regret. I was beginning to find my way in this new world and to understand the hopes and aspirations as well as the fears of the people who dwelt in it. One had the feeling of being in at the making of history. The revolution which, within a decade, was to transform the British Empire into a Commonwealth was already gathering momentum. Even during that brief period of twenty months, eleven colonies had won new constitutions which were landmarks on the road to independence. It is interesting, in retrospect, to recall the names of the eleven: Trinidad and Tobago, Gold Coast, Sierra Leone, North Borneo, Nigeria, Dominica, Grenada, St Lucia, St Vincent, Singapore and Gambia. All of these have since reached their goal as independent states, or as constituents of federal states.

One of the privileges, and pleasures, of a Colonial Secretary was that of meeting the new leaders who were soon to attain to positions of power and responsibility in their countries. For many of them, the journey from the carefree joys of the agitator to the burdens of government had been so very short. I remember one of them saying to me, half in earnest, half in jest: 'It is an uncomfortable feeling, not being able to pass the buck to you.' And it must have been; for the achievement of independence was not only the end of one road but also the beginning of another, and harder, road along which they would face many hazards. In the struggle for freedom from colonial rule, they had aroused expectations, and now they had to strive to fulfil them. They had to try to make two blades of grass grow where one grew before. They had to promote rapid industrial development to establish a diversified and viable economy. More and more schools and colleges had to be provided to enable their young people to acquire the knowledge and skills needed to earn their own livelihood and that of their country. The conquest of the diseases which plagued their people and decimated their lands was an essential prerequisite to the progress they so fervently desired. The war on want was an even more formidable challenge than the conflict with the imperial power had been. For many of them the task was rendered more difficult by the necessity of welding people of differing languages, customs and deep-rooted tribal loyalties into one nation. Some of the new leaders have risen magnificently to the challenge, whilst others have proved unequal to it.

For myself, and those who share my views, there is no regret that we regarded our mission as one of not only ending colonial rule but also of endeavouring to replace it with democratic self-government. That the Westminster model has been, and will be, modified and adapted to meet the different circumstances of each country I fully recognize, but I am sure that the foundations of democratic government which we laid will remain and that, in the fullness of time, new and virile democracies will arise.

In the years following my brief stay at the Colonial Office, I have kept an abiding interest in the countries which I strove to serve. I have had opportunities of again visiting them and meeting their ministers. I have rejoiced with them at their independence celebrations, and have shared in their triumphs, as well as endeavouring to understand their tribulations. The young men who, less than twenty years ago, were students at our colleges, are now the presidents or prime ministers of their countries. I enjoy a real thrill to find them attending the conferences of Commonwealth Prime Ministers, and sitting at the same table as our own Prime Minister. I have joined them at the conferences of the Commonwealth Parliamentary Association and argued with them by day and night. Whenever I go to one of our universities or colleges I seek out the students from the Commonwealth and talk with them, and am aware that I may be exchanging views with a future prime minister.

All the time the conviction grows within me that the future of our world may be determined not in what we are pleased to regard as the corridors of power but on the paddy-fields of Asia and in the *shambas* of Africa. With that conviction comes the desire, and the hope, that the Commonwealth which we in Britain have shared in creating may yet provide an example of how people of different races, colours and creeds can live together in equality and dignity.

9

THE ROLE OF THE RECONCILER

FOR twenty years from 1939 to 1959 I served in the higher
counsels of the Labour Party at Westminster and at Transport
House. In 1939 I was elected a member of the National Executive
of the party and in the course of my service was a member of
some of its most important committees. In the same year I was also
elected as one of the Parliamentary Labour Party's front bench
spokesmen, and I sat on the front bench for the next twenty
years—the Government and Opposition front benches in turn.
The twenty years covered a period of mixed fortunes for our
party. There were days of triumph and nights of despair; of
controversies over policies and conflicts for the leadership;
of left-wing revolts and right-wing ripostes; of bitter dissensions and reconciliations. Every party in turn shares these
chances and changes of fortune, and each profits from its rivals'
misfortunes.

Throughout this period I was often described as a middle-of-
the-road man. For myself I prefer to think of my role as that of a
reconciler, ever seeking to promote unity, and to prevent rival
factions and personal antagonisms from tearing the party to
pieces.

It is a role which suits my temperament, and which my
experience in trade union work had moulded into a pattern of
behaviour. If a man is to serve his cause he must be true to himself. When I joined the I.L.P. I did not regard it as just another
party thirsting for power, but as a cause akin to a religion. The
meaning of socialism for me was best expressed by James Bruce
Glazier: 'Socialism means not only the socialization of wealth,
but of our lives, our hearts, ourselves. Socialism consists not in

getting but in giving, not in being served but in serving.' This was the socialism which inspired our service and enriched our lives in fellowship.

For me, as for countless others of my contemporaries, the spirit of those early years is a precious heritage. The Labour Party owes much to those for whom it is a cause. They are the folk for whom the meanest task is a mission, the comrades who only ask, 'What can I do to help?' They rejoice in the party's triumphs and are steadfast in times of disaster. It was their loyalty in 1931 which made 1945 possible, and their steadfastness in the years of strife was at long last rewarded in 1964. I shall feel honoured if I am counted as one of their company.

I served on the National Executive from 1939 to 1959 and, apart from the three years when I sat ex-officio as Deputy Leader, served throughout as a constituency party representative. The press regarded the elections to this section of the executive as a contest between the left and the right, and there was some justification for their view. It was certainly the case at the Morecambe conference of 1952 when the left, led by Nye Bevan, won six of the seven seats, and such stalwarts as Herbert Morrison and Hugh Dalton were rejected, leaving me as the sole survivor of what was labelled 'the old guard'. The Morecambe conference rocked the party from top to bottom. The prophets of gloom emulated their predecessors of 1931 in predicting the end of the Labour Party as a political force in the country. The conference left a legacy of bitterness which threatened to justify their prophecy. Morecambe was indeed the low-water mark in the morale of the movement, following as it did the resignation from the Government of Nye Bevan and Harold Wilson and the defeat of the party in the 1951 election. The Constituency Labour Parties, especially those in Tory strongholds, love rebels. The hopelessness of their electoral prospects, and the scorn with which they regard the entrenched Tory establishment, combine to make them responsive to the man who kicks over the traces. The isolation of the rebel strikes a deep chord in the life of comrades who themselves feel isolated in their communities. At the same time they fear the effects of dissension on the harmony of their parties, and on their electoral prospects. Yet, though they support the rebels, they also have a warm regard for the reconciler. I think it was because they looked on me as fulfilling this role that even at Morecambe they re-elected me as one of their representatives on the executive.

The defeat of Herbert Morrison was deeply regretted by the old members of the executive. For many years, as chairman of the policy committee, he had been the architect of Labour's policy. It was Herbert who had led in the framing of the programme set out in 'Let us Face the Future' upon which the party had won the 1945 election; and it was he who, as Leader of the House, had organized its implementation. He was always a brave fighter who would volunteer to put the executive case on sticky issues to conference. His defeat at Morecambe left a big gap in the ranks of the executive, and the question then arose as to who should take his place as chairman of the policy committee. This was a key position and many of my fellow members pressed me to accept nomination, and I was appointed because they felt that I could help to bridge the gulf between right and left.

Before the committee began its task I gave much thought to planning its work. In this I collaborated closely with our general secretary, Morgan Phillips, as I knew he shared my views on the way ahead. The Labour Government had by 1950 carried out the heavy and comprehensive programme set out in 'Let us Face the Future'. The period following the election of 1950 had not been noteworthy for its legislative achievement. This was understandable because of the handicap of a small majority. Even more serious in its effect upon the morale of the party was the threat to the achievements of the 1945 Government, and especially to our major achievement, the Welfare State, from the worsening economic situation at home and the burden of rearmament. On the committee devolved the responsibility of framing policies designed to deal with Britain's basic economic problems, the burden of rearmament and the perilous international situation. In this we co-operated with the international committee under the chairmanship of Sam Watson.

The policy committee immediately settled down to its task and, although there were disagreements on some issues, not always as between left and right, we secured a larger measure of agreement than at first had seemed possible, and I was able to present an agreed policy statement entitled 'Challenge to Britain' to the 1953 conference at Margate. Political programmes can be quickly outmoded by events, and nine years were to elapse between the publication of 'Challenge to Britain' and the formation of Harold Wilson's administration in 1964. Yet 'Challenge' was as relevant to the situation in 1964 as in 1953—as these excerpts will prove:

> If fifty million people, crowded on these islands, are to earn a decent living without relying on foreign aid, we must discard the prejudices and privileges of the past and plan the work of our mines, our fields and factories for the common good. . . . We import half the food we eat, and with few exceptions all our raw materials. To pay for these essentials we rely on selling our manufactures. . . . The world's manufacturing capacity has greatly increased. Not only are the industrialized countries producing more but the primary producing countries have started to manufacture as well. . . . Moreover, all countries are tending to become increasingly self-sufficient in manufactures of the kinds which are simplest to produce. . . . Our best prospects lie in the export of goods which require a high degree of technical experience. This means we must change the whole emphasis of our production and export effort. . . . The plan we outline will involve sacrifices not only of material benefits but of many cherished habits and traditions. . . . The British people will accept these sacrifices once it is realized that only by so doing can we regain our economic independence, defend our living standards and play our full part in saving the peace. . . . In a tight corner the British people are unbeatable. Our weakness as a nation is our unwillingness to face the facts until the crisis is on top of us.

Our party conference, with its delegates representing a fair cross-section of the British people, seldom fails to rise to a challenge, and the debate on the new programme was worthy of our movement. The debates were lively, as they should be, but they were free from personal rancour, and fulfilled the hopes I had expressed in opening the debate, and appealing for unity:

> We who are at this conference did not create the Labour movement: we inherited it. It is a precious heritage. It is our duty to preserve it and keep it, and hand it on inviolate and stronger to the boys and girls who are growing up. At the end of this week let us go out with all the resources of this great movement, trade unions, co-operative, constituency parties, all sections, speaking with one voice, commending 'Challenge to Britain' to the nation. That is the way to be worthy of the movement . . . and the way to gain the confidence of the British people.

At the end of the conference I had the satisfaction of knowing that I had served the party in the role for which I am best fitted—that of a reconciler. This was the role I still endeavoured to fill in the controversies within the Parliamentary Party in the years which followed that conference of 1953.

2

The trade unionist turned politician has often been treated as fair game for the gibes of the slick commentator, a political equivalent to David Low's 'white nag', stodgy if solid, conservative if loyal, and holding on to a safe seat which would be so much better used as a launching pad for the younger and more ambitious. I am one of the fortunate, who has enjoyed for over thirty years a safe seat in which, as a wag once remarked, the votes after the poll could be weighed rather than counted! It is often forgotten that many of us, including myself, were in at the beginning and helped to make the seat safe by extending loyalty to the union to loyalty at the ballot box. It has also to be borne in mind that, with rare exceptions, our entry to Parliament was the beginning of a second career. We had first to win our spurs in the service of our union before we could hope to gain the nomination of the union for a constituency; and our second career did not begin until we were in the forties, or even older. By then our approach to public life, its opportunities and responsibilities, had been moulded in the furnace of industrial conflict and strife.

My own life followed this pattern. I came to Parliament in 1936 after ten years as an officer, and for a period as president, of the South Wales Miners' Union. I had worked in the coal-mine for seventeen years. Life in the mine is hard and perilous. It would be hell without the loyalty of man to man, and the fellowship of kindred spirits. To curry favour with the boss was a heinous crime, to betray a comrade an unforgivable sin. Loyalty became the supreme virtue. It was our rule never to argue with one another in front of the management. Policy and attitude would be settled in the privacy of the committee, and once settled called for one voice and one voice only. If this meant the sacrifice of personal liberty, then that was the price of survival. Within a few months of my election to my trade union post came the grim ordeal of 1926—and for the rest of my tenure of office we had to tread warily along the hard road to recovery. I knew how dissension among union leaders had disheartened members, and how it had been exploited by our enemies. I had also lived through 1931 when, but for the steadfastness of the trade unions, the Labour Party could not have survived.

When a trade unionist, trained in this hard school, enters Parliament he brings with him these virtues of loyalty and steadfastness. One of my first concerns on entering the House of Commons was to join the miners' and the trade union groups. The work of these groups does not attract much attention and seldom even gets a mention in the press, but their influence is always powerfully if quietly exercised. Their members provide the solid core of loyalists which a political party needs to sustain it through all the vicissitudes of fortune in government and opposition.

The Labour Party had its full share of these vicissitudes in the fifties, and there were times when they were aggravated and embittered by the clash of personal ambitions. This was understandable, for at that time the long reign of Clem Attlee was drawing to its close. He had been elected leader in 1935, a few months before I joined his team, and he held the confidence of the party, and especially of the trade union members, without any serious challenge for twenty years. I know that this will be questioned by some who will cite episodes in which attempts were made to depose him. The first was the one which failed to get off the ground because of the loyalty of a colleague, and it deserves to be recalled as an example of personal ambition subordinated to a sense of honour.

When the Second World War broke out in 1939 Clem Attlee was in hospital undergoing an operation. The responsibility of leading the party during those crucial days of September 1939 fell upon his deputy, Arthur Greenwood. He rose to the occasion magnificently, and became Britain's voice when Neville Chamberlain faltered and failed. Arthur was greatly loved by the party in the House and the country, and his prestige soared in those days. Some members pressed Arthur to stand for the leadership, but he immediately declared his loyalty to his leader and the move petered out. Politics are tough at the top and it is all the more gratifying to be able to record an occasion when loyalty was stronger than ambition.

There were two other occasions when there might have been a challenge to Clem Attlee's leadership, and it is interesting to recall that the decisive part in defeating them was played by one of the greatest of trade union leaders—Ernest Bevin. The first of these was in 1945 when, following our victory, the question arose as to whether Attlee should wait until the Parliamentary Party had assembled and had an opportunity of selecting its leader before accepting the invitation to form a Government. All this took place at Transport House, and like most of my colleagues I heard of it afterwards, but it was generally believed that Ernest Bevin, in a few stern words, had settled the issue there and then. The second was during the lifetime of the 1945 Government and is reputed to have been made by some of the ministers serving under Clem Attlee, and to have been aimed at replacing him with Ernest Bevin, only to be quickly consumed in the fires of Bevin's wrath the moment he heard of it. I had no knowledge of this attempt to displace our leader until after the event. What I am certain of is that if it had reached the stage at which the Parliamentary Party would have been called upon to decide it would have been overwhelmingly defeated—and the trade union members would have been solid in support of Attlee.

It was those of us who worked closest to and served longest under him who most fully appreciated his great qualities. He had few of the outward trappings of a great leader. He did not have an imposing appearance. He was not an orator, though some of his speeches were models of logical argument and incisive language. In his Cabinet he would listen, and doodle, but in his summing up would get to the heart of the matter in a few sentences and there would be no ambiguity about his decision. The six years of his premiership will have their place in our history. He will be remembered as the head of the Government which created the Welfare State and began the transformation from Empire to Commonwealth. Within the party he was revered as the man who stood firm in 1931, who came to the leadership in a time of tumult within the party and who, through all the controversies of the forties and fifties, remained the steadfast leader who rallied our forces and held us together. He is one of the rare examples of a political leader who became more revered in his retirement than he was in the period of his active life. Those who have been present at our conferences and witnessed the spontaneous demonstration which greeted him whenever he came on to the platform during his years of retirement will have appreciated the depth of the affection felt for him.

It was inevitable that after such a long period under such a

leader the choice of his successor should have given rise to rival
factions. There were some who held the view that this could have
been avoided if Attlee had retired following the 1951 election. I
was one of those who urged him to continue in the leadership. I
did so because I believed that at that time only Clem Attlee could
hold the party together. Our defeat in that election had been
partly attributable to the dissensions within the Government.
The first priority was to heal the wounds which our party had
inflicted upon itself, and I felt that to involve the party in the
strains and stresses of a contest for the leadership at that time
would be more likely to aggravate than to heal the wounds. There
were others who took a contrary view, but I was convinced that
in urging Clem Attlee to remain at the helm I and those who
joined me in our representations were expressing the desire of
the majority of our colleagues in the Parliamentary Labour Party.
Unfortunately Herbert Morrison interpreted our action as one
designed so to delay Attlee's retirement as to prejudice his
prospects for the succession, and he suspected that this was in
accord with Attlee's wishes. In his autobiography Herbert wrote:

> I have been asked more than once if I feel that it is true that Attlee
> deferred retirement until it was over-late for me to succeed him.
> My answer has always been, regretfully but inevitably, in view of
> the evidence, that this is in my view a correct interpretation.
> Quite apart from any consideration of my own future, both Attlee
> and the party would probably have found it a wiser policy if he
> had retired after our defeat in 1951. . . . There were influential
> Labour M.P.s who talked to him on this line and I was told by
> them that their point of view had found a receptive ear. They were
> presumably misled into believing taciturnity meant agreement.

The truth is that Herbert was misled into believing that the
influential M.P.s to whom he refers represented the prevailing
view of the Labour M.P.s. I know that the colleagues who joined
me in persuading Clem Attlee to remain as our leader would all
have been glad to see Herbert succeed him. Herbert had rendered
devoted service to the party and was entitled to claim, as he did
in his autobiography, that he had often, in the executive and at
conferences, taken over burdens and responsibilities which
normally would have fallen on the leader. He had rendered
notable service to the country as Home Secretary during the war,
and his work in London during the blitz was an important contribution to the country's survival and ultimate victory. In the

1945 Parliament he had proved a highly successful leader of the House of Commons in carrying through Parliament an immense programme of legislation. This made it all the more regrettable that his relations with Attlee became strained. It was accounted for mainly by differences of temperament, on the one hand to what Herbert calls Clem's 'taciturnity' and on the other to his own exuberance. There is no doubt that this temperamental strain was aggravated by the action of Herbert in 1945 when he sought to delay Attlee's acceptance of the commission to form a Government.

There is another episode which reflected this lack of complete confidence between Attlee and Morrison, and in which I was involved. It relates to the choice of a successor to Ernest Bevin when he retired from the post of Foreign Secretary on account of his failing health. Bevin had suggested to Attlee that I should succeed him. When I was called to No. 10 to talk over this suggestion with the Prime Minister I at once made it clear that I did not want to be considered for the post. I had then served for a year at the Colonial Office. I had experienced the ordeal of undertaking responsibilities in an over-seas department after years of concentration on domestic problems. For the first months it had been a tough job to adjust to new tasks and I was beginning to find my feet, and to find deep satisfaction in my new and wider sphere of service. Moreover, I thought that there were others who were more fitted than I was to fill this immensely important post, including Herbert, who was eventually appointed. In the course of his all too short tenure of office he had some difficult problems to face, not least of them the intractable problem of West Germany and its place in the European defence organizations then being developed within the North Atlantic Treaty Organization. These are problems which present great difficulties and arouse deep passions. Before Herbert could establish himself firmly in the new office the 1951 election had brought the Tories back to power. The defence and foreign affairs controversies were to cause repercussions in the party after our defeat in 1951 and to provide the background to the More-cambe conference and to the loss by Herbert of his place on the National Executive. This was deplored by most of us and led to two attempts to bring him back. The first, when he stood for election as treasurer, failed when he was defeated at the conference ballot by Arthur Greenwood; the second proved successful when the rule was changed so as to provide that the Deputy Leader of the Parliamentary Party should serve ex-officio on the National Executive Committee. Meantime, two younger men had forged ahead in Parliament and the party—Nye Bevan and Hugh Gaitskell.

Nye Bevan was one of the outstanding parliamentarians of my time, and the only one who stood equal to David Lloyd George and Winston Churchill, and there were many who placed him above both of them as a parliamentary debater. I count the speech he made in the House following the Suez disaster as not only his best but the finest I heard in my years in Parliament. He had a remarkable gift of word and phrase. I say 'gift', for he had none of the advantages of education which most of his political adversaries had enjoyed. He could command his audience, whether friendly or hostile. He combined the arts of the platform orator and the skilled debater, equally at home in Trafalgar Square and in the parliamentary arena. He possessed two gifts, as did our famous compatriot David Lloyd George—that of being able to think quickly on his feet, and to seize upon some word or phrase uttered by an opponent and turn it back upon him with devastating effect.

He was a rebel who could not bear to be harnessed, impatient of authority, all authority, including that of his own party. This is the reason why, though he was outstanding in his gifts, the leadership of the party eluded him. It had been said that to attain to the leadership of the Labour Party it is essential to be left of centre, but it must be remembered that the centre is of paramount importance and that the solid core of the centre is to be found in the trade union group. If Nye had played a more active part in that group and cultivated the friendship of its members the succession to Attlee would have been his for the asking. Without their support even a man of Nye's talents and abilities could not reach the top in the Labour Party. Hugh Gaitskell succeeded because he won their allegiance. It is something of a paradox that a man of Gaitskell's background—Winchester and Oxford— should have gained the confidence of the trade union members who, it was often remarked, do not look with too much favour upon those who are described as 'intellectuals'.

Hugh Gaitskell was one of the brilliant galaxy of young men who came to Parliament in the glorious July of 1945 and which included, among others, Harold Wilson. With Hugh came his close personal friend Evan Durbin, whose tragic death at the age of forty-two was a sad loss to our party and the nation. Evan Durbin's book *The Politics of Democratic Socialism* was the testament of the kind of socialism which inspired the generation to which he and Gaitskell belonged. In the foreword to the 1953 edition of the book, Gaitskell expressed his own as well as his friend's political faith when he wrote:

> It [the book] reflects an outlook on politics which was shared by many of his friends and contemporaries in the Labour movement, an outlook which marked, in its way, a new phase in socialist thought, different from that of the early Fabians and from the ideas associated with the stormy period before the First World War. It marked, one might say, the transition from the pioneering stage to that of responsibility and power. The most fundamental ideal of those who shared this outlook was social justice, but it was an ideal in no way inspired by class hatred. They were equally devoted to democracy and personal freedom. They believed in tolerance and they understood the need for compromise. They were realistic in politics and critical of armchair politicians who, not understanding what the British electorate was really like, were forever making bad political judgments. Above all, while accepting the ultimate emotional basis of moral valuation, they had great faith in the power of reason both to find the answer to social problems and to persuade men to see the light. They were for the pursuit of truth to the bitter end through the patient and unswerving application of logical thought. They wanted no barriers of prejudice to obstruct the free working of the mind or blunt the sharp edge of intellectual integrity.

'This', Gaitskell concludes in the foreword, 'was Evan Durbin's outlook,' and, as I learnt from my close association with him, it was also the outlook of Hugh Gaitskell.

It represented an approach to politics, and to the role of the Labour Party in the Britain of the mid fifties, which suited our mood and found a ready response in our ranks. The party had fared badly in three successive general elections. From the decisive victory of 1945, when we held a majority of 186, we had slumped to a majority of eight in 1950, and in 1951 we had fallen further, giving the Tories a majority of sixteen, and then in 1955 to 277 seats and a Tory majority of fifty-nine. There were many factors which had contributed to the decline in our electoral fortunes, but the overwhelming majority of Labour M.P.s were convinced that one of these—and many thought the most important—was the effect of our internal dissensions. Ever since the resignations of Nye Bevan and Harold Wilson from the Government of 1951 the party, in Parliament and in the country, had been torn by controversy. Rival groups had been formed within the Parliamentary Labour Party, the 'Bevanite' group on the left and counter groups on the right. These divisions were reflected in the constituency parties, and the activists in all the constituencies were disillusioned and disheartened by the endless wranglings; many of them gave up active participation in the work of the party. Both the Parliamentary Party and the National Executive had sought to impose discipline by expulsions, but these only added fuel to the fire and further embittered relations. There was an intense desire among the Members in the House to make a fresh start and to look for a new leader among the younger men. This was the major factor in the choice of Hugh Gaitskell to succeed Clem Attlee when he retired shortly after the 1955 election. In the ballot to elect the new leader Hugh Gaitskell came first with 157 votes, Nye Bevan second with 70, and Herbert Morrison third with 40 votes. The decisive character of the ballot reflected the wish of the party to see an end of fratricidal strife, and its resolve to get on with the job of winning our way back to power. Herbert Morrison was deeply hurt by his defeat, and though pressed to remain as Deputy Leader he felt that, in view of the low vote he had polled, he could not continue.

In the choice of a new Deputy Leader the party was more evenly divided. I was asked to stand for election by those who thought that it would be advantageous to choose a deputy who could bring a wider experience to the service of the new leader and who would co-operate loyally with him. They feared a recurrence of trouble if a struggle for power broke out between the leader and his deputy. They recognized that, as chairman of the policy committee and as a member of the Shadow Cabinet, I had endeavoured to reconcile the rival factions, and thought that I could render the same service to the party as Deputy Leader. There were others who argued that to choose Nye Bevan as deputy to Hugh Gaitskell would ensure that the two wings of the party were represented in its leadership. When the ballot was held in February 1956 I was elected by 141 votes to 111 cast for Nye Bevan. Following the excitement of the election for leader, that for the deputy leadership was conducted quietly and without personal bitterness. I was naturally pleased with the result, and felt deeply honoured by the trust reposed in me. In the annual elections for the Shadow Cabinet I had topped the poll from 1951 onwards, though in 1954 had shared the top place with Hugh Gaitskell. I believe that the confidence I enjoyed among my parliamentary colleagues was a recognition of the role I had fulfilled in the party.

3

When Hugh Gaitskell came to allocate responsibilities to the members of the Shadow Cabinet he consulted me about the choice of front-bench spokesmen. Nye expressed his desire to serve as spokesman on foreign affairs, but this was difficult as Clem Attlee had, before his retirement, appointed one of our able young members, Alf Robens, to this post. I volunteered to give up my position as front bench spokesman on colonial affairs, so that Nye Bevan could take over from me. I had been very sorry to relinquish the post, for I found real satisfaction in the work, but I recognized how important it was to make full use of Nye's gifts and abilities. After a period Nye again asked to be appointed as spokesman for foreign affairs. Alf Robens generously agreed to stand down.

During the three years in which I served as Deputy Leader I endeavoured to foster a partnership between these two men, Gaitskell and Bevan. In their abilities and temperament they complemented and supplemented each other. I recognized that the future of our party was in their hands. In partnership they could lead it to triumph and achievement, in rivalry they could destroy it. In some ways they resembled that other partnership which turned sour and destroyed a party—that of H. H. Asquith and David Lloyd George.

Hugh Gaitskell possessed a massive intellect allied to a remarkable capacity for work. He also had the quality which he attributed to his friend in the words I have quoted: '. . . the pursuit of truth to the bitter end through the patient and unswerving application of logical thought'. He would never commit himself to a snap decision, not even on the least important matter. He would subject every issue that confronted him to the most searching analysis and would argue the pros and cons with his colleagues, never letting us get away with a superficial judgment. When he had made up his mind he was like a rock, and would hold to his considered judgment with unyielding tenacity. Nye once referred to him as a 'calculating machine'. It was far from the truth; if he had been more calculating he might have saved himself from the personal attacks which caused him deep anguish. Once he made up his mind there was no calculation of the consequences to himself. For him, as for Durbin, there was to be 'no barrier . . . to obstruct the free working of the mind or to blunt the sharp edge of intellectual integrity'. Integrity, absolute integrity, this was the essential quality of Hugh Gaitskell's character. I remember a long talk, indeed a series of long talks, I had with him before he launched his attack upon the famous Clause Four of the party's constitution, with its demand for 'the common ownership of the means of production, distribution and exchange'. He knew that I belonged to the old tradition in socialist thought and practice, and that Clause Four was an article of faith to me and to my generation. When I reminded him of this he replied sternly: 'Maybe, but you know that we do not intend, any of us, to implement Clause Four fully, and I regard it as my duty to say so to the party and the country.' When he considered it was his duty to say or do something then nothing could change him. The sharp edge of intellectual integrity would cut through all barriers.

He abhorred the colour bar in every form and every place, and he would have been very unhappy at some of the more recent developments with regard to immigration. On education he was convinced that one of the barriers to the creation of a truly democratic society in Britain was the existence of a privileged system. I remember when we were considering the educational policy of the party how strongly he urged the view that one of the first priorities should be the integration of the public schools into the state national system. He would become impatient with those of us who argued that our first priority should be the expansion and raising of the standards in our state system rather than to find room for a few of our children at the public schools.

Many of his friends were disappointed and some even shocked at his attitude to the entry of Britain into the European Economic Community. His speech at the party conference was notable not only for its sustained argument but also for the passion he imparted into the discussion. From my many talks with him on this question I understood how he came to resist the proposal. To him the major problem in Europe was how to ensure the peaceful unification of West and East Germany. He was deeply concerned lest the mystique of German unity might some day lead to a resurgence of Nazism, and an attempt by force to restore the pre-war Reich. He was equally convinced that the Soviet Union would resist this and that the world would be plunged into a third world war. He feared that the Common Market would freeze the division of the continent and accentuate and aggravate these perils. He had thought deeply over this problem and his plan for the 'disengagement' of Central Europe from the rival military alliances of N.A.T.O. and the Warsaw Pact was designed to provide a solution for what he regarded then as the major threat to the peace of the world. There was another feature of that speech at the conference which surprised many people: his fervent declaration that he would not join in the surrender of what he described as 'a thousand years of history'. It did not surprise me, for I had lived with him through Suez. In the early days of that crisis he had adopted what some regarded as an equivocal attitude. The responsibility of dividing the country weighed heavily upon him. It was only when he became convinced that the Conservative Government was intent upon the use of force, in violation of our pledge to the charter of the United Nations, that all hesitation vanished. When the path of duty was clear, then no consideration of pride or popularity would deter him from following the dictates of conscience.

The Suez crisis brought him and Nye Bevan closer together. From that time they came to appreciate each other's qualities more fully and to understand each other better. The issues which had divided them most acutely, and at times bitterly, were those of defence and foreign affairs. Hugh had been a staunch adherent and advocate of the Atlantic Alliance. Nye had never shared this view. He feared the consequences of dependence upon and subservience to the United States. He regarded Foster Dulles, the American Secretary of State, with his ideas of creating an anti-communist block to encircle Russia and China, as a dangerous man. He feared that Dulles's policy would lead to a world confrontation of the communist and capitalist powers, which could end only in catastrophe. Britain could play a decisive role in preventing this if she was freed from any commitment to the policies of Foster Dulles. These were the considerations which led him to give warning against 'sending a British Foreign Secretary naked into the conference room'.

With Hugh Gaitskell and Nye Bevan coming closer on these issues, the hopes and prospects of a fruitful partnership between them improved. We worked together on the preparation of our programme for the 1959 election, and entered the campaign full of hope that victory would be ours. We were sadly disappointed when the party suffered another defeat. I would so much like to have seen a Government with Hugh Gaitskell as its Prime Minister. He had in him the making of one of our great prime ministers. He was a greater statesman than politician, and high office would have brought out more fully than did opposition the gifts with which he was so richly endowed. When the 1959 election was over I went to see him and told him that I had made up my mind to retire from the position of deputy leadership. I was then sixty-nine years of age, and with a Conservative majority of a hundred, five years would elapse before another general election. I felt that I had done my job as his deputy in helping to establish him as the undisputed leader of the party. Some of my friends indeed thought that I had done so almost to the point of self-effacement. We both realized that with my retirement the obvious choice for my successor was Nye Bevan, and I told Hugh that the party was now anxious to see Nye serving as his deputy and that I was confident that the partnership would develop and grow. When nominations were invited for the deputy leadership the only name submitted was that of Nye Bevan, and he was elected unanimously. To those who had lived through the turbulent years of party strife this was a great relief. We hoped that the party would now settle down to its work. But fate had in store a cruel blow, for within a few months Nye was struck down by a fatal disease. The whole nation mourned the passing of one of its gifted sons and grieved at the loss of a courageous and colourful leader. When tributes were paid to his memory in the House of Commons I was asked to pay tribute for all my compatriots, and I quote from what I said in Parliament on 7th July 1960:

> I was privileged to know Aneurin Bevan over very many years, and I know that if he were here today he would want to say how much he owed to the community in which he was reared. I know that he would want me to say a word about Tredegar. He was deeply rooted in the life of his valley and deeply attached to his native town. The valleys and villages, torn and scarred by a century of industrialism, are nothing much to look at, but they are wonder-

ful places to grow up in. They are communities with a deep sense of neighbourhood, where one man's success is everyone's joy and one man's adversity is everybody's burden. In paying this tribute to this greatest of the sons of the valley, I pray that our beloved valleys may yet, in the years to come, have the privilege of producing men of the calibre of Aneurin Bevan.

4

Once again the party had to choose a deputy leader, and I supported George Brown. I had admired George from the days when I first met him at our party conference. His warm humanity and Celtic temperament made a strong appeal to me. In his blunt forthrightness he was reminiscent of his old chief, Ernest Bevin. I felt sure that he would work well in co-operation with Hugh Gaitskell. Moreover I was anxious that the trade union element in our party should be represented in the top leadership. Prior to his appointment George had served as chairman of the trade union group, and had restored it to the position of influence in our counsels, which the party was to need in the months that followed, when the controversy over unilateral nuclear disarmament plunged it into disarray.

When the conference passed a resolution in favour of unilateral nuclear disarmament, and Hugh Gaitskell made his 'fight and fight again' speech, the Parliamentary Party stood firm by the leader and sustained him through the greatest crisis of his career. Our support for him was all the stronger because some of those who opposed him on this issue had descended to bitter personal attacks, and had even questioned his integrity. I saw him regularly during those difficult days and realized what a strain they were on him. After a full week's work in the House he would spend almost every week-end addressing conferences and meetings in the country, and every speech was most carefully prepared. In the last weeks before his illness he had been preparing for a visit to Moscow. The invitation to meet Khrushchev had pleased him so much. He felt that by a frank exchange of views with the Russian leader he could make a real contribution to the improvement of relations with the Soviet Union. When I saw him a few days before Parliament broke up for the Christmas recess, I was distressed to see how tired he was. I urged him to take a rest but he would not hear of it—he had set his heart on the

Moscow visit. That visit was not to be, for the illness which must then have been developing rapidly was to take him away from us. In the last year of his life I had the feeling that the whole country had come to regard Hugh Gaitskell as a man they would feel proud to have as Prime Minister. The whole nation felt it had suffered a grievous loss.

The loss of two men of the calibre of Hugh Gaitskell and Nye Bevan was a serious blow to the party. They had both reached the stage in their careers at which they had made the breakthrough from being party leaders to that of acceptance as national leaders. The universal grief felt and expressed at their passing was abundant proof of this.

Once again we had to face the difficult task of choosing a new leader. It was clear from the outset that the choice lay between Harold Wilson, George Brown and James Callaghan. All three of them had entered Parliament in the election of 1945, and had soon won recognition by appointment to ministerial posts. In the long years in opposition they had given ample proof of their ability and there was general recognition that they all possessed the qualities of leadership.

In the contest each of them had his supporters, who expressed their preference publicly. I supported George Brown and confess that my choice was not uninfluenced by the hope I had cherished that the party would find a leader from the ranks of the trade union members. However, all of us were resolved that when the ballot was over we would join in closing ranks behind the new leader.

The first meeting which Harold Wilson addressed, following his election as leader, was held at Cardiff. I joined him on the platform and pledged my fullest support for him. The warm-hearted Welsh audience received this declaration with enthusiasm. For thirty years, at every election, Wales had returned a majority of Labour Members to Parliament. Now with unity amongst the leaders they felt we were on our way to victory.

Remembering the days when the role of a reconciler had often seemed fated to end in failure, I left the gathering at Cardiff with hopes rekindled that the future might yet bring its reward.

10

FROM MY NOTEBOOK

MANY times, as the New Year came in, I have resolved to keep a diary, only to find my resolution fail within a few weeks. To make up for this I would chronicle in my notebook the most important episodes, either at the time they happened or at the end of each year. I have drawn on these records in writing this book.

Below are excerpts from my chronicle for 1955 and 1956 which I think may be of more interest reproduced as recorded at the time.

NINETEEN FIFTY-FIVE

Another troubled year for the party!

Early in the year Nye B. became a problem once again. Ever since 1951 and his resignation he had seemed to alternate between a desire to work with us and the passion to be different. He is, I believe, influenced by the life of Fox and the careers of Winston and L.G., the rebels who eventually came out on top. If we were involved in a war again, I would not be surprised to see him emerge—as L.G. did in 1916, and Winston in 1940—as a P.M. whose ruthlessness suited the time of stress and conflict. The '55 episode began one day in the House when he got up from the Front Bench and strode across to the box to put a question following Clem A. It was so obvious, in gesture and spirit, a pushing of Clem out of the way, that it aroused deep feelings. This and some further episodes led to a decision by the Parliamentary Committee to withdraw the Whip. At the committee meetings we had heated arguments on this decision. I was convinced that it was against our interests in a year that seemed certain to see a general election. I was supported by Harold Wilson, Hugh Dalton and Clem—on the other side the chief protagonists were Herbert M., Hugh G. and Willie Whiteley. At the party meeting the parliamentary committee only just by a narrow majority got their decision confirmed. It was an empty victory as I had predicted in the Shadow Cabinet. Later on the N.E.C. rejected a motion for expulsion by one vote—Clem A. supported my resolution not to do so—so Nye stayed in the party. I remembered the incident when my E.C. (of the South Wales Miners' Federation) wanted to expel Arthur Horner for having supported Pollitt in the General Election of 1935 against Bill (W. H.) Mainwaring, the miners' nominee. I persuaded them not to on the ground that this would have involved the S.W.M.F. in fatal internal strife when we were only just beginning to climb out of the slough of despond after 1926. I still think I was right in both cases.

Early in 1955 rumours began to circulate that the 'Old Man', Winston, would soon go. It was said that now Eden was recovered and seemingly fit Churchill could vacate the throne for his chosen prince. Yet it seemed he was reluctant. He loves power and office—all of it, including the trappings; the 'Garter' made him feel and behave like a schoolboy who had won all the prizes. It was said in the lobbies that Eden, Butler and Salisbury had become tough and had forced him to go. As soon as Eden came in a general election became inevitable. We were caught rather unprepared. The 'Nye row' earlier in the year—indeed the trouble ever since 1951, and in particular since the Morecambe Conference in '52—had split us badly. We did not have the appearance of an alternative government. There was no real life in it from the word go. It was a half-hearted fight—it was bound to be after years of internal strife. Our feuds had also entered deeply into our life—in Parliament, at the N.E.C., at conference and in the country.

After Morecambe (when I became chairman of the Policy Committee of N.E.C.) we went to work to prepare a programme, partly to get away from the split but also to seek some unity in policy if not in personal relations. Out of this came the policy embodied in 'Challenge to Britain'. It was largely based on the premise supported by all our economists—Hugh G., Harold

W., Tom Balogh and all of them—that the fundamental *malaise* of the balance of payments could not be redressed, let alone be cured, except by (*a*) seeking a new 'bed' for our economy in a Commonwealth plan, and (*b*) a recasting of the pattern of our industrial life. The proposals in 'Challenge to Britain' stemmed from that thesis.

Events had not, by the spring of '55, justified that diagnosis, at any rate on the surface. The Tories had a lot of luck. The terms of trade turned in their favour. The death of Stalin created a new hope for the easement of tension between East and West. All this helped the Tories to prepare the ground, and Butler's budget was a brazen piece of electioneering—sixpence off the income tax, etc. etc.

So we were in the battle—handicapped on all fronts. I made one of the party's broadcasts, mostly on the colonies and the two-thirds of the world in poverty. Technically one of my best I believe. Did it touch a chord? I am afraid not, though I am glad I made it. There were few appeals to sacrifice in this election—it was an appeal to material interests, not to the spirit. And there was deplorable complacency. There was scarcely a ripple on the even surface of the pond! Meetings were poor in attendance and spirit. I spoke at Gravesend, Lewisham, Wandsworth, then on to Stroud, Gloucester, Flint, Anglesey, Cardigan, Pembroke and Swansea. And of course the rally at the Cory Hall, Cardiff—still the old hall of memories. We were the victims of the success of our policies from '45 to '51—and of the Tories' behaviour in refraining from making frontal attacks on the Welfare State. There was no deep felt or widespread grievance. Full employment, overtime, increased earnings—all this outweighed the increase in cost of living. In the event we did not do too badly. Wales was solid—27 seats out of 36 once again, though in Wales, as elsewhere, the vote slumped in those seats, like mine, which are traditional strongholds. We came back to Westminster 270 strong, a much better result than seemed possible at first.

As soon as we were back things began to move. Hugh Dalton wrote a letter to Clem (which he also sent to the press) saying that he was not proposing to stand for re-election to the Shadow Cabinet—as he believed the old ones should clear out to make way for young blood. The same day (6.5.55) he wrote me:

My dear Jim,

I have written a letter for publication in which I urge the need for a much younger Shadow Cabinet in the new Parliament, and draw attention to the number of members of our Parliamentary Committee at the end of the last Parliament now over sixty-five and even over seventy. I didn't, of course, mention any names. I then say that I have decided not to be a candidate for the Shadow Cabinet in the new Parliament, and that I hope a number of my fellow veterans will decide likewise, so as to allow some of our very good younger men to have their chance. I repeat that I mention no names in my letter but I write to *you* to say that I very definitely do *not* have you in mind. You are the youngest of us nine veterans who are sixty-five or over this year, maybe some not sixty-five yet —the books only say you were born in 1890, but not the month. Anyhow you have in my judgment and in my affection a very special position. Four or five years hence, if the tide turns our way, you could still be a most valuable and effective Cabinet Minister. Not so, I fear, some of our other older colleagues. And there are so many good younger comrades waiting their turn. The procession must move on. Till next week.

Yours ever,

Hugh Dalton

The letter which Hugh D. sent to the press was sharply commented upon by Chuter Ede and Manny Shinwell and others. Eventually both Chuter and Manny announced their decision not to stand. Clem A. wanted to give up. The Parliamentary Committee said, 'No—go on'—not all the members but most, including myself. He (Clem) went to the party meeting and placed himself in the hands of the party and said that he was prepared to go on for a year. At this Nye B. got up and urged Clem to stay and leave the time-table out of it. The party acclaimed all this and Clem stayed.

Meantime I was pressed to stand for deputy against Herbert M., who had shown signs of ageing rapidly and losing grip. I think there was delayed reaction from his earlier thrombosis. It was clear that age was telling on him much more than on any of his contemporaries and even than on Clem A. On 8th June I was asked to come to a meeting in one of the interview rooms in the House of Commons to meet a group of M.P.s—drawn equally from centre and left—and asked to accept nomination for the deputy leadership. They told me that they spoke not only for themselves but

143

for others who had sent messages to the convenors. That same evening I saw Hugh Dalton and some of my Welsh and coal-mining colleagues, all of whom pressed me to stand, and they all joined in saying, 'Don't give an answer at once—consider the matter and then let us know.'

When later the party meeting so warmly acclaimed Nye Bevan's pleas to Clem to go on, and coupled this with the announcement that he (Nye) would not stand for either leader or deputy, I felt that if I stood I should be acting out of character, having all the time worked to keep us together and united. So I declined. I stood for the Parliamentary Committee and came out on top with 186 votes, followed by Hugh Gaitskell with 184, and then a drop to 148 for Jim Callaghan and Alf Robens and 147 for Harold Wilson. Nye came seventh with 118 and George Brown was elected for the first time with 101 votes.

Clem A. told us (at the first meeting of the newly elected Parliamentary Committee) that he proposed to name members of the committee to have charge of subjects, it being clearly under-stood that this would be without any commitment to that—or any—office in the future. This is the origin of the term 'Shadow Cabinet'. The most important appointments were H.G. for finance, Alf R. for foreign affairs, Nye B. for labour, Harold W. for trade and Jim Callaghan for fuel and power. I remained in charge of colonies. So we were off again to another spell in opposition. It looked as if we were fated to be there for a full Parliament—unless a crisis blew up.

Late in July (1955) Clem had a mild attack of coronary throm-bosis. It was kept a secret for some time. I did not know for some time, nor as far as I know did any of my colleagues in the Shadow Cabinet. He came to Malta (to the Round Table Con-ference on Integration) in September and to party conference in October. He was obviously affected—one noticed this as he got up and sat down. (One saw the same effect on Winston after he had the same kind of stroke.)

Rumours began about his retirement. He denied them again and he was in his place when the House resumed in October. But the press reports continued. Percy Cudlipp (Editor, *Daily Herald*) had an interview with Clem when he talked of his looking forward to a rest and that the party should make up its mind about his successor. Suddenly, in late November, Clem A. made up his mind to retire. Like Clem! It was a sudden decision in the end.

When he decides, he decides quickly, definitely and irrevocably.
So after twenty years he retired. One felt like the cockney in
Noel Coward's *Cavalcade* who, on hearing that Queen Victoria
was dead, exclaimed: 'It will be funny without her.'

And now began the contest. It seemed to me clear (1) that
the party had made up its mind to settle the leadership for a long
time, and (2) that of the younger men Hugh Gaitskell stood out.
He had added enormously to his prestige in the movement by his
speeches at the party conference and in Parliament attacking
Butler's autumn budget. Herbert, on the other hand, whilst
being in good form at conference had failed lamentably in the
House. He had had to wait too long. In the last days of the contest
he was not helped by Nye B. attempting to give him a clear run
by offering to withdraw if Hugh G. would do the same. It was
altogether too Machiavellian and created cynicism, and finally
decided many to turn and vote for Hugh G., who won easily with
157 votes to Nye's 70 and Herbert's 40. That meeting of the
Parliamentary Party, when the result was declared, was deeply
moving. Herbert's best friends had urged him not to stand. It was
difficult for him not to, and yet there were none who would not
have spared him the humiliation of those 40 votes and being
bottom of the poll. He had rendered immense services to the
party—for twenty-five years he was the most influential man on
the N.E.C. The Government of '45 owed so much to him in preparing 'Let us Face the Future' and in carrying it through as
Leader of the House. His greatest mistake was to go to the F.O.
in 1951. I was pressed to stand for 'deputy'. The only alternative
was Nye, and many thought—at that time—the partnership of
H.G. and N. would not work, that both would be uneasy and
would run separate empires. There were others who felt that the
best and quickest way to unite the party would be for Nye to be
made deputy. This feeling was very strong in the ranks of the
middle-roaders who had opposed Nye for the leadership. The
result of the ballot showed the strength of this feeling, for it was
not as decisive as was at first expected. I was elected by 141
votes to 111, a majority of thirty.

So, for me, it was the climax of a career that had begun with
the I.L.P. in our branch at Ammanford, gone on to secretary of
the trades council, then two years at the Labour college; three
years as political agent at Llanelly; ten years as miners' agent,
and on to the president's chair of the South Wales Miners'

Federation; and then to Parliament in 1936. Now Deputy Leader at sixty-five—with no more ambitions. Ten years off that age and I might have reached the top, though all through the years I have doubted if I had the toughness—perhaps the ruthlessness—which is required to reach the top and stay there.

I have now spent fifty-two years of working life since June 1904. I have been richly blessed with health, with good parents and home, with fine colleagues in my old S.W.M.F. days and more recently in Parliament—but beyond all in my wife, Win. She has some of the qualities I lack—real tenacity and courage, and the ability to live within herself and let the rest of the world go by, completely untouched by the lure of 'Society': she has always fought shy of it. She has the deep strength of her Dad. And we have been fortunate in our children. Sometimes the desire to spend what time remains on the sidelines rather than in the centre of public life becomes strong.

MEETINGS WITH BULGANIN AND KHRUSHCHEV

At Chequers. Sunday, April 22nd, 1956. Hugh Gaitskell, Alf Robens and I were invited to lunch at Chequers by the P.M. (Eden). We travelled up together from H.G.'s house in his car. At lunch the party included Bulganin, Khrushchev, Gromyko, Malik (Soviet Ambassador) and the interpreters; the Prime Minister (and Lady Eden), the P.M.'s son Nicholas with young Khrushchev, R. A. Butler, Selwyn Lloyd, Sir William Hayter (U.K. Ambassador in Moscow), Sir Ivone Kirkpatrick (Permanent Under-Secretary at the Foreign Office) and Mr Barber (of the British Embassy at Washington).

At lunch I sat next to Khrushchev, who had the Prime Minister on the other side, and Mr Barber sat the other side of me. A bearded young man—a Mr Orchard of the F.O.—acted as interpreter, sitting on a chair behind us. Khrushchev had been told that I was an old coal-miner, as he had been—and his father too. I told him that I had been a coal-miner for seventeen years, which he said was longer than he had been. He told me that the Donbas was not now their most important coalfield but the Urals and Siberia, where the coal resources were unlimited, and that the 'gasification experiments' had not developed far. 'It won't do—we've got to get the coal out,' were the words he used.

After lunch H.G., A.R. and I went with B. and K. (and their interpreter) into the White Parlour and had thirty-five minutes' talk until they were whisked away to Windsor to take tea with the Queen. We broached the question of the Social Democratic leaders imprisoned in the Eastern satellite countries, but at this stage we were interrupted, so we had to leave this and other questions till the next evening (Monday 23rd) when they were to dine with the N.E.C. and Parliamentary Committee. They agreed to our suggestion that at this meeting there should be an opportunity of putting questions to them informally and of their putting questions to us.

Impressions. . . . K. is obviously the key man, B. the silent watcher and occasional prompter. K. is a big-shouldered, broad-chested collier type, with a slow smile. Neither K. nor B. has the engaging personality of Malenkov. Hayter said that Malenkov made a fatal mistake when he followed Stalin. He had been told to choose between P.M. or secretary of the party. He chose to be P.M. and K. became secretary. And now M. is in a minor post and K. is the boss. Molotov (it seems clear) is now a retired elder statesman. Gromyko, at the official level, is the man who now counts. He is shortish, dark—could be a Welsh collier. K. says at times, 'Gromyko will have to work out one of his compromises', but G. does not compromise easily it seems. Malik was cordial, but when he asked me what we wanted to talk about and I mentioned, among other topics, the Social Democratic leaders in prison, he frowned and was obviously displeased at the idea of our raising such questions. I said to him: 'They are our comrades.' Monday's meeting promises to be interesting. . . .

Monday, April 23rd. Dinner at the Harcourt Room, House of Commons. 8 for 8.30 p.m. Present: Members of the N.E.C. and Parliamentary Committee.

B. and K. were late in arriving—8.45 p.m. It was ten o'clock when Edwin Gooch (chairman of N.E.C.) rose to propose the health of our visitors. Bulganin responded in a happy speech, about fifteen minutes. Then as he sat down someone called out 'Khrushchev'. This was taken up by others and K. got to his feet. He began slowly and amiably, then somehow he began to show an aggressive tone and to drift into the past. I was not sure whether it was an interjection by George Brown that set him going, but anyhow he launched into a long recital of the pre-1939 Munich days and why they were driven into the Hitler pact, and then into the post-war period and N.A.T.O., and the Labour Party being more difficult than the Tories—that kind of strain. There were some notable (and forboding) things he said, or implied, by tone as much as language. Those that left the deepest impression on my mind at the time were his references to Germany. The purport of these was that Germany is getting stronger, and she had chauvinistic tendencies; Dr Adenauer was an old man and would soon be gone. Germany will be our competitor for markets; she will want to come East, and then she will turn to us, the U.S.S.R., and will want an agreement with us. 'History', he said, 'has its own laws'—and he said this in a context which seemed to suggest that a pact between the U.S.S.R. and Germany is the logical outcome of this historical process. He said this with all the certitude of a Plymouth Brother speaking of the Second Coming. On disarmament he said that their new proposals to the 1956 Disarmament Commission were proposals the Western powers had made at various conferences. 'Now *we* put these up and *you* turn down your own proposals.'

Later, when he returned to this question, he dismissed 'control' as impracticable and foolish. 'Flying over each other's countries—what good is it all? We in our immense country could easily conceal an atomic plant.' It was confidence not control that was important. H.G. referred to this and said that confidence must be built up and inspection and control would build up confidence—but he (K.) would have none of it. As he went on he became more truculent and eloquent; it just poured out. He spoke for over an hour (about sixty-five minutes). 'We are strong; we have beside us, and behind us, the People's Democracies and China. We do not need to beg—we can stand on our own feet. We have the H-bomb; it's our having it that has saved us from war. We want peace; we would like to give more to consumer goods—your peasants have better homes than ours, your industrial workers are in some things better off—but we have to give priority to heavy goods industry. In 1917 when the October Revolution came we had a small unorganized proletariat, and a mass of illiterate peasants. We've changed all that and now we are strong; we are united; we are not afraid; we can win through. If you want to be friends, all the better; if not—well, it's all right, we'll manage.' These are not his actual words, but this is my memory of how it all sounded.

H.G. got up to reply—at about 11.25 p.m. (K. took from 10.20 to 11.25.) There was an amusing incident just after he (K.) began his speech. At 10.30 p.m. the bell rang at end of sitting—and he stopped speaking till we waved him on. Then, a minute after, the House policeman put his head in and shouted: 'Who goes home?'

H.G. said there were many things in K.'s speech with which we could not agree. He was not going to argue all these now: in particular he was not going into the past—though K. must remember that we also fought the Munich policy. Then H.G. said that there were two things we felt that we must say and put to them.

(1) The plight of our Social Democratic comrades in Eastern and Central Europe.

(2) The position of the Jews in these and in the U.S.S.R. Up jumped K. as soon as H. sat down and said: 'Nyet.' In the U.S.S.R. they had no social revolutionaries; in the old days they had been enemies of the working class—had even tried to assassinate Lenin. As for Poland, and C. Slovakia, they were independent countries. To H.G.'s suggestion that we would give a list (of the prisoners) in the hope that they would use their influence to secure the release of these Social Democrats, he said: 'Nyet'—he would take no list. Sam Watson and Nye Bevan intervened; there were sharp exchanges, there was a good deal of talk and cross-talk. The whole evening became charged with tense feeling and once again we heard the cry: 'The Conservatives are easier to get on with than Labour.' We heard this on Sunday (at Chequers), and the next day—April 24th—at the Speaker's lunch. While B. was speaking of talk about good relations and more meetings and visits, K. interjected to say, 'More visits with the proviso that Labour is more amiable.'

It wasn't a happy evening. K. was tough, and blunt, and at times arrogant. I left feeling disturbed, unhappy; I thought we were regarded as less amiable because Social Democracy is the real alternative to Communism—and we meddled about Social Democrats in prison. And more important, these German references struck me as being really sinister. Co-existence seems the only chance; co-operation seems far away; real co-operation and confidence far, far away. (Early the next morning Morgan Phillips came to see H.G. and me at the House of Commons and told us that he had talked to Malik after the dinner and again that morning and had arranged for a final meeting with K. and B.)

Thursday, April 26th, 1956. 11 a.m. at Claridges. Present: B., K. (and his son) Malik and the young interpreter, H.G., J.G., Edwin Gooch and Morgan P.

H.G. said we had come to wish them well and *bon voyage* and hoped that the talks (with the Government) had been successful. Regarding Monday night's dinner he expressed regret that it had ended as it did. He said that we felt that it was our duty to raise the question of the S.D. (prisoners) and that it had been done in a blunt but friendly way. In regard to the interruptions during dinner and his speech—it was all in a good spirit if at times rather brusque in manner. K. said that they had been disappointed and hurt on Monday evening. They felt that all that happened had been arranged and each one given a role, that they felt antagonism to them, and that they had wanted to establish friendly relations with us as with the other Socialist parties. He had not intended to speak—was asked to, and then provoked by interruptions into making a long speech. I then took it up and said that he had been under the wrong impression, that our intention had been—as we had said to Malik on Sunday—that after formal and short interchanges from Edwin Gooch and B. we would have a mutual question-and-answer session. I then went on to say that I had lived through all that period of the Soviet Union, that we were Socialists and Democrats and whilst we would fight for our way of life we had fought against all the attempts to isolate Russia. I recalled the *Jolly George* [1] and Ernest Bevin's strike, 1924, and the Labour Government's being the first to recognize the U.S.S.R., and that we wanted them to be left to work out their way of life and we would stick to ours.

On Monday (the dinner) I said that H.G. had raised the question of the imprisoned Social Democrats in a courteous but frank manner and that George Brown's boisterous humour was but a tough docker talking to a tough miner. I took up the part of his speech where he seemed to me to lump us with the men of Munich and said that we had fought Chamberlain; that it was we who took the step to defeat him and had refused to serve under him. K. said that he was aware of this and was not thinking of the Labour Party but of the Government of that time. He said that

[1] The *Jolly George* contained cases of ammunition consigned to the 'White Russians' and when the London dockers refused to handle them they were strongly supported by Ernest Bevin, then general secretary of the Transport and General Workers' Union.

they had read reports in our press (including the Labour press) on Monday's dinner, and were particularly concerned at the impression given that they had refused to discuss relations with Socialist parties. They had not; they were anxious for discussions, witness their invitations to the French, Norwegian and other Socialist parties. So-called revolutionaries and Trotskyites were imprisoned as enemies of the working class. Towards the end of the meeting it became more cordial. K. said that after the quarrel things were better. The last few minutes were spent in cordial exchanges and handshakes and we parted in a good mood. They wanted us to visit Russia and we said that we would discuss this with Malik.

THE SUEZ CRISIS

From the notes on the events during 1956, written on 27th December 1956, the following account of the Suez crisis is extracted as written at that date.

The crisis is well documented in *Hansard*, press and pamphlets, notably the *Manchester Guardian* pamphlet and that written for us (the Labour Party) by Sidney Jacobson of the *Daily Mirror*, 'The truth about Suez'. For my part in it there is the broadcast (8th November 1956) and my speech moving the vote of censure. I record here some of the off-the-record events of the crisis.

(1) The early days. August 1956. Hugh Gaitskell and I talked over the issue of the nationalization of the canal. We saw Eden before the 2nd August debate in the House, and made it clear to him that we could not and would not support force except in accordance with the charter, while agreeing that some precautionary measures were wise.

(2) In the debate on 2nd August H.G. in his speech rather overdid the Nasser-Hitler line, though he made it clear that on force we were adamant, as we had told the P.M. in our private interview.

(3) H.G. went for a holiday immediately after the debate. I stayed on. On the Friday, 3rd August, I saw Morgan Phillips at my request in my room in the House. It was clear that the press had given a distorted view of H.G.'s speech of 2nd August and the party reaction was already evident. Morgan and I agreed to

have the full speech reprinted at once and sent to M.P.s (Labour), candidates, and all affiliated organizations including constituency Labour parties, calling attention to the latter part of the speech.

The part of the speech which many newspapers highlighted was the following:

> I have no doubt myself that the reason why Colonel Nasser acted in the way he did, aggressively, brusquely, suddenly, was precisely because he wanted to raise his prestige in the rest of the Middle East. He wanted to show the rest of the Arab world: 'See what I can do.' He wanted to assert his strength. He wanted to make a big impression. Quiet negotiation, discussion around a table about nationalizing the company would not produce this effect. It is all very familiar. It is exactly the same that we encountered from Mussolini and Hitler in those years before the war.

In the latter part of the same speech Hugh Gaitskell said:

> Last of all, I come to a matter which cannot be ignored at this moment just before the recess. There has been much talk in the press about the use of force in these circumstances.
>
> First, I would say that we need to be very careful what we say on this subject. It is unwise to discuss hypothetical situations in present conditions. Obviously there are circumstances in which we might be compelled to use force, in self-defence or as part of some collective defence measures. I do not myself object to the precautionary steps announced by the Prime Minister today. I think that any Government would have to do that, as we had to do it during the Persian crisis.
>
> I must, however, remind the House that we are members of the United Nations, that we are signatories to the United Nations Charter, and that for many years in British policy we have steadfastly avoided any international action which would be in breach of international law, or indeed contrary to the public opinion of the world. We must not, therefore, allow ourselves to get into a position where we might be denounced in the Security Council as aggressors, or where the majority of the Assembly were against us. While force cannot be excluded, we must be sure that the circumstances justify it and that it is, if used, consistent with our belief in and our pledges to the Charter of the United Nations and not in conflict with them.

Thursday, August 9th. The news of the military precautions began to create the suspicion that they were on an extensive scale. I phoned Hugh Gaitskell (on holiday in Pembrokeshire) and we agreed that I should see the P.M. about it, and arranged to take Alf Robens with me.

Friday, 10th August. I saw the P.M. with Alf Robens in the Cabinet Room at No. 10 at 3 p.m. With him was Salisbury. We stressed these points:

(1) That the military precautions were, it seemed to us, on a scale that created fears that war was contemplated.

(2) That we again wanted to re-affirm that we would not support force except in accordance with the Charter.

The P.M. explained that:

(1) Assembling our forces took some time—that they were only what the military (advisers) thought essential to meet possible contingencies.

(2) On force, he did not go beyond what he had said in the House—could not rule out etc. . . . .

Both Alf R. and I thought that Salisbury looked worried and anxious at this interview. P.M. asked us to agree to a short press release—merely a statement that we had been to see him. We told him that we should be reporting to H.G. and to the Shadow Cabinet and that we would want to see him again. We returned (to my room in the House), wrote report which we sent to H.G. and arranged for the Shadow Cabinet to meet on Monday—the 13th.

Monday, 13th August. Shadow Cabinet met in Hugh Gaitskell's room in the House of Commons. I reported fully on the interview which Alf R. and I had with the P.M. on Friday the 10th, and we decided to issue a statement in these terms: 'In view of public anxiety the committee (Shadow Cabinet) call upon the Government to make plain that the military precautions taken in the last ten days are purely precautionary, solely intended for defence against possible aggression and not preparation for armed intervention outside and inconsistent with our obligations under the Charter of the United Nations.' We also decided to call on the P.M.

Tuesday, 14th August. Hugh G., Alf Robens and I called on P.M. and again put our view (as set out in statement) and demanded the recall of Parliament, and repeated the demand until eventually Parliament was recalled on 12th September.

Thereafter the course of events in the crisis is fully reported in *Hansard*, but I must put on record, first, how disturbed Hugh G. was after a talk he and Morgan Phillips had with Guy Mollet during one of his visits to London (I was at Llanelli at the time); secondly, the concern we felt at the rumour as to what took place, particularly as to what was talked about and planned at the secret meeting between the two P.M.s (Eden and Mollet) on 16th October; and thirdly, an account of the short interview Hugh G. and I had with the P.M. on the fateful day of the ultimatum, 30th October.

30th October. Hugh G. and I met that morning in his room at the House and decided to put down a private notice question to the P.M. that afternoon. Butler (Rab) later informed us that as the discussions with Mollet and Pineau were still proceeding the P.M. desired to put off his statement till 4.30 p.m., and if H.G. put his question in at 3.30 p.m. as per custom he (Butler) would reply that the P.M. would make a statement at 4.30 p.m. He also told us that the P.M. had asked him to say that he would see us at 4 p.m. At 4 p.m. Hugh and I went along to the P.M.'s room in the House and were told that the statement was not yet completed, and were asked to wait in the adjoining room. We were called in to the P.M.'s room at about 4.15 p.m. Selwyn Lloyd was with him. The P.M. apologized for keeping us and said that the discussions with the French had only been concluded after lunch. Then he gave us a copy of his statement to read. The last part (of the statement) contained the ultimatum, and when I read it I said to Hugh: 'Good God: this is war.' There was no time to say more than that we stood by what we had said on force, before we had to go to the House. This was how the Opposition— representing half the nation—was consulted about an act of war. The full statement made by the Prime Minister can be seen in *Hansard* for 30th October 1956; this is the last part to which I have referred:

> As a result of the consultations in London today, the United Kingdom and French Governments have now addressed urgent communications to the Governments of Egypt and Israel. In these we have called upon both sides to stop all warlike action by land, sea and air forthwith and to withdraw a distance of ten miles from the canal. Further, in order to separate the belligerents and to guarantee freedom of transit through the canal by the ships of all nations we have asked the Egyptian Government to agree that Anglo-

French forces should move temporarily—I repeat temporarily—into the key positions at Port Said, Ismailia and Suez. The Governments of Egypt and Israel have been asked to answer this communication within twelve hours. It has been made clear to them that if, at the expiration of that time, one or both have not undertaken to comply with these requirements, British and French forces will intervene in whatever strength may be necessary to secure compliance.

While this ultimatum was being dispatched the Security Council was meeting in New York, and Gaitskell sought to persuade the P.M. to hold his hand pending consideration of the situation by the Council:

> The matter [he said] is being considered now in the United Nations and we do not know what decision will be reached there. Would it not be extremely unwise, therefore, for Her Majesty's Government to reach any irrevocable decision until they know what decisions are taken by the United Nations?

Eden replied:

> I am sorry I cannot give that undertaking, and I must explain why to the House. The fighting is going on at this moment; I do not have the very latest information, but in all likelihood there is air and other fighting in the very close vicinity of the canal, perhaps over the canal . . . That is why we and the French Government thought it absolutely imperative to ask for this temporary measure to be taken now, and why we have asked for the replies by the early hours of tomorrow morning. Therefore, with the best will in the world, I could not give an undertaking to the Rt. Hon. gentleman that we would not act.

There was no time to wait—not even for a few hours. There seemed to be some compulsive force driving Eden to declare war. In the debate which took place later that day, the same feverish anxiety to 'act' was expressed by the Foreign Secretary, Selwyn Lloyd, when he said:

> There have been some complaints today from the Opposition benches about the Government's failure to consult the Opposition before taking action. The facts are that the moment the Prime Minister had finished his discussions with the French Ministers he at once spoke to the Leaders of the Opposition. Really, the idea that the Government of the day can take action only after prior agreement with the Opposition . . . !

For the Foreign Secretary, as for the Prime Minister, it seemed there was no time to wait for the decision of the United Nations; no time to consult the Opposition, even though it represented half the nation; in a few hours we were plunged into war. . . .

A week later, on 7th November 1956, Selwyn Lloyd broadcast to the nation, and on the following evening, 8th November, I followed him with a broadcast for the Labour Party, in the course of which I said:

> Last night Mr Selwyn Lloyd spoke of the seven fateful days. He seemed to speak of them with pride. I regret that I cannot—and that many of you, my fellow citizens, do not—share his pride. We think of those days—yes, and we shall remember them, as the seven days of humiliation for our country, the days in which we lived through the bitter experience of witnessing a British Government—Mr Selwyn Lloyd's Government—waging war in violation of our solemn pledges under the Charter of the United Nations; defying the resolutions of the General Assembly, using the veto—the first British Government ever to use the veto in the Security Council; tearing up the Tripartite Declaration which bound us and France to act in unison with the United States in the Middle East; bringing the Commonwealth to the brink of dissolution.
>
> Mr Selwyn Lloyd complained impatiently last night that the Security Council has held nearly two hundred meetings on Palestine. But the paramount duty of a Foreign Secretary is to learn to be patient. In this age of the H-bomb, we cannot afford ministers whose patience becomes exhausted. . . .
>
> There is but one redeeming feature in this week of gloom, and it is that you—the people of Britain—have won a great victory. It will be recorded that when this Government took us to the brink of a third world war, you by your moral force helped to turn them back. You have proved that you can change a Government's policy when you know it to be wrong.

Many years have gone by since I spoke these words on 8th November 1956, and thousands of words have been written and spoken since then on the tragic events of that fateful week of the Suez crisis, but there is not a word I said in that broadcast that I would want to change now.

11

FIRST SECRETARY OF STATE FOR WALES

WHEN I was appointed to the new office of Secretary of State for Wales in October 1964 many of my compatriots, at home and in exile, greeted the creation of the Welsh Office and the inclusion of its ministerial head in the Cabinet with the cry of 'At long last. . . .'

Nearly a century had gone by since the nationalist movement 'Cymru Fydd' had raised the banner of Home Rule. The fervour with which it had been acclaimed by the people of Wales gave promise of its early achievement. The emergence of the two young dynamic leaders, Tom Ellis and David Lloyd George, to positions of power and influence in the Liberal Party induced a feeling of assurance that the day was near when Wales would become a self-governing nation. The movement gathered momentum and the demand for Home Rule seemed to be irresistible. But the years rolled on and still Home Rule became more and more elusive. William Ewart Gladstone was preoccupied with the claims of our Celtic neighbours, and as his endeavours to win Home Rule for Ireland were continually rebuffed, the prospects for Welsh Home Rule receded. Meantime the Scots, having stubbornly clung to their Church and law, had been rewarded with a Scottish Office and their own Secretary of State. If the Welsh had emulated the Scots instead of the Irish we might not have had to wait for a century for Wales to catch up with the Scots. It is an example of how a policy of 'all or nothing' often ends up in nothing. . . .

In the nineteen-thirties the Welsh Parliamentary Party

launched an endeavour to persuade successive governments to establish a Welsh Office and to give Wales a voice in the Cabinet. This endeavour was to continue for the first thirty years of my parliamentary life, as I will now relate.

The first of these efforts, in my time in Parliament, was made in 1938. Neville Chamberlain had succeeded Stanley Baldwin as Prime Minister. It was thought that the new Prime Minister might look with more favour than his predecessors upon the proposal for a Secretary of State for Wales. In any case, his response to a request to receive a deputation was immediate, and on 30th June 1938 a deputation, led by the then chairman, Morgan Jones, Caerphilly, put the case to the Prime Minister.

The deputation reported that they had been cordially received, and that Neville Chamberlain had undertaken to examine the case and to send a considered reply to the chairman. He was as good as his word, and on 27th July 1938 this was received by Morgan Jones.

Neville Chamberlain's letter is important in that it sets out the two arguments that had been, and were to be, advanced as reasons for the rejection of the demand.

This was not the first, or the last, time that I was to hear these arguments from governments of my own as well as other parties. For these reasons Neville Chamberlain's letter is of such interest that I publish it here in full:

> 10 Downing Street,
> S.W.1.
> 27th July 1938

DEAR MORGAN JONES,

I send you this letter in fulfilment of my promise to the deputation from the Welsh Parliamentary Party which I received at the House of Commons on the 30th June. As you will remember, I undertook to consider the arguments advanced on that occasion in support of the request for the establishment of a Welsh Office, with a separate Secretary of State for Wales, and to communicate my decision in due course. I have had an opportunity of thinking the matter over and I can now give you my considered reply.

Let me say at once that I am not lacking in sympathy for the argument from national sentiment which was presented by yourself and others, and that I recognize the existence in certain quarters of a feeling that the administration of Welsh affairs should, as far as may be possible, be concentrated in a single department. But it is my duty, in considering the matter, to have regard also to the practical considerations, and after examination of all the governing factors I have reached the conclusion that the request is not one which can be sustained.

Under the present system, while Welsh affairs are dealt with in the appropriate Government offices in London, arrangements have been made—where this is possible—for their concentration in a separate division; and there are, of course, offices in Wales itself which handle individual questions, of a nature to be dealt with locally. To this extent, therefore, Wales is receiving the special treatment which was one of the objects of the deputation. I am satisfied of the efficiency of these arrangements, and I do not consider that Wales would receive any practical advantage from co-ordination of the various activities in a single department.

Such co-ordination would, moreover, involve considerable expenses in the establishment of a new office, the provision of staff, etc., and I do not feel, particularly at the present time when the calls on the Exchequer are many and heavy, that Parliament could justly be asked to vote money for it.

The analogy of Scotland has been advanced not only by the deputation but on other occasions. I think, however, that it must be recognized that the two cases are not parallel. For Scotland has always had different systems of law and administration from those in force in England; indeed, even before the institution of the Scottish Office, most of the Scottish administrative work was performed in Scotland and the Lord Advocate was, for all practical purposes, the head of a distinct Scottish Department in London. Wales, on the other hand, since Henry VIII's Act of 1535, has been closely incorporated with England and there has not been, and is not now, any distinct law or administrative system calling for the attention of a separate minister.

In these circumstances, while I fully appreciate the motive which led the members of the deputation to approach me, I fear that I must ask you to inform them that I do not feel able to comply with the request which they made when we met.

Yours sincerely,
(Signed) N. CHAMBERLAIN

Within a few weeks of the receipt of this reply the Munich crisis was upon us, and this made a further approach inadvisable. Indeed it was not until 1943 that the matter was again considered by the Welsh Parliamentary Party. By this time Parliament and the country were sufficiently confident of the outcome of the war for our attention to be increasingly turning to post-war problems. The Welsh advisory committee on post-war problems had been inhibited by its terms of reference from considering constitutional questions. It was understood that these would be examined by the Government's own committee on post-war reconstruction, and it was therefore decided to make another approach, this time to the Coalition Government headed by Winston Churchill.

There was almost complete agreement on the proposal for a Secretary of State with a seat in the Cabinet. There was, however, considerable difference when we came to consider administrative devolution. The prevailing view was that we should restrict our demands for the transference to a Welsh Office of those departments of administration in which there was already some degree of devolution in the form of the Welsh Department of Education and the Welsh Board of Health. It was then decided to make representations on these lines to the Government. A letter was forwarded to the Prime Minister, signed by all the officers of the party, in the following terms:

WELSH PARLIAMENTARY PARTY

7th July 1943

DEAR MR PRIME MINISTER,

The Welsh Parliamentary Party represents all the Members of Parliament for the Principality and we meet to discuss all matters affecting Wales and to further, by joint effort, its interests.

At the meeting of the party held on Tuesday, 6th July, we had under consideration the replies given by you and the Deputy Prime Minister to questions in regard to the establishment of a Welsh Office with a Secretary of State as its head.

The party decided unanimously some time ago to examine the problems of the future government of Wales, and in particular the establishment of a Welsh Office with a Secretary of State.

A committee of the party is preparing concrete proposals. This work is being continued and it is hoped to have our proposals ready in the near future. When they are completed it is our intenttion to forward them to you for the consideration of the Government, and to ask you kindly to receive representatives of the Welsh Parliamentary Party to discuss the proposals.

We hope this course will be convenient to you.

Yours sincerely,

(Signed)

ARTHUR EVANS	*Chairman*	
MEGAN LLOYD GEORGE	*Vice-Chairmen*	
ANEURIN BEVAN		
D. O. EVANS	*Hon. Treasurer*	
JAMES GRIFFITHS	*Hon. Secretary*	

The only response was that our proposals would receive consideration. In 1944, when Megan Lloyd George was the chairman, another approach was made to the Prime Minister, which elicited the following reply:

10 Downing Street,
Whitehall
2nd January 1945.

DEAR MISS LLOYD GEORGE,

Thank you for your letter of 10th November regarding the proposals of the Welsh Parliamentary Party for the establishment of a Secretary of State for Wales. The matter is, as you know, receiving consideration. The difficulty is that a proposal of this nature has such far-reaching implications in the administrative sphere that detailed consideration has to be given to it by the many authorities concerned. These authorities are of course heavily burdened with war tasks.

Yours sincerely,
(Signed)   WINSTON S. CHURCHILL

By this time the end of the war in Europe was within sight and Members were more and more turning their minds to the election which everyone expected would follow upon victory. On taking office as Minister of National Insurance I had to relinquish the post of secretary of the party and hand over to my successor, the new member for Brecon and Radnor, Tudor Watkins.

For the first three years of the 1945 Parliament ministers were heavily engaged in the implementation of a massive programme of legislation, and none were more fully engaged in this task than those Welsh members who were serving in Government. The only specifically Welsh interest which came under our consideration during those hectic years was that of the administration of the social insurance and health services. Many experts sought to persuade Nye Bevan and me to establish separate administrative machinery for the north and south of Wales.

We rejected their advice, and created a unified system for the whole of Wales. In this we were following the example already set by some Government departments, which was to be followed by others, so that by the fifties there were no fewer than seventeen departments which had established administrative units in Wales.

The Welsh Parliamentary Party had not been idle in those years, and Tudor Watkins, with characteristic doggedness, had been pressing for more tangible recognition of Welsh nationality than was provided by these administrative innovations, welcome as they were. The Welsh Council of Labour had also been urging the Government to action. In the discussions which took place within the Government the key figures, with whom I had many arguments, were Herbert Morrison and Nye Bevan.

Herbert, as Home Secretary in the war-time coalition, had been sympathetic to Welsh claims and to him we owed the first relief from the oppression of the Tudor ban on the use of the Welsh language in the courts. However, when we came to consider the establishment of a separate Welsh Office with a political head, whilst acknowledging the strength of the case on grounds of the recognition of national sentiment, the administrator in Herbert made him a kindly but resolute opponent. His argument was that to break up the administration of departments most closely concerned with the economic and social life of Britain would be a retrograde step, and would be to the disadvantage of the people of Wales. He had supported the decision to treat Wales as a unit for administration of the new welfare measures, but only as part of, and subordinate to, the central administration and under the authority of a United Kingdom minister.

Nye's doubts about the wisdom of the creation of a Welsh Office went beyond considerations of administration. He has related how he came to realize that if he was to achieve his objectives, and his burning desire to create a Socialist society, it was imperative to reach out from the valley, and beyond the county, to the centre where the levers of power were operated. He was impatient of nationalisms which divided peoples and enslaved nations within their narrow geographical and spiritual frontiers. He feared that devolution of authority would divorce Welsh political activity from the main stream of British politics, as he felt was already happening in Scotland.

However, both he and Herbert agreed that the wishes of the Welsh M.P.s and the Welsh Council of Labour called for some response, and in the course of the next year we adopted a number of measures which have their importance as stages on the way to the creation of the Welsh Office and the appointment of a Secretary of State. Herbert Morrison as Leader of the House provided for an annual debate on Welsh affairs. This was followed by the convening of periodic meetings of the heads of the regional offices of Government departments in Wales. Then in 1948 came the decision to establish a council for Wales and Monmouthshire, composed of persons appointed by the Prime Minister, representative of local government, industry and cultural institutions within the principality. The council, through the publication of a number of well-prepared and documented reports, was to influence the subsequent development of the Welsh policy of successive governments.

The success of the council was in no small measure due to the leadership of the first chairman, Huw T. Edwards, a well-known and widely influential figure in Wales. The chairmanship of the council gave him an opportunity which he used to the full. His background of work in the coal-mines in South Wales, allied to his trade union and local government experience in North Wales, had made him equally well known in the south and in his native north. Under his leadership the council made an intensive study of a number of Welsh problems and produced several valuable reports. The most important were those on the problems of rural depopulation and on government administration in Wales, and the latter provided detailed proposals for the setting up of a Welsh Office, with considerable devolution of authority, and headed by a Secretary of State.

When the Conservatives returned to power in 1951 they kept the promise they had made during the election to appoint a Minister of Welsh Affairs, but they kept it in a curious manner. It had been expected that they would appoint one of their Welsh Tory M.P.s even though their choice was limited to the half-dozen who held Welsh seats. However, what they did was to designate the Home Secretary as Minister for Welsh Affairs. In the thirteen years of Tory rule, 1951–64, there were five designated ministers for Welsh affairs. The most successful move the Conservatives made to try to meet Welsh demands was in the appointment of Lord Brecon, a South Wales industrialist, as Minister of State for Wales. He had no executive responsibilities and was able to devote his time to maintaining contact with the local authorities and voluntary bodies.

Another development of interest came as the result of a proposal, made to the Select Committee on Parliamentary Procedure by Ness Edwards, the Member for Caerphilly, for the setting up of a Welsh Grand Committee on the pattern of the existing Scottish Committee. The Select Committee recommended that this be done and the Government accepted their recommendation. The first meeting of the committee was held on 11th May 1960 under the chairmanship of George Thomas, Cardiff. My Welsh Labour colleagues did me the honour of inviting me to make the opening speech.

In the years between 1945 and 1964, under successive governments, a number of steps were taken which, if not dramatic in their impact, yet led to a fuller consideration of, and increased opportunities to debate, Welsh affairs in Parliament.

Welcome as all these measures were, they did not satisfy the desire for fuller recognition of our nationhood nor the demand for devolution of administration. While I had opposed the proposal for a Parliament for Wales, I was convinced that both on grounds of national sentiment and the necessity for further devolution of administration, the appointment of a Secretary of State and the creation of a Welsh Office were desirable. The majority of the Welsh local authorities and the Welsh Council of Labour had declared their support for this proposal.

Hitherto the majority of my colleagues in the Labour Party had been opposed. However, a fresh opportunity came to give further consideration to the question when in readiness for the 1959 election the National Executive of the party set up a special committee, under my chairmanship, to prepare a Labour programme for Wales. I was, at the time, the deputy leader of the party and I had discussions with Hugh Gaitskell and my Welsh colleagues and urged them to agree to include it in the programme.

To my intense satisfaction they unanimously agreed and for the first time the Labour Party pledged itself to include a Secretary of State for Wales in the next Labour Government. When Hugh Gaitskell came to our Welsh Labour conference and added his pledge as leader of the party it was received with enthusiasm. The pledge was reaffirmed in the 1964 manifesto and by Harold Wilson at Cardiff in his first speech as leader.

2

When I retired from the position of Deputy Leader in 1959, I agreed, at Hugh Gaitskell's request, to remain on the front Opposition bench to be responsible for Welsh affairs. Hugh had asked me before the 1959 election whether in the event of Labour being returned to power I would be willing to serve as Secretary of State for Wales, and I agreed. The years were rolling on and I had reached the allotted span—and, as an old collier friend used to say, I was living on the 'bonus'. For a year or so after 1959 I had felt unwell, but after hospital treatment I made a good recovery.

With my vigour restored I made up my mind that if my good friends at Llanelli agreed I would stand again at the General Election of 1964. They were not only willing but anxious that I should, for they had made up their minds that with a Labour victory I would become the first Secretary of State for Wales.

During the 1964 campaign, as in all the election campaigns since 1945, I made a speaking tour of Wales. In my speeches I concentrated on Labour's policy for Wales, and found that wherever I went the proposal to appoint a Secretary of State was warmly welcomed.

Wales gave its approval to our policy by increasing the Labour representation to twenty-eight out of the thirty-six seats, and once again Llanelli returned me with a large majority.

For thirty years Wales had returned a majority of Labour M.P.s to Parliament, a remarkable example of political loyalty and stability. We rejoiced in the return of a Labour Government even if the majority was small. The day after the declaration of the poll I was called to No. 10.

Harold Wilson greeted me cordially and invited me to become —in his own words—'the Charter Secretary of State for Wales'. I at once raised the question of my age, but he said that it was his desire, as he felt sure it was the desire of the people of Wales, that this honour should come to me. We came to a mutual under-standing that I would stay long enough to establish the new Welsh Office on a firm foundation and then give way to a younger man. It was in this spirit of mutual regard and frankness that we then, as later when I retired, discussed the matter.

When the announcement came I received messages of goodwill from Welshmen at home and in exile. There was one message which deserves a note: it was from a Cornishman who wanted to reunite Celtic Cornwall to Wales and to make me Secretary of State for a new Celtic kingdom!

I was pleased by the appointment of Goronwy Roberts as Minister of State and Harold Finch as Under Secretary. I first met Goronwy when he was a lecturer at University College, Swansea. I was impressed by his qualities of mind and character and that first impression had deepened during the years in which we had served together in the House of Commons. He brought to all his work a deep love of Wales, its language and culture.

When I was president of the South Wales Miners' Federation I had brought Harold from the valleys to our office at Cardiff to serve in our workmen's compensation department. He had an almost unrivalled knowledge of the field of social service. I was fortunate to have two such splendid colleagues. And all three of us were equally fortunate to have as our P.P.S. Tudor Watkins, the Member for Brecon and Radnor. We made a Welsh quartet, bringing together north, mid and south Wales, and ensuring unity by bringing in Monmouthshire.

There were some who held the view that it would be best to begin without any specific transfer of powers, and that we would serve Wales the better by acting as watchdogs over the work of all departments. I did not share their view. I had some experience of government and was convinced that a minister without a department is seriously handicapped in his work; moreover that a roving commission is almost bound to create friction between him and his colleagues. This conviction was strengthened by the message I received from Sir Thomas W. Phillips, who was the permanent secretary to the Ministry of National Insurance when I was the minister. I had kept in touch with him, and when I was appointed to my new post he sent me a cordial letter of good wishes accompanied by this note of advice:

> You must be, of course, a watchdog for Wales as a whole, but in order to do this effectively you ought to have a department of your own, with a competent civil service staff. This will help to give you the professional assistance you will need and avoid the risk of being regarded as a tiresome busybody who is always interfering with other people's business without having any business of your own.

Fortified by his advice, I sat down with my two colleagues to prepare our proposals for submission to the Prime Minister. In 'Signposts to the New Wales' we had envisaged that 'in addition to his overall supervision of Welsh affairs, the Secretary of State will have executive responsibilities over a wide field, including education, health, housing and local government and agriculture'.

I had prepared a scheme which provided over a period for a phased transfer of power of the departments specified in our policy statement, the first transfer to be of those powers which were then vested in the Department of Housing and Local Government. It was a tribute to the Prime Minister's interest in our work that he was able to make the following statement on the transfer of powers to the Welsh Office within five weeks of my appointment as Secretary of State:

> As the House knows, the interests of Wales are now represented in the Cabinet by my right hon. friend the Secretary of State. My right hon. friend will have a Welsh office in Cardiff, which will be adequately staffed, and a small ministerial office in London. He has already taken over responsibility for all issues affecting Wales which do not fall within the responsibility of any other department. He will now take over virtually all the executive responsibilities of the Ministry of Housing and Local Government in Wales.
>
> In particular, my right hon. friend will be responsible for housing, new towns, town and country planning and the organization of local government. In view of the close link between policies on urban planning and on road planning he will also take over from my right hon. friend the Minister of Transport responsibility for roads, including trunk roads, in Wales.
>
> In the vital field of regional planning my right hon. friend the Secretary of State for Wales will co-operate closely with my right hon. friend the First Secretary of State, and his department will provide the chairman of the Planning Board for Wales. The formulation and implementation of the plan for Wales will be done in conformity with the overall national policy for which the First Secretary of State is responsible.
>
> With reference to the work of other Government departments, the application of national policies in Wales will be for the ministers centrally responsible; but my right hon. friend will have oversight within Wales of the execution of national policy by the Ministry of Agriculture, Fisheries and Food, the Department of Education and Science, the Ministry of Health, the Ministry of Transport, the Board of Trade and the Ministry of Labour. For this purpose my right hon. friend the Secretary of State will maintain close and regular contact with the heads of the Welsh Offices.

In the course of the next few months I had further consultations with the Prime Minister on the development of our work, and in a speech at Newtown on the 24th July 1965 he said:

> As I said in the House of Commons when I described the new arrangements, we shall keep on reviewing the position in the light of experience. Indeed we are doing this all the time because there have been important additions to your Secretary of State's executive

duties, such as forestry, national parks, water resources, and, following a meeting I had with him this week, I think he is going to have new and real functions in connection with higher education in Wales.

Step by step, the province of the new Welsh Office was being enlarged and its authority strengthened. Of course, I could have wished for the transfer of powers over a wider field, and I have no doubt that this will come in the fullness of time. Meanwhile I was resolved to lay a firm foundation upon which further devolution could be justified.

In this spirit, and with this resolve, I set to work. The first job was to man the ministerial office in London. We were provided with accommodation in Parliament Street. The building had at one time housed the well-known firm of civil engineers, Cowdray-Pearson, and as I walked up the steps to my room I would often glance at the stained-glass window which depicted some of the projects of these famous engineers, including the Port Talbot Dock in 1895.

A minister leans very heavily upon his permanent and private secretaries and, as in my previous offices, once again I was fortunate. The first permanent secretary of the Welsh Office was Goronwy Daniel, who came to us from the Ministry of Power. He had already distinguished himself in his civil service career and he was the obvious choice for the post. In addition to bringing to his new responsibilities his considerable talents and wide experience he provided a link with the Wales of yesterday. His father was a colliery manager with whom I had negotiated many settlements as a miners' agent, and his wife was a grand-daughter of David Lloyd George. From the Admiralty came my private secretary, Ken Pritchard, whose father was a railway worker at the Severn Tunnel. These two were soon joined by another Welshman, Lloyd Thomas, who at the Home Office had worked with the earlier ministers for Welsh affairs.

In carrying out my 'oversight responsibilities' I had the cordial co-operation of the heads of other government departments in Wales, and was pleased to find that the practice of bringing them together at the conferences of heads of departments had created a real team spirit in their ranks.

From the outset I made up my mind that I would use every moment I could snatch away from Westminster to visit Wales. This was none too easy as our majority of three necessitated constant attendance at the House of Commons. Virtually every week-end was spent in journeys to Wales. In the first year I visited each of the thirteen counties, most of the towns and many villages and hamlets. Everywhere I found pride in the recognition which the appointment of a Secretary of State and the establishment of the Welsh Office had brought to our nation. From these journeys I returned with a renewed awareness of the many urgent problems which face my country.

12

WORKING FOR WALES

1 BUILDING A NEW ECONOMY

WALES has still to recover from the wounds of the thirties. What was then experienced was not only material poverty but also the indignity of idleness, the frustration of human hopes and the dissolution of a society and a way of life. Notwithstanding all that has since been attempted and achieved, the fears persist, the doubts remain and the wounds are unhealed.

It all came so suddenly and caught us unprepared. In those halcyon days before 1914 everything had seemed so settled and sure, the economic base so firm, the livelihood of our people secure and our communities so prosperous. Year by year the basic industries expanded, there was work for all and life was becoming better and fuller.

We never paused to ponder on how narrow was the base of the economy which had developed since the first industrial revolution, nor gave a thought to what might happen if its foundation crumbled. Three out of every five of our people depended for their livelihood, directly or indirectly, on coal, steel, tinplate and slate. Then came the 1914 war and within a generation all was changed. 'King Coal' was dethroned, the old tinplate mills gave way to the new strip mills, and slate was replaced by the cheaper if more brittle tiles as a shelter over our heads. A thriving community needs a balanced population with the young, middle-aged and the elderly in due proportion. Wales, with the rest of the kingdom, suffered grievously from the loss of the young men who did not return from across the sea, and then in the years of the great depression a quarter of a million people, mainly the young, left Wales in search of work. For a small nation of two and a half million this was a cruel blow.

In the mid thirties the Conservative Government began to recognize, reluctantly, that the industrial areas of Wales, and those of England and Scotland which had been similarly affected, could not be left to sink ever lower into depression and desolation. They appointed commissioners to investigate and report on their plight and in 1936 provided a million pounds to assist in the rehabilitation and reconstruction of the afflicted areas. This was but tinkering with the problem, and it was not until rearmament and the war brought munition work that the downward slide was halted. In 1945 came the first major endeavour to build a new economy to replace the old by means of Hugh Dalton's Distribution of Industry Act, with its control over the location of industry, and its positive inducements to attract new industries, supplemented by Government-built factories, and trading estates. A new economy began to develop, more firmly based and widely diversified. In every valley there are to be seen the new industries that are a tribute to the work of Hugh Dalton. The Conservative Government were to substitute for the bold and imaginative Act of 1945 the Local Employment Act with its scheduling of smaller areas where unemployment was high and persistent. This measure made a contribution to the provision of new industries in some of the localities which came within its scope. However, with all the successes to their credit, these measures fell short of what was needed and desired. Aid did not come until unemployment had already reached a high level, the criterion was too narrow and rigid, for it took no account of that hidden unemployment we describe as depopulation.

I had given a good deal of thought to the problem of the Welsh economy ever since the warnings of the Barlow Commission in 1940 against the absurd concentration of population and industry in the south-east and London. While the commission's recommendations had been influenced by considerations of defence and the dangers of over-concentration of industry and people in modern warfare, there were other considerations which impressed me and which had their relevance to Wales. The first industrial revolution had, as one of its consequences, crowded three-quarters of our population into three of the South Wales counties. The growth of industry in this corner of Wales had relentlessly drained the most virile section of the community away from the rural areas, leaving behind an ageing population. This is socially bad for any community, but in particular it endangered the

171

foundations of a rural society which was Welsh in character and language. Some of my compatriots saw in this a devilish plot by the English to destroy our nation and our way of life, whereas it was the inevitable result of allowing economic and commercial considerations to be the sole determinant of the location of industry. In the old economy location had of necessity been determined by geological factors and the paramount need to be near the coalfields. Now, in the age of the second industrial revolution, whilst coal was losing its magnetism, the opportunities of a planned distribution of industry based on civilized concepts of town and country planning were within our grasp. However, I could discern the trends in the new revolution which would, unless consciously guided and directed to serve the needs of sensible planning, result in a different but equally dangerous concentration. The growth of a wide range of light industries producing the gadgets we all want would tend to be located near to their markets. In Wales this would give to the eastern half a decisive advantage over the western. Unless we could create a counter-pull I could see the emerging Wales being divided not into north and south but into a prosperous east and a languishing west.

With these considerations in mind I welcomed the publication of the national plan in 1965, and of working with George Brown in the creation of the machinery within Wales to achieve its objectives. The plan was a bold and imaginative effort to set Britain on the road to solvency by ensuring continuous economic growth. It recognized the key role of the regions in the achievement of its target, and especially the paramount importance of the underdeveloped areas of the country. It was for this purpose that regional planning machinery was established. The distinctive position of Wales and Scotland was recognized by the responsibilities delegated to the Secretaries of State.

I had to decide what form the regional machinery should take in Wales. There were then, and still are, some who argue that I should have created a number of separate planning regions within Wales, in particular that the north and south-east corners should be linked with the industrial areas beyond in England. But the opening of the new Severn Bridge brings Bristol within easy reach of the Newport/Cardiff area, while the Mersey tunnels, and the prospect of a barrage across the Dee estuary, provide close links between north-east Wales and Merseyside. I was confident that these border areas in the north and south would develop under their own momentum. It was the economic prospects of west and mid Wales which gave cause for concern. I therefore decided that Wales should be treated as one unit for economic planning, with its own Planning Board and Economic Council.

The board's functions being to advise the Government on current problems, and to co-operate with the Economic Council in the formulation of plans for future development, I was anxious that its membership should be representative of both the old and the new industries, and of town and country. I had long felt the need to bring the university and colleges into closer relationship with industry. The studies already undertaken by members of their staff could make a valuable contribution to the work of the Economic Council. It was desirable that the Welsh ministers should be closely associated with the council, so I appointed the Minister of State, Goronwy Roberts, as its chairman.

I regard the decision to set up a single planning board and council for Wales as an important step forward. In their work they will be confronted with difficult problems, e.g. the future of the valley communities, the problem of rural decline and depopulation and the provision of a co-ordinated system of communications. In both south and north the pattern of road communication was determined by the need of the old industries to have access to the overseas markets. Now the paramount need is for improved communication from all parts of Wales to the markets of the midland conurbation and the metropolis. In the south we now have the two-road system, from the Severn Bridge and along the coast, and the Heads of the Valleys road. I promoted schemes to carry the Heads of the Valleys road westwards and to link it to the coastal road where the two converge upon Swansea. In the north, the road will run from Anglesey and Arfon to the barrage and the tunnels. In mid Wales the projected new town will provide both the need and the justification for improved roads to the midlands. When these west–east road systems are completed we may go on to realize the dream of many of my fellow countrymen of a highway to link north and south.

There are some who fear that these economic changes, and the communications they necessitate, will open the door to the invader, and to the undermining and destruction of our traditional way of life. In my view there is far greater danger to our tradition, and most of all to our language, in the invasion which comes over the air! We cannot escape any of these dangers: we have already reached the point of no return. What we must now do is to face up to the dangers and resolve to turn the challenge of change into an opportunity of building a new economy, on firm foundations, and of creating a society which will combine what is precious in our inheritance with the new vigour and strength the scientific and technological revolution can provide.

Our workers have already given ample proof of their capacity, and ability to learn new skills. The young people at our schools and colleges have both the qualities needed and the resolve to dedicate them to the service of the country. The destiny of Wales can be safely entrusted to them. What I sought to do was to provide Wales with the administration and machinery which would enable its people to participate in the building of a new economic and social order.

When I set up the planning board and council I expected that there would be criticism on two grounds. First, that its members were appointed by and subservient to ministers and, secondly, that it did not have executive powers. I understood, and shared this view, and I had in mind the possibility of creating a democratically elected council for Wales to which the responsibilities of the Economic Council could be transferred, and to which executive powers could be entrusted in this all-important sphere of economic planning.

2 REORGANIZING LOCAL GOVERNMENT

In a long career in public life there is one experience which I regret having missed—that of serving on a local authority. However, my work in the trade union movement and later as a Member of Parliament had brought me into close touch with local authorities and in particular with my friends who were serving as members. During the years of the depression I had been deeply impressed by the services rendered to our people by our councils. It is not too much to say that their salvage work saved our community life from complete dissolution. I understood how my Labour friends had become so closely attached to the councils on which they served that they almost resented any suggestion that local government should be reorganized. When, as Secretary of State, I was entrusted with the responsibility for local government reorganization, one of my friends expressed sympathy with me. 'You ought to know', he said, 'that Welshmen are eager to change the world—providing you do not interfere with their parish.' Experience has shown that there is some justification for his cynicism. In private everyone agrees that a radical reconstruction of local government is both necessary and urgent, but when proposals are put forward the usual reaction is: 'Leave us alone to do our work—all we want is more money.'

Just before I took over my new office a commission, under the chairmanship of the late Sir Myrddin Evans, a Welshman with a notable career in the civil service, had completed a thorough investigation into local government in Wales. The commission recommended that the number of county councils should be reduced from thirteen to seven, and the county boroughs from four to three. As an exercise in drawing boundaries for enlarged county councils the commission's proposals had merit, but unfortunately the limitations placed upon the commission by the terms of reference precluded them from considering the reorganization of the lower tiers of local government within the counties or of venturing into the new field of regional government. On this account, and even more because of resistance to any change, the commission's plan was given a frigid reception. The then Minister for Welsh Affairs, Sir Keith Joseph, whilst accepting some of the proposals with regard to the county boroughs, rejected the other recommendations and intimated that he would set out his own proposals in a White Paper.

When I came to consider the matter the White Paper was far from being ready and I decided to make a fresh approach. I came to the conclusion that it would be futile to appoint another commission to produce another report—the waste-paper baskets at Government departments and council offices were already full of discarded plans. My colleagues responsible for local government in England and Scotland decided to appoint royal commissions, but I secured the full approval of the Government to set up a working party under the direction of the Permanent Secretary of the Welsh Office, Goronwy Daniel. Their instructions were to prepare plans for the reorganization of local government at all levels from the parish to the county, and at the same time to consider whether a regional council for the whole of Wales was desirable and, if so, to prepare proposals for such an authority.

I was anxious to secure the co-operation of the existing local authorities in the preparation of my plan. In the past, apart from giving evidence to the commissions, the members serving on the councils had not been asked to come in at the preparatory stage and I felt that it would be an advantage if their knowledge and experience could be made available to the working party. I invited the associations of the various councils to send representatives to meet me at the Welsh Office. They welcomed the invitation and appointed about fifty to come to meet me. I outlined the procedure I had decided to follow and asked them if they would agree to nominate a number of persons of experience to be available for consultation with the working party. I was gratified to find my suggestion warmly approved by the associations' representatives, who expressed their pleasure at being brought into consultation at the preparatory stage. The work was well on the way to completion when I retired from office. I felt satisfied that we had got away to a good start. I was anxious that we should not miss the opportunity of pioneering in this important sector of our democratic system of government. I hope that we shall not stop at making changes in the existing structure but will also venture into new fields.

It seemed to me that fundamental reform might mean the creation of an elected body to administer certain services throughout the principality. Experience had shown that both central and local government had found it necessary to create *ad hoc* bodies to serve regional needs which could not be adequately met by existing machinery. The Welsh education authorities had established the Welsh Joint Education Committee; the central government had appointed the Council for Wales; and I had appointed the Welsh Economic Council. In these circumstances the logical and democratic step would be to change local government boundaries and set up an all-Wales authority rather than set up more unrepresentative bodies. I am also satisfied that some form of regional government will be established in England as a result of the current examination by the Royal Commission on Local Government. To all those who, like myself, desire to maintain the identity of Wales the reform of local government presents both a challenge and an opportunity. If we have the courage to act, and the wisdom to look beyond our parish, we can now create a new organ of government which will improve the well-being of our people and which will be at the same time an embodiment of our nationhood. My friend Gwilym Prys Davies has produced a plan for a central council for Wales.

Without accepting all its details I commend it to the consideration of my fellow countrymen. We pride ourselves on our
radicalism. Here is an opportunity for us to be worthy of our
radical tradition.

3   A NEW TOWN IN MID WALES

We are a nostalgic people. A longing for some lost paradise is
woven deeply into our character. We are peasants who have never
become fully reconciled to industrialism. I remember the colliers
I worked with who had left their home in the countryside in
search of a livelihood in the mines. While they toiled in the pit,
they dreamed of the day when they would return to spend the
eventide of their lives back home, and kept the dream alive by
returning each year for their summer holidays. 'If only we could
have stayed,' they would sadly say when they came back to work.
Alas, there was no room for them on the farm. The foundation of
the Welsh rural society was the family farm of twenty acres or so,
with grazing for the sheep on the nearby hillside. One of my predecessors as M.P. for Llanelli, Llewellyn Williams, has given us a
moving picture of the Welsh rural society in his book *Slawer
Dydd* ('Long Ago'). How times have changed. The family farm
has become just a part of a bigger holding, and the old farmhouse
is in ruins. The smithy is closed and the carpenter, bootmaker
and saddler made redundant by the stores in the town. There are
so few children that the village school has to be closed. The
chapel is half empty and the members so few that they cannot keep
a minister. Without a schoolmaster and a minister the community
has lost its natural leaders. The young men and women have gone.
There is no work for them on the farm, and there is now nothing
to do but to follow the others who have gone away in search of
work and livelihood. Now it has got to be England—the midlands
or London—for even down in South Wales they have enough to
do to find work for their own people.

The five counties which lie at the heart of rural Wales—
Brecon, Radnor, Montgomery, Merioneth and Cardigan—have
suffered grievously from the loss of their people. In the first half
of this century their combined population declined by fifty
thousand—a thousand lost each year; enough people to sustain
five thriving village communities. There appears to be no end to
the drain. Each year the number of workers in full employment

in agriculture in Wales goes down by a thousand and the five counties lose more in proportion than any of the other counties in Wales. The young go away, leaving the old behind. In the five counties the proportion of the population of pensionable age is 20 per cent higher than in England and Wales, and the income per head is £1 a week less than that of the rest of the population. The whole of this lovely countryside is caught in a vicious circle—depopulation drains it of its youth, the community is impoverished, and this accelerates the drift away from the villages and the rural society is left to decline. I had heard Clement Davies so often in Parliament pleading for 'my people, my county', and imploring governments to come to their rescue. He had advocated the building of a new town to restore economic vigour and to revive hope. I had joined him in the campaign to rid the Welsh country-side of that other 'decline' (as they called T.B.) and had seen how, by bringing to our aid the marvels of modern medicine and the developments of the health and social services, the country-side had been saved from that scourge. What was now needed were the resources and the resolve to combat this 'decline' called 'depopulation', which was undermining the whole fabric of society in the rural areas of the five counties.

I was under no illusion that this would be an easy task. I was convinced that the situation in mid Wales was so serious that only a blood transfusion could save it from decay. Already in some areas the death rate exceeds the birth rate. It follows from the age structure of the population that a policy designed to restore vitality to mid Wales must provide for bringing in people as well as industry. I therefore made up my mind to initiate steps for the building of a new town under the provisions of the New Towns Act. When I announced my decision there was a furore. All kinds of people, for all kinds of reasons, violently attacked the project. The only reason advanced which I treated seriously was that a new town would, by attracting people from the midlands, tend to undermine the rural society, and threaten the future of our language and way of life. I thought it was rather an irony of history that this agitation should coincide with the centenary of Patagonia, that brave venture of our forbears to establish a new community in far-away Argentine. I am as proud of our language and way of life as any of my critics are, and as anxious as they to preserve them. But we cannot preserve any of these in a deserted land.

When I came to appoint consultants to advise me on the project I made clear in the terms of reference that the new town should, architecturally and culturally, have a character in keeping with the area. I was fortunate to secure as consultants a group of people who were not only technically competent but who shared my desire to preserve the distinctive character of the area. They produced a plan which fully justified my hopes and the claim they make that:

> The site we have chosen [Caersws, Llanidloes, Newtown] gives scope for a striking design for the town, which can be made not to mar but to enhance the natural beauty of the Severn Valley. It will be attractive in itself, combining as it does the features of a resort and recreational settlement with the requirements of manufacturing industry. Add to this its close relationship to our proposed national park (the Plynlimmons) and we have something entirely new in urban planning—the deliberate location of industry close to an area where the people who work in the factories can join with the visitors from outside in the enjoyment of the country-side. This, we believe, is the pattern people will increasingly demand in the rest of this century, and it cannot be provided in the overcrowded regions of Britain.

I still hope that we shall have the courage to carry out their plans. Here is an opportunity for us to be pioneers in town and country planning. In the past we have allowed greed to dictate the pattern of our urban development, so that our land is full of horrible examples of the failure of man's handiwork to match the beauty of the natural setting, and even worse, to mar it with ugliness and dirt. Of course it would mean bringing industry from England and workers with the industry. If we had not done just this in South Wales our towns and valleys would have sunk into decay. The obvious area from which to attract industry and people to mid Wales is the midlands conurbation. The movement from the midlands is already westwards. The new town of Dawley is within twenty-three miles of the border—and other projects will bring development nearer still. There are many people who believe that the need for the overspill of the midlands can best be met by new developments just across Offa's Dyke. This will further accelerate the drift away from mid Wales. I share the view of the consultants that a new town in the Welsh part of the Severn is the answer to the related problems of rural decline in Wales and urban congestion in the midlands, and that 'given imagination and sensitivity in its execution, it could prove to be Wales's showpiece to the world', and 'dispel the deeply rooted belief that Welsh culture and economic decline are inseparable'.

4 FLOOD AND DROUGHT

On a Monday afternoon in the winter of 1964 I found myself strapped to a helicopter with my feet dangling out, and having a panoramic view of the Wye and the Severn valleys in flood. The two valleys were like a sea. Above Newtown the pilot lowered our machine, we circled around and eventually landed in the playground of a school. The town was a heartbreaking sight. The river makes an S turn around the centre of the town and the flooded waters of the Severn had gushed in from all sides. Water, like fire, can be a welcome friend and a devastating enemy. Many of the houses had been rendered completely uninhabitable, and some were too dangerous even to enter. The fortitude of the people impressed me deeply. In one house I found father, mother and their three children clearing the filth from floor and walls. The father shook his head and said: 'Well, there it is, it's happened; all there is to do now is to pitch in and clear it all up.'

Having arranged for the Welsh Office officials, in co-operation with the local authorities, to tackle the salvage work, I returned to my London office to consider how we could prevent floods in future. Together with our colleagues we got down to the problem. It was ironical that just before the floods occurred I had been considering what steps could be taken before the next summer to prevent drought, which earlier that year had led to severe rationing of water in Swansea. Flood and drought in the same land and the same year, and not for the first time!

Earlier in the year the Water Resources Act, 1963, had come into operation. The Act provided for the setting up of new machinery. This machinery consists of a Water Resources Board to advise ministers, including the Secretary of State for Wales, on the action needed for the conservation, redistribution and augmentation of water resources, and at a lower level of river authorities to control the abstraction of water from rivers. This is not the ideal machinery. I should like to see all the distribution undertakings being brought under public ownership, and conservation and distribution brought under a unified service which would be administered regionally. In Wales the service could be administered by a Welsh Water Board, under the aegis of a regional council.

Meanwhile I had to turn to the machinery already established. The chairman of the Water Resources Board, Sir William Goode, readily agreed with my suggestion that a Welsh Water Committee should be set up to advise me on the complex water problems in Wales. My first request to the new committee was to make a survey of the resources of the Severn and to recommend how these could best be harnessed to prevent flooding and to meet the ever-increasing demand for water.

If we are to solve the twin problems of the increasing demand for water and of preventing the desolation caused by flooding we shall have to formulate a scheme whereby the interests of the 'givers' and the 'takers' of the water are reconciled and at the same time to design our conservation policies in such a way that the blessings of water in abundance are fairly shared and its perils prevented.

5 THE WORKER'S CASTLE

More than one half of all the houses in Wales are owner-occupied. In some of the industrial valleys the proportion is as high as seventy-five out of every hundred. Wales was a property-owning democracy long before the Tories coined the phrase.

Behind the ambition, indeed the passion, to own the 'worker's castle' lies a story.

In the forty years between 1871 and 1911 the population of the three industrial counties, Monmouth, Glamorgan and Carmarthen, trebled. The people who came to work in the mines and mills had to find a house near to their place of work, and the choice before them was to live in a 'company house' or to build their own. To live in a company house was to be at the mercy of the employer and to risk eviction if one dared to come out on strike. To own one's own home was one of the defences of the worker against the tyranny of the boss. To build the house one had first to find a plot of land, and in some valleys all the land belonged to one landlord, and, with the powerful aid of a feudal legal system, the landlord was able to exploit the situation to the full. Most landlords refused to sell a plot freehold but carved up their estates into small plots and leased them for ninety-nine years. To the lease would be attached a covenant which decreed that when the lease expired the house would 'revert' to the landowner, and most of these covenants also contained a clause that the leaseholder had to repair and rehabilitate the premises to the landowner's requirements. Under this system the worker who had saved and sacrificed to build his own home found that it was taken away from him when the lease ran out and, in addition, he must pay for repairs.

The evils of this system had spread from the valleys to the new suburbs around the towns, and in Cardiff and other towns voices were raised in the demand for leasehold enfranchisement. As long ago as 1884 a Royal Commission on the Housing of the Working Classes had recommended leasehold enfranchisement on fair terms, but as in the case of so many other royal commissions their report and recommendations had been forgotten. The Liberal Party had included leasehold reform in their programme since the days of Gladstone and had kept it in their programme ever since. The Labour Party likewise had pledged itself to bring about the end of the evils of leasehold. *Hansard* contains the record of the many private bills for leasehold reform, none of which came anywhere near the statute book. As a member of the 1945 Government I had learnt that the stumbling block to the enactment of this measure of justice was what was described as the principle of the 'sanctity of contract'. The lawyers held that a lease was a contract entered into by two willing and equal parties, and for Parliament to intervene and to force one of the partners to surrender his rights under the contract was unthinkable. It would be a blow at the sanctity of contract.

The assumption upon which this 'sanctity' was based bore no relation to the circumstances in which our forbears made the contract of the ninety-nine years' lease and built their cottages on the hillsides in the eighteen-seventies. To describe that contract as one between 'willing and equal parties' was a travesty of the real situation.

By the nineteen-fifties some leases were running out, and even the Conservative Government could not resist the demand to do something. They provided that when the lease expired the worker could stay in his 'castle' as the tenant of the landowner and pay rent to him. This only added insult to injury by making the owner-occupier a rent-paying tenant in the house which he or his forbears had built and paid for.

With the return of a Labour Government in 1964 the first steps were taken towards the long overdue reform of the leasehold system, and as Secretary of State I was privileged to take part in the framing of the policy which was eventually set out in the White Paper.

My colleagues and I realized that the best way to overcome the obstacle which had in the past frustrated every effort at reform was to lay down a new principle as a basis for legislation to secure enfranchisement which would be fair and equitable to both parties to the lease. This was set out as follows: 'The basic principle of a reform which will do justice between the parties should be that the freeholder owns the land and the leaseholder is morally entitled to the ownership of the building which has been put on and maintained on the land.'

The principle was later embodied in the Leasehold Reform Act of 1967. It had taken Parliament eighty years to translate into legislation the recommendation of the royal commission of 1884. I was pleased to be in at the end, and to help to realize the hopes of so many of our best citizens.

6 EQUAL VALIDITY

'When a language dies—as die they do—something irretrievably precious is lost.' Every Welshman, at home and in exile, will share this feeling expressed in the editorial column of *The Times* when commenting upon the Hughes Parry report of 1963–5 on the legal status of the Welsh language. The fear that we would lose our language has aroused deep emotions in Wales, not only among those of my compatriots who understand and speak Welsh. Its loss would be felt as grievously at Cardiff Arms Park as at the national Eisteddfod, and in Monmouth as in Merioneth. The survival of our language is the proudest victory that Welsh democracy has ever gained over the 'Establishment'. As I said at the Welsh Grand Committee: 'Since the time of Henry VIII, there have been powers who have sought to destroy the Welsh language. They all failed because the people willed their language to live.' It survived the ban of the Tudors, but will it survive the growing anglicizing influence of the economic, social and cultural changes of our time? It is these influences rather than the dictates of authority which are the most to be feared. Indeed the attitude of the authorities has in recent years been more sympathetic. The first measure to modify the Tudor ban was approved by Parliament as recently as 1942 with the passing of the Welsh Courts Act. It was my privilege, as Secretary of State, to make the next and most important change in the official status of our language when I accepted the major recommendation of the Hughes Parry report:

> That after all legislation now affecting the use of the Welsh language in law or administration had been replaced or amended, there should be a clear, positive, legislative declaration of general application, to the effect that any act, writing or thing done in Welsh in Wales or Monmouthshire should have the like legal force as if it had been done in English. The effect of such a declaration would be of course to raise the status of the Welsh language in Wales to one of equality with that of English. The legal status of English in Wales would not be affected.

I had no hesitation in accepting the principle of equal validity. I share the view expressed by the Council for Wales in their admirable report on the Welsh language that:

> the task of statesmanship in Wales is to foster the growth of the Welsh language, and to do this in ways acceptable to all Welshmen who themselves, for the most part, are proud of the language and desire to see it survive. At the same time measures must not be such as to inflict any hardship upon any group within the community.

The embodiment of the principle of equal validity in legislation will ensure both of the objectives set out in the Council for Wales report. To go beyond this, as some desire, will lead to divisions between the Welsh-speaking and the non-Welsh-speaking people in Wales, a division which, far from helping to foster and sustain our language, would create antagonisms which would impede its growth and hasten its demise. To do less than this would be to deny to our language the status which justice demands and the place in our life which its riches deserve. It is my view that the survival of the language will depend more on other measures and endeavours than on its status in legal and official life, welcome as this will be.

The fate of our language is in our own hands. Our forbears preserved it and sustained it against all the powers of State and Church because they willed it to live. Its future will be ensured if we and our descendants also will it to live.

13

THE WILSON ERA

IT WILL be for the historian to assess the place which Harold Wilson will finally occupy in the ranks of British prime ministers. What is already established is that he ushered in a new era in the annals of the Labour Party. I have known every one of Labour's leaders, from the founding father James Keir Hardie. Each will be remembered for the distinctive qualities which he brought to his task, and each has his own niche in the story of the party's pilgrimage to office and power.

I have sought in these pages to record the impression each of them made on me and my contemporaries. If I were asked to pronounce an interim judgment I would say that Harold Wilson is the most accomplished parliamentarian of them all. He is a superb politician and a master of the debating forum. He was lucky enough to be born with the gifts and attributes so essential for the craft, and he has worked hard in developing and perfecting them. He has fluency of speech and a racy style rather than the sweep of the orator. He is endowed with a prodigious memory, and this allied to his other gifts, a quick and biting wit and instant reaction to the loaded question, combine to make him a formidable debater. He enjoyed considerable advantages as he entered upon his leadership. Following a brilliant academic career he had served in the war-time civil service, first as economic assistant in the War Cabinet and later at the Ministry of Fuel and Power. It was during his period at this post that I came to know him, when he was writing a book on the coal industry and I had written a book in Welsh and a pamphlet in English on the same subject.

It is a considerable advantage to a politician to have served in the civil service and so to have become familiar with the corridors of power. This is an advantage which, in a measure, the P.P.S. enjoys. I applaud heartily the initiative taken by some ministers in recent years in inviting back-bench M.P.s to visit their departments and see how the work is done. Experience as a civil servant was to prove highly valuable to Harold Wilson, who went straight from the poll to ministerial office. What a flying start for a young politician! Wilson has never looked back. Two years later he was a member of the Cabinet as the holder of one of the senior posts, the President of the Board of Trade.

He resigned with Nye Bevan in 1951, and then followed long years in Opposition. From his first day on the Opposition front bench his reputation as a debater grew, particularly during the period when he served as 'Shadow Chancellor'. In 1963, when he was yet under fifty, he became leader of the party. By any test this was an achievement, and with a quarter of a century of active life before him he has the best chance of any prime minister of beating the Grand Old Man's record of four times in that office.

Beside the advantages of his early promotion there were two others which he enjoyed in a measure denied to his predecessor as leader, as I am sure he would acknowledge. First, he was the nominee of the 'left', that is, of the old Bevanite left, and was ensured of their support, and at the same time of the traditional loyalty of the centre and the right. Secondly, he entered into the inheritance bequeathed by Hugh Gaitskell. One of the major contributions which Hugh made to the party was the assertion of the supremacy of the Parliamentary Party in matters of day-to-day policy in the House of Commons and an assured place for the leader in the party's hierarchy. Harold Wilson's path as leader has been all the smoother because Hugh Gaitskell trod the hard road.

Harold Wilson's gifts and qualities are revealed at their best in the Commons debating chamber. He is the first prime minister to turn the question hour into a confrontation with his political foes. He transformed the twice-weekly session of parliamentary questions to the Prime Minister into a personal combat. The Tories, if unwittingly, helped him both by the election of Edward Heath as their leader, and by Heath himself persisting in intervening with supplementaries. This half-hour of confrontation became the star event of the parliamentary week.

The Prime Minister trained hard for this duel, took immense pains in the preparation of his replies to questions, and thought up all the possible supplementaries. His memory, allied to his quick reaction, skill and wit, made him the master of the supplementary. His performance at the dispatch-box delighted our side and infuriated the Tories. I have witnessed many confrontations between rival leaders in Parliament, but none which was so uneven as that between Wilson and Heath. It was generally thought in the Lobbies that the Conservative Members had voted for Ted Heath, the first leader they had been allowed to choose for themselves, because they believed that he would be the nearest match to Wilson. This made it all the more galling to have to confess that their man generally came out second best.

'Image' has become all important in modern political life. If the centre of power is at No. 10, the image-makers are to be found in the parliamentary press lobby and the television studios. Television has become the most effective and dangerous weapon in political warfare. This image-maker can make or wreck the reputation of a politician. Harold Wilson is as effective in the studio as he is in Parliament. Even his most rabid critics—and he has many—have to admit that he comes over well on television and presents himself and his policies with consummate skill. Labour's new leader is the completely equipped and fully armed political protagonist.

2

When Harold Wilson began his career as leader of the Labour Party the reign of Harold Macmillan was drawing to its close. Leaving Winston Churchill out of the reckoning, Macmillan was the ablest leader the Tories had had, in my time in the House, since Stanley Baldwin. Taking over the leadership when the Tories were in complete disarray following the disaster of Suez, he had done a first-class salvage job. In the 1959 election, sensing the prevailing mood, he had inaugurated the 'never had it so good' era and cleverly exploited it to win a decisive victory. By 1963 the tide had turned against him and he had lost his nerve. In a panic he discarded some of his old colleagues. He was rebuffed by de Gaulle. Thereafter he was but a pale shadow of the confident 'Supermac' of the cartoonist. When ill health compelled his retirement he bungled the arrangements for the appointment of his successor. All this had its impact on the morale of the Tory Party, and on its image in the eyes of the electorate. Britain was ready for a change. Harold Wilson sensed this and was ready to seize the opportunity it presented. Labour's election manifesto for 1964 opened with this clarion call:

> The country needs fresh and virile leadership. Labour is ready, poised to swing its plans into instant operation . . . impatient to apply the new thinking . . . a new Britain, mobilizing the resources of technology under a national plan; harnessing our national wealth in brains, our genius for scientific invention and medical discovery; reversing the decline of the thirteen wasted years, affording a new opportunity to equal, and if possible surpass, the roaring progress of other Western powers while Tory Britain has moved sideways, backwards, but seldom forward. . . . The Labour Party is offering Britain a new way of life that will stir our hearts, rekindle an authentic patriotic faith in our future, and enable our country to re-establish itself as a stable force in the world today for progress, peace and justice.

This vision of a new Britain in which Socialism, allied with science and technology, would release the pent-up energies of our people and lead Britain to greatness found a real response among the electorate.

In the 1964 election the massive Tory majority of over a hundred was wiped out, and Labour returned to office, but with a majority of only three! Within two years of his election as leader of the party Harold Wilson had led it to its first electoral victory for thirteen years. Undismayed by the smallness of the majority he had boldly proclaimed that, the nation having returned it to power, this Government would govern. On the day that he entered No. 10 he was confronted with the financial crisis the Tories had left unsolved and with a balance of payments deficit which threatened the country's solvency. The new Government took immediate action to save the pound and to concert plans which would put the country firmly on its feet.

While Jim Callaghan, as Chancellor of the Exchequer, was fighting for the pound, George Brown, at the new Department of Economic Affairs, was preparing a national plan to mobilize the nation's industry for economic growth, and Frank Cousins was harnessing technology for the battle. At the same time the Government remembered its pledge to the people by raising pensions, removing the evils of 'Rachmanism' and promoting legislation to end profiteering in land. The nation warmly welcomed the new and resolute leadership of Harold Wilson and his

Government, and admired their courage in governing despite the small majority.

The Prime Minister realized that he could not carry on for more than a year or so before he would have to go to the country and seek a renewed mandate and an adequate majority. The timing of the election was a delicate exercise. If he went too soon he might be charged with running away from a difficult situation; if he delayed too long the tide might turn against him. He kept all the options open and his judgment in timing was vindicated when in March 1966 Labour won its greatest triumph since 1945 and was returned with an overall majority of ninety-seven.

3

When early in 1966 it became virtually certain that a general election was imminent my first inclination was to retire altogether from active politics. I had been vouchsafed a long innings. I had completed thirty years as Llanelli's M.P. During most of that period I had been at the centre of politics in Parliament and in the counsels of my party. I had enjoyed the privilege of serving in the three departments of National Insurance, the Colonial Office and, in the autumn of my life, the great pleasure of serving as the Charter Secretary of State for Wales. I had already been blessed with what in Welsh we speak of as *Dyddiau'r Addewid* (the promised span), and was now living in the years of grace. Sixty-two years had gone by since I started my working life in the coal-mine, and they had been years of hard toil and endeavour. My wife, who had shared forty-eight of these years with me, urged me to call it a day.

However, there were two considerations which pulled the other way. First, I was anxious to give my constituency party ample time to choose my successor. The Llanelli constituency had been so generous in its loyalty and support that I felt it incumbent upon me to play fair with them and not to force them to a rushed decision. Secondly, I had cherished the ambition to help to win all the constituencies in Wales for Labour, and this time I felt we had a real chance of achieving this record. I consulted my good friends at Llanelli, who wanted me to fight one more battle for the cause. This clinched the matter, and in March of 1966 I fought my eighth contest.

In each election since 1945 I had been released from the calls of my constituency for all but the last three days of the campaign to help others in Wales and across the border. This time I felt that I should devote all my spare time to a tour of Wales, speaking to my compatriots about my work as Secretary of State. So off I went once again on an election tour, starting at Brecon, travelling north along the eastern side, around the north Wales coast and back along Cardigan Bay to Llanelli. As an old campaigner I rejoiced to find that the meetings were well attended and enthusiastic. There was real fervour in the approval for what Wilson had done in according Wales fuller recognition of its nationhood.

As I travelled through the Beacons, Plynlimmons, Snowdonia and by the shores of Cardigan Bay, I remembered what a parlia-mentary colleague—a much travelled man—had once told me: that, in the variety of scene and landscape, Wales is a miniature of all the loveliness and grandeur of nature. In this spring of 1966 I made many calls on my journey from one meeting to another, talking to people in the village squares and over a cup of tea at wayside cafés. One day when I was lunching at the hotel at Pentrefoelas the landlady recognized me and insisted that I should sign the special leather-bound visitors' book which she had inherited from her father. She brought the precious book for me to sign as Secretary of State for Wales, and proudly pointed to the signature of two notables who had lunched at the hotel in May of 1908, David Lloyd George and Winston Churchill. As had happened in all my tours of Wales, the last assignment was at Fishguard, staying overnight at the little inn where the French had surrendered on that famous occasion when the women of Fish-guard, dressed in colourful native costume, had marched round and round and frightened the enemy into surrender.

I returned to Llanelli, where this time I faced three opponents —Tory, *Plaid Cymru* and Communist. Then came three days of touring the constituency in a loudspeaker car, ending up as usual with our rally at the market hall, Llanelli. On to the count, or, as one of my fervent supporters used to say, the 'weighing' of the votes, with the following result:

Griffiths, J. (Lab.):	33,674
Peel, J. C. (Con.):	7,143
Davies, P. (*Plaid Cymru*):	5,132
Hichon, R. E. (Com.):	1,211
Majority:	26,531

Once again my vote and my majority were both up, and Llanelli, for the eighth time in thirty years, had reaffirmed their loyalty to Labour and their faith in their Member. My pride in my own victory was all the greater as other results came in. We had come very near to achieving my ambition, winning thirty-two of the thirty-six Welsh seats. This is the largest number of seats won by any single party in Wales. In 1906 Liberals and Lib.-Labs. combined had won all the seats except one, but that one—how significant—was won by James Keir Hardie for Labour, plain Labour, without prefix or suffix.

Travelling back to London the day after the poll I was cheered on my way by the news that Labour was back in power, and with a majority which with ordinary luck would give it five years in office. The next election might not be until the seventies, when I would be in my eighties! Memory turned the pages back to the elections of the past: to 1910, when with a thousand votes we had celebrated our moral victory; to 1922, when we had first won Llanelli; to the scare elections of 1924 and 1931, when Llanelli held the fort; to 1936, when I was first returned with a majority of 16,000. Now I was on my way back to St Stephen's with a majority of 26,000!

I fell to thinking about the call which would come from No. 10.

When I see the Prime Minister [I told my wife], I shall thank him for the privilege of serving as the Charter Secretary of State for Wales, and for all the support he has unfailingly given to me in my work. I have fulfilled the task he entrusted to me in October 1964. I have established the new Welsh Office on firm foundations and have initiated measures which in the fullness of time will be of service to my country and my people. I now feel that I can lay down the burden of office and hand over to a younger colleague.

When the Prime Minister called me to No. 10 I told him at once of my desire to retire. He was most generous in his tribute and later that day sent me a letter, the reading of which moved me deeply:

10, Downing Street,
Whitehall.
4th April 1966

MY DEAR JIM,

When you came to see me this morning you said that you felt that you would now like to step down from the position of Secretary of State for Wales.

As you know, when we discussed this last October, I asked you then to continue for a few more months.

When you came to see me in October 1964, I told you that I was anxious that you should be the Principality's first Secretary of State, and I said that I hoped you would act, as it were, as the Charter Secretary, to see the new Office into operation before handing over to a younger successor.

Your appointment was welcomed throughout Wales, and all my visits there since have shown the deep affection in which you have been held and the appreciation of what you have done during those eighteen months.

The Office is now accepted throughout the Principality and more widely. I cannot imagine that any future Cabinet will ever be without its Secretary of State for Wales.

May I thank you for all you have done in these years. As I said in Cardiff last week, you have brought to our counsels at every level of Government the needs of the Welsh people.

But more—you have brought to all our discussions, even those going far beyond the problems of Wales, the imagination and vision which have carried you throughout a great political career, and the sagacity and experience which you have accumulated in all your many years of public service.

In this new and, I am sure, exciting Parliament you will have a big part to play, so this is no question of retirement. But I want to wish you and Mrs Griffiths all the best for the future.

Thanks again,

Yours ever,

HAROLD.

Back in the Welsh Office I called to my room the two men who had been my constant companions in the exciting work of building a new department—the Permanent Secretary, Goronwy Daniel, and my private secretary, Ken Pritchard, and together we toasted the future of the Welsh Office. I thanked my two ministerial colleagues, Goronwy Roberts and Harold Finch, knowing that no minister had been more loyally supported than I had been by my minister and under secretary. I stayed to welcome my successor, Cledwyn Hughes, and to pledge him my full support; and then I left that quaint building, tucked in between corridors of power, and went home to begin the writing of these memoirs.

4

When the 1966 Parliament assembled its first task was to proceed
to the appointment of a new Speaker. I was accorded the honour
of moving that the Member for the Itchen division of Southampton
be elected, and my motion was seconded by the Father of the
House, R. H. Turton, the Member for Thirsk and Malton. I
rejoiced in the election of Dr Horace King for both personal and
party reasons. He was an old and valued friend and deserved the
honour of being the first Labour Member to be appointed to the
chair.

The new House evoked memories of 1945. Our benches were
crowded with eager Members, no fewer than forty-nine of them
having won former Tory seats. With a substantial majority for the
Government all seemed set fair for a full period of five years of
endeavour and achievement. The Prime Minister entered the
House to receive the plaudits of his supporters for what we all
recognized had been his greatest personal triumph. The Chancellor, Jim Callaghan, had shared the experience of Hugh Dalton,
with 'the balance of payments gnawing at his heart by day and
night'. With half the deficit he had inherited already wiped out
we hoped that the wind would now be set fair for him. George
Brown, by dint of hard work and boisterous friendship, had persuaded the Confederation of British Industry and the Trade
Union Congress to co-operate with the Government in the dual
task of ensuring stability of incomes and prices and in measures to
promote economic growth. All the other ministers had their
legislation ready to present to the House. Our Labour benches
were pervaded by a gala atmosphere on that first day of what
promised to be a fruitful session. Alas! Within three months all
was changed. Once again we were reminded that the only certain
thing in politics is uncertainty.

Within three months of the glorious electoral victory in March
of 1966 the Prime Minister had to announce in Parliament that,
faced with yet another balance of payments crisis, the Government felt compelled to introduce a series of severe deflationary
measures in an effort to save the pound sterling.

As I listened to Harold Wilson on that sad day, memories of
1949 came vividly back to mind. That was the year in which I was
privileged to serve as the chairman of the party's National
Executive and to preside over the annual conference at Blackpool

during Whitsun week. In my presidential address I had invited the
1,500 delegates to share my pride in the achievements of the 1945
Labour Government:

> During the past four years you and I have been privileged to take
> part in a silent revolution in Britain. We have ensured the transfer
> from private to public ownership of some of the key industries and
> services. To have accomplished this change, and by democratic
> methods, is by itself an achievement of immense importance and
> significance.
>
> We are living in an age of economic and social transition. The
> old economic systems have broken down over a large part of the
> world. The fundamental problem of our day is not whether but
> how there shall be brought about the change from an unplanned to
> a planned economy. The people will not tolerate a return to the
> economic anarchy of the thirties with its mass unemployment, its
> poverty and its frustration of human hopes.
>
> There can be, there must be, no going back, but which way
> forward? That is the major issue of today. It is my conviction that
> in these past four years the Labour Government has shown the way
> forward. We are privileged to take part in the creating in our
> country of a new economic and social order which will be a com-
> bination of planned economic prosperity, social security, democratic
> freedom and human dignity. If we succeed—as we shall, and as
> we must—we shall not only create a better Britain: we shall
> provide an example to the others who are at the crossroads.
>
> If we succeed they will choose our way.

The conference demonstrated, by voice and vote, that it shared
my pride and my hopes, and at the end of the conference the
delegates stood to pledge themselves to work by day and night to
ensure the return of the Labour Government in the general
election of 1950.

Three months later I was called on a Saturday evening in
September to a ministerial meeting at No. 10 to be informed by
the Prime Minister that the Government had decided to devalue
the pound as against the American dollar, and that the Chancellor,
Stafford Cripps, would be announcing the decision in a broadcast
on the following Sunday evening at nine o'clock.

It so happened that I was due to travel north to address three
thousand young Socialists who had assembled at Butlin's Camp at
Filey, Yorkshire, on the Sunday afternoon. I consulted Clem
Attlee, who said: 'Go and make your speech, but remember—
not a word about all this until Stafford has spoken.'

When I reached Filey I was besieged by campers and pressmen, all of whom wanted to know what Stafford would say in his broadcast, and I had to stall them in true Yorkshire character and say 'nowt'. We all gathered together in the assembly hall at the camp to listen to the broadcast, and as soon as it was over I was asked to comment. The jargon of the City has always been beyond me and I told the eager young Socialists that it was better to devalue money than men, and ever since I have had the feeling that I was right.

I had been more fortunate than Cripps, for in the weeks before the decision to devalue he could not fall back on 'nowt' but had to deny that the Government had any intention of devaluing. He was later to suffer agonies as he was taunted by Churchill and the other Tories with having prevaricated. I had noted how strained Stafford looked at that Saturday evening meeting. I feared that he would break under the tension and the taunts. The constant worry about the balance of payments had broken Hugh Dalton, for I am sure that it was the strain which had led to the unfortunate lapse which ruined his career.

Looking back over the years I can see that it was the devaluation of 1949, and all that followed, which marked the beginning of the troubles in the party which finally led to our defeat in 1951, and to thirteen years in the political wilderness.

Following the resignation of Hugh Dalton the Government had been sustained by the mutual confidence and close collaboration of the triumvirate, Clem Attlee, Ernest Bevin and Stafford Cripps, who in their varied gifts and temperaments supplemented and complemented each other. I remember how one day during the post-devaluation debates my good friend George Tomlinson remarked that he feared that our top three were in danger of drifting apart, and we went to see Ernest Bevin, whose confidence we both enjoyed, to express our concern. Ernie listened to us and again his massive common sense came to the rescue of the party. Alas, both Ernie and Stafford began to break under the strain, and ill health soon compelled them to relinquish their posts.

I was at that time in close touch with the constituency parties for, during my year of office as chairman of the party, I devoted most of my week-ends to attending conferences in the regions and addressing public meetings. The sudden halt in our progress following devaluation and its consequent cuts had disheartened the faithful. The dedicated members of our party are not interested in political power for its own sake. This is one of the basic differences in the approach to politics between our party and the Conservatives. The Tories have inherited the tradition of a ruling class for whom power is a divine right. For the dedicated Socialist political power is only of value as the means by, and through, which we can advance towards a Socialist society. And when from 1949 onwards the Labour Government was confronted with the task of making both ends meet, and that in a threatening international situation, the movement lost its dynamism, the Parliamentary Party lost its cohesion, and two years later was to be driven into the political wilderness for thirteen years.

Was Wilson's era to end in the same way? Like Attlee's, his Government had been built around a triumvirate—Wilson, Brown and Callaghan. It was these three who in 1964 had taken the decision to fight through the balance of payments crisis they inherited, and to save the pound. Harold Wilson's resilience, Jim Callaghan's steadfastness and George Brown's exuberant energy had carried the Government through the difficulties of the first stage of the battle for solvency. Their team work had won the admiration of the party in Parliament and the country, and generated the enthusiasm which won the electoral triumph of March 1966. When in July 1966 the Government was compelled to introduce further deflationary measures and so virtually abandoned the National Plan, trouble began. George Brown had begun with zest the creation of the new Department of Economic Affairs and the preparation of the plan. It was a cruel blow when the crisis laid his plans in ruins. In his chagrin he threatened to leave the Government, but was persuaded to stay, and his disappointment was assuaged by his appointment to the Foreign Office—the post once filled by his mentor, Ernest Bevin. In his short tenure of the office he was to suffer further disappointment when his hope of securing Britain's admission into the E.E.C. was frustrated by the 'General'. His subsequent resignation had something of the inevitable about it. The loss to the Government was serious as he was regarded by the party as one of the last survivors of the 'cloth-cap' brigade. He will come back. The party needs its George Browns to rekindle the old spark in the rank and file of the movement.

If the July measures had succeeded the Government would have recovered its confidence and the party its enthusiasm. But—

as has often happened in British politics—when a government runs into heavy weather its luck deserts it. Harold Macmillan could write with feeling on this theme!

As Harold Wilson and Jim Callaghan fought valiantly to balance payments and save the pound, trouble after trouble befell them, and with strikes at the docks, the members of the Seamen's Union refusing to sail and de Gaulle's 'Non', all their efforts were in vain, and the Government were compelled to devalue.

Like Stafford Cripps, Jim Callaghan found himself charged with having broken his pledge and he resigned from the Treasury, but in such a dignified manner that the party warmed to him.

With Callaghan moving over to the Home Office, and Douglas Jay leaving the Government, Harold Wilson had to find new men for the key posts at the Treasury and the Board of Trade. He found them in two of Hugh Gaitskell's protégés. Hugh had been confident that in Roy Jenkins and Anthony Crosland we had two young men who by their ability and character were destined for high office. The promotion of Roy brought me special pleasure, for his father, Arthur Jenkins, had been my deputy when I was president of the South Wales Miners' Federation.

When I was a student at the Labour college I studied Marxism and tried very hard to understand it. I could not bring myself to accept the materialist concept of history: my Welsh temperament recoiled against such an arid doctrine. At the end of each lecture on the M.C.H. I would join a fellow student, who shared my revulsion, in singing: 'I am the master of my fate, I am the captain of my soul.' Even so I had then, even if reluctantly, to accept that the 'Old Man's' economic analysis of capitalism had some validity. Marxists can still make out a formidable case that capitalism, even when diluted by Keynesism, has failed to find a way to use the productive forces it develops without running into recurring crises.

It is a sad commentary upon our Western civilization that we have failed to manage our affairs without subjecting so many of our workers to the misery of unemployment, and that our only way to put the country on its feet is to put the workers on the road. It does not make sense to me to witness the rich countries taking measures to hold back the production of wealth while millions of people in the poorer lands are enslaved by hunger and disease.

The Marxists assert that capitalism generates the economic strains and stresses that inevitably end in war. It is my conviction that we can, if we have the wisdom and the will, solve our difficulties by a new kind of war—the war on want. The 'Old Book' is right: it is by turning swords into ploughshares that mankind can find the way to prosperity and peace.

14

AT CLOSE OF DAY

I FEARED the consequences of deflation upon Wales. I had pinned my hopes upon building a new economy as part of the national plan with its provision for regional regeneration. I had dreamed of a new town in mid Wales to rejuvenate our languishing countryside. I had even chosen the name I wished to give to it—Treowen ('Owenstown'), in commemoration of one of Wales's greatest sons, Robert Owen. My dreams have been disappointed, but I still cherish the hope that when the present difficulties are overcome, as overcome they will be, they may yet come true.

Economic recession and financial stringency soon had their repercussions in our towns and valleys. The rise in unemployment aroused old fears. My old industry, coal, was fast running down and the new industries planned to provide new jobs were slow in coming. Discontents found their expression in electoral setbacks. We lost Carmarthen and came dangerously near to losing two of our strongholds in the Rhondda and Caerphilly. The by-elections took place when things were going wrong for the Labour Government, and it was inevitable that there should be a massive protest vote. In the old days one would have expected that this would have gone to a party of the left, at least in the Rhondda, where in the forties the Communists had come within an ace of winning one of the Rhondda seats. What surprised most people was that it was the nationalist party, *Plaid Cymru*, which gained from the protest vote against Labour. Their electoral success caught the headlines and aroused speculation as to whether we were witnessing the emergence of a new political force, which might displace Labour as the dominant influence in Welsh politics.

The Welsh Nationalist Party was founded in the nineteen-twenties by a group of writers, nonconformist ministers and laymen. Its first leader was Saunders Lewis, born into a nonconformist home, a son of the manse. The philosophy of Calvinism was too arid for his romantic temperament and he found a spiritual home in the Roman Catholic Church. He is a passionate lover of the Welsh language, which he has enriched by his poems and dramas. He rose in revolt against those forces and influences which threatened the language, culture and way of life. He saw these threatening influences as the consequences of the Protestant and industrial revolutions. The first had led to the subjugation of Wales to an alien rule, and the second to the destruction of the peasant society in which our way of life was nurtured and sustained. He dreamed of a return to the golden age, with the Welsh chieftain in his castle, the minstrel in the hall, and the peasant in the cottage, all sheltered within the sanctuary of the ancient Church: a society of ordered unity where each man had his secure place.

This is Saunders's dream, and if to many it seems an idle one, it has its fascination for those who can find no abiding place nor joy in the materialist society of the Western world.

His successor as leader of the Nationalists, Gwynfor Evans, is cast in a different mould. He is not a dreamer but a successful business man, a pillar of nonconformity and a pragmatic politician. His first important decision was to change the name of the party, discarding 'Nationalist' for *Plaid Cymru*, the Party of Wales. He has built up the membership of the party by an appeal to three sections of the Welsh community: the traditional Liberals who must, with the decline of their own party, find a new one; the young people who are the products of the 'all-Welsh' schools; and those others who see in '*Plaid*' the only hope of defeating Labour. It was by mobilizing the votes of all three elements, together with those of the discontented among Labour's traditional supporters, that '*Plaid*' gained its electoral successes.

The alliance will not endure and the Nationalists will not threaten Labour's hold in Wales, provided we learn the lesson so dramatically presented by our unexpected setback.

When the Labour Government overcomes its financial and economic problems—as it will—the disgruntled will return to the fold. But there are more permanent and deeper discontents to which as Socialists we have to find the answer. These arise from the feeling of ordinary men and women that our modern society has become so complex, and its problems so baffling, that they are victims of forces beyond their control. The worker in industry is caught in a whirl of machines which dominate his working life. He is swallowed up in a big industrial plant which makes him feel that he does not count as a human being, that he is only a cog in the machine. The old intimate relationship between the place where he works and the community in which he lives is broken. He is becoming a commuter among commuters whom he seldom meets except in the rush to and fro by train or bus. Grass-root democracy withers as power and responsibility move ever further away from the town and valley.

The growth of nationalism in Wales and Scotland, and that of regionalism in the north and west of England, are protests against the over-centralization of authority in the remote corridors of power. But nationalism has no real answer to these deeper discontents which are to be found in every country which comes under the influence of our modern industrial system.

It is on these deeper discontents and their challenge that I ponder as life draws nearer to its close.

In the spring of 1967 I made two special journeys to my valley: the first to attend a gathering to commemorate the fiftieth anniversary of the Trades and Labour Council, the second to intimate to my comrades of the Llanelli Constituency Labour Party that I would not again be standing for election to Parliament.

We have a hymn for every mood, and at these gatherings I felt like the old saint in the hymn in which, having reached the summit of Mount Zion, he looks back nostalgically to the winding road he has travelled on life's journey. I went again to the village where my life's journey had begun. The old home still stands guard over the bridge which spans the Amman River and leads out to the world. The smithy is silent and the village politicians no longer gather around the anvil to argue about life's problems. The village school is still housed in the same building in which I learnt the three R's; the only change is in its name. When I first attended it was known as the board school, then Balfour's Education Act changed it to council school and now it is the county primary school. As I went around the classrooms with the headmaster I saw that there had been another change since my day—there was no standard X-7. When the pupils reach the age of eleven they leave the primary school and together cross the bridge to Ammanford, and having crossed they part, some to go to the grammar school and the rest to the secondary modern. How presumptuous of us to divide our children into successes and failures at this tender age and to send them in their different coloured blazers on their separate ways. I was very glad to know that the education committee is planning to reorganize secondary education on the comprehensive principle.

I watched the children at play and was delighted to see how well they looked. What a transformation higher living standards, supplemented by the expansion of the social services, have wrought in children's physique. The mid-morning milk and the midday school meal are some of the best investments the nation ever made. I was proud of these children of the Welfare State. I remember Margaret McMillan coming to our valley to campaign for the provision of school meals for necessitous children, and it is a sad commentary on our boasted affluent society that there should still be such children at some of our schools.

From the school I made my way to the mine at which I had started my working life in 1904. I reached the pit-head just as the men were coming up from the morning shift. There was the familiar rush to hand over the safety lamp at the lamproom, but then came the change from our days. Instead of rushing for home, taking with them, as we used to do, the dirt and grime of the mine to add to Mother's burden, they made for the pit-head bath and, after a shower, on to the canteen for a cup of tea and the luxury of that first smoke at the end of shift.

As ever with the miners when the day's work is done, the talk was fast and furious. They welcomed me to their fellowship around the tables and we talked about the changes in the methods of mining since the time when we worked in the headings and stalls of the 'Little Vein', cutting and filling with hand-tools. The machine has now taken over some of the heavier work at the coal-face but has added its noise to the discomforts which we suffered. And the perils remain, the roof falls still take their daily toll and the dust the machine churns up chokes the lungs.

But it was not of these perils that we talked that day, but of the fear that the mine would close down. It is a tragedy that just as life was beginning to get better for the collier the future of the industry should be threatened by its rivals—oil, atomic energy and sea-gas.

That evening as we enjoyed in retrospect the memories of fifty years ago at the anniversary gathering we could not escape the anxiety felt over the prospects for the future. When we founded the Trades Council in 1917 there were twenty coal-mines at work in the valley; now only two of those survive, and these, even with the three new mines sunk since then, cannot absorb the men made redundant by closures. The unwanted men have now to seek work elsewhere. The National Coal Board is anxious that those made redundant should move to the mines which have the prospect of a long life, but the miners in the valleys are loath to leave the homes they have stinted and saved to build and the community in which they are so deeply rooted. The word redeployment trips so easily off our tongues that we sometimes forget that it means a painful uprooting for the workers and their families. At the anniversary celebration the cry was: 'Bring us new industries. We have done our full share of the nation's hard work and deserve a break. We want to keep the old place going and live out our lives with our neighbours.'

I hope the powers that be will listen to this cry and have the grace to provide a smooth passage for my old industry as the country moves over to the era of the new fuels.

The men who have risked their lives to produce the coal upon which our industrial might was founded deserve well of the nation, as do the communities they created. In these valley communities almost every house is owned by the family who lives in it and, with leasehold reform at long last achieved, the land on which it is built will soon be theirs as well. In the long years of the great depression the houses had come to look bare—the 'cement boxes with slate lids' as someone once described them. With full employment in the years after 1945 the worker and his wife set about cleaning them up and today they are a pleasing sight, painted, and coloured in bright hues. The housewife has been relieved of the back-breaking toil of clearing the dirt and grime the collier used to bring from the pit. He now comes home from work dressed like a bank clerk, to a house furnished with many modern amenities and gadgets such as a bath and a fridge, a washing machine and television. The whole family enjoy escape to the coast and country in the small car. As one miner said to me:

'For the first time in my life I am discovering what a lovely land ours is.'

Life is fuller and better—or is it? As the local mines and mills close down the men have to seek work farther away from home and become commuters. The close relationship between work and community is broken. Once the men of the village were fellow workers and fellow citizens, their whole life spent in toe intimacy of the community. How to preserve this neighbourliness in a mobile society: this is one of the problems which change has brought to the valley. The changes in industry have also brought problems. In the small industrial units every worker would know his mates by their Christian names. They would walk together in the morning to their work at mine and mill and share each other's company in the leisure hours of evening. Work, home, community were all linked in unity and fellowship. Now this unity is broken by the demands of modern technology. The machine calls for continuous operation in a cycle of shifts which move all round the clock each day for seven days a week. In the giant new plants the individual worker's contribution is swallowed up in the collective process. Industrial relations become depersonalized and the manager a remote person he seldom sees. As one of the workmen who had moved from a small to a big unit said to me: 'I hate these giant corporations—they have neither a body one can kick nor a soul one can damn.'

In his rough words he expressed one of the major problems of modern industry: how to humanize industrial relations, and to find a way to give the worker the feeling that he counts, not only as a producer but also as a human being. The guild Socialists had a point of real importance when they sought to provide a new status for the worker in industry. As a lifelong trade unionist one of the disappointments I have experienced is the failure of the movement to take more positive action to promote and develop industrial democracy, and, as a vital step towards its achievement, to reorganize the structure on the lines of one union for each industry.

In the social and cultural life of the valley communities the most notable change is to be found in the decline in the membership and influence of the nonconformist chapels. In my boyhood days the chapel was the centre of the life of the community. We all grew up under its wing. We learnt Welsh at the Sunday

school, took our part in the cantata, joined the choir and cultivated our gifts at the Young People's Guild. All of these are still
there but their influence has weakened, whilst the 'clubs'
multiply. There seem to be ample resources readily available to
build palatial club buildings, and these are full every evening and
crowded on Sundays. Even the miners' welfare institutes, built
out of the magic pennies of the miners' welfare fund, now find
that they can keep going only by adding a bar to their other
attractions. The clubs provide good fellowship, they give
generously to local causes and help the afflicted and distressed.
Whether they will produce leaders for the community, as the
chapels did in my time, remains to be seen.

What reassures me, and gives me confidence for the future of
the valley and its communities, is meeting the young people at
school and college. They have a self-assurance that my generation
lacked, they enjoy wider opportunities and are better equipped
for life at work and in leisure. At my meetings with them I was
pleased with the frank manner in which they talked about the
problems of their individual lives, and the ability which they
revealed in discussing the problems of the country and the world.
If new opportunities can be provided which will enable them to
find work in the valley then these young people will not only
maintain the best traditions of the community but will enrich its
life by their gifts and service.

At one of the gatherings of young people which I attended I
asked a question: 'If you reach my age you will live to the two-
thousands. What kind of world will it be then?' Their answers
revealed their awareness of the rapid changes that are taking
place, and, most important, the fact that the scientist and
technologist are transforming the world into a parish and its
people into next-door neighbours. The 'telly' has become their
window on the world. They see how other people live and recognize the challenge of the population explosion and of world
poverty. One of them, in his answer to my question, said:
'President Kennedy was right when he told us that today man
holds in his mortal hands the power to abolish all forms of
human poverty—and the power to destroy all forms of human
life'—to which my young friend added: 'It is our responsibility
as young people to ensure that we make the right choice.'

Their grandfathers devoted their savings to provide the means
to send missionaries to Asia and Africa, and they would willingly

give their life to service in helping the peoples of these continents to overcome the poverty which holds them down. I am proud of these young people, and because I remain convinced that the principles and the spirit of socialism hold the key to the solution of the problems of our country and the world, I fervently hope that we can attract them to our movement.

These were the thoughts in my mind as I went to meet the delegates at the conference of the Llanelli Constituency Labour Party. Thirty-one years had gone by since the party had selected me as their candidate, and throughout the years they had supported me loyally. We had campaigned together at eight elections and I was sad that now the time had come to relinquish my candidature and to ask them to choose my successor.

The delegates at this 1967 conference were the sons and daughters, and some of them the grandchildren, of the men and women who had selected me as their standard-bearer in 1936. The changes of the past thirty years have eroded the rigid class divisions of the old days and the delegates at this conference were sons of toil and members of the professions in almost equal numbers. Their discussions covered the whole range of our domestic and international problems. They were naturally deeply concerned about the industrial future of the communities they represented. They realized that they had to build a new economy to replace the old. They welcomed the steps taken by the Labour Government to attract new industries to the area, but were firmly of the view that a more radical approach was called for, and hoped that the Government would not hesitate to establish publicly owned and operated industries if private enterprise could not be induced to bring industry to the valleys. With their experience of the depression they regard the establishment of the Welfare State as Labour's major achievement and they were concerned at the talk of 'selectivity'. To them the Welfare State is not a luxury to be sacrificed in times of stress but an essential attribute of a civilized society.

They were wholeheartedly in support of Harold Wilson's stand on Rhodesia, but were equally resolute in their opposition to America's intervention in Vietnam and in calling for more positive action to end the war. The younger delegates, whilst taking part fully in the discussions on these topical issues, were especially concerned with the more fundamental problems which arise as we enter the age of the scientific and technological revolution, and the kind of society which is emerging. They show a real concern about the changed attitudes of this materialistic age and the false values of the affluent society.

As I sensed this deep concern at the conference, as I had done at my meeting with the young people at school and college, I remembered how, in 1952, I had joined with Clem Attlee in commending to our movement a new 'Statement of Socialist Principles' formulated by the group of dedicated comrades who sponsor the journal *Socialist Commentary*. In this statement they too were concerned with, and gave expression to, these deeper discontents in these words:

> Modern discontents, even though they cannot be stated as simply as those of previous generations, are none the less real, and keenly felt. Discontent today is linked up with the growth of the centralized, highly organized managerial society which is enveloping us.
>
> It arises out of such imponderables as the status of the worker in industry, whether his work gives him satisfaction, his loneliness in the atomized society of the big cities and his difficulty in expressing himself in the face of the remoteness of the centres of power. So much of the individual's experience brings home to him his littleness in a big world, and seems to detract from his own value and to diminish the significance of his efforts.
>
> We know already that it will not be enough to construct a society which does no more than guarantee material wellbeing; it must also be a society which provides men with the conditions in which they may use their possessions and abilities in a creative way, to live out their lives in freedom and fellowship.

When this new statement was published I was invited to write a foreword, and in it I recalled what I said in Parliament when I introduced the National Insurance Bill in 1946:

> As I have worked on this Bill I have often recalled an experience of the grim days of 1940. I went down to my native village after our party conference of that year. We had decided to enter Government and see the war through. After my speech an old collier came to me and said: 'Yes, you are right; we have to see this thing through to the bitter end, but,' he added, 'after this, what?' I believe that security will release our people from the haunting fears of yesterday, and their gifts and energies for the service of the nation.

Yet, as security removes those fears, there emerges a longing for something beyond, for an outlet through which these creative energies can find expression and fulfilment.

I remember reading some time ago about an unusual kind of strike that had taken place in a factory in the U.S.A. It was not a strike over wages or any of the usual grievances. This was a strike in protest against the dehumanizing conditions and the intolerable boredom of the assembly line. In a demonstration those who led the procession carried a banner inscribed:

WE WANT BREAD—AND ROSES TOO

Bread and roses: the symbols of the ideal Socialist society which inspired me in the morning of life—and still beckons me on at the close of day.

INDEX

Index